WISDOM
OF THE
CEO

WISDOM
OF THE
CEO

**29 Global Leaders Tackle Today's
Most Pressing Business Challenges**

G. William Dauphinais

Grady Means

Colin Price

Introduction by Klaus M. Schwab

John Wiley & Sons, Inc.

New York • Chichester • Weinheim • Brisbane • Singapore • Toronto

Published by John Wiley & Sons, Inc.
Published simultaneously in Canada.

Library of Congress Cataloging-in-Publication Data:

ISBN 0-471-35762-6

Printed in the United States of America.

10 9 8 7 6 5 4 3 2 1

Contents

Contents

Acknowledgments

A book such as this comes together only with contributions from many. We are grateful to the 29 chief executive officers who, by contributing so generously to this book, have made it their own. We acknowledge the patient participation and incisive thinking of the following PricewaterhouseCoopers colleagues across our organization, who contributed content, cases, and counsel for our introductory chapters:

Martin Aked

Pierre Anglade

Steve Arbeit

Robert Avila

George Bailey

John Barry

Bill Bax

Ray Bromark

Robert Brooke

Frank Brown

Nigel Buchanan

Denis Collart

Dennis Conroy

Steve D'Arcy

Trevor Davis

Abeer Embaby

Matthew Faulkner

John Ferron

John Frankovich

John Gauntt

Tig Gillam

Michael Hanley

Tammy Hanna

Jay Henderson

Vivek Kapur

Michael Katz

Ellen Knapp

Mike Korotkin

Adrian Lamb

Susan Lotwin

Roger Marshall

Frank Milton

Bob Muir

Barry Nearhos

Mark Ondash

Bill Powell

Frank Pringle

Steve Redwood

Chuck Robel

Marco Rochat

Muriel Rosenberg

David Shaw

Pat Sherry   Nigel Vooght

Bob Strickler   Paul Weaver

Bill Trahant   Peter Weibel

Paul Turner   Dorothy Yu

This book was made possible by the perseverance and dedication of a transatlantic project management and editorial team:

Ana Cardenas, Maryline Damour, and Chris White brought outstanding project management skills and goodwill to the entire process.

Carol Ballock, Gene Zasadinski, and John Thackray edited many of the chapters, always with skill and discretion.

Our editor at John Wiley & Sons, Linda Witzling, entered the current at the halfway mark and provided the fullest possible support.

Helen Rees, the literary agent who truly knows the agenda of business, has provided valuable guidance for this, as for many other PricewaterhouseCoopers books.

George Fasel drew the manuscript into a whole that retains the distinctive voice of each author. We are most grateful for his participation.

As final editor for PricewaterhouseCoopers, Roger Lipsey again added inexplicable patina.

And Lisa Silverman stood at the center. Her insights and single-minded determination to keep this project on track are why you have this book in your hands now.

G. William Dauphinais

Grady Means

Colin Price

Foreword

Discerning the Agenda
of the Global Economy

For nearly three decades, The World Economic Forum has been fostering dialogue among leaders in government, business, academia, and other dimensions of society. In recent years, we have been compelled by rapidly moving events to focus on the globalization of the economy—the increasing interdependence and integration of world economic life, which, while still in process and in many areas uneven, affects growing numbers of people every day.

One unmistakable by-product of globalization is that the challenges and opportunities facing business decision makers everywhere are becoming increasingly alike. The CEO in Texas is grappling with some of the same problems as his counterparts in Zürich and Tokyo. The head of a telecommunications giant may find himself profiting from the insights of an international financial services institution or an Internet search engine. The brokerage business with a new online unit may have lessons of value for the video rental corporation or the automotive manufacturer. In these circumstances, the critical importance of high-level dialogue is even greater; the rewards it may bring, even richer.

PricewaterhouseCoopers has understood these rewards and brought together what the editors and authors—leading partners of that firm—appropriately call the wisdom of 29 CEOs of global companies. The editors and authors have structured the contributions of these outstanding business leaders into eight broad topics, which, taken together, can safely be called the agenda for the global economy in the next few years. PricewaterhouseCoopers analysts, working under the direction of the three general editors, have also contributed introductory essays on each of the following eight topics:

Globalization

Growth

Shareholder value

Organization

E-business

Disruptive technology

Innovation

Knowledge management

The introduction that follows this brief foreword stresses that our planet is experiencing a level and pace of change that is without precedent and unlikely to abate in the foreseeable future. Change is by no means confined to the world of business, but the steadily integrating global marketplace is playing an ever larger role in the lives of all human beings. I am unshakably committed to the position that we will cope effectively and productively with that reality to the extent that we maintain open, effective communication among all sectors of civil society. *Wisdom of the CEO* is a valuable contribution to that communication. We will all grow from reading it.

Klaus M. Schwab, President
World Economic Forum
Geneva, Switzerland

INTRODUCTION

Warp-Speed Change

The Challenge to Business Leadership

Within very recent experience, the half-life of change has collapsed. Global eras of fundamental change—geopolitical, technological, economic—that might once have taken centuries are now completed in a few years. Corporations that mapped out five-year strategic plans now review their strategies monthly.

What is going on? Why is the pace of change sliding down the catenary curve to the point of "instant"? How do CEOs understand this pace of change? How do they sort out what many call volatility into understandable and manageable trends? What principles, wisdom, and processes do they employ to confront this era and prosper? These questions have prompted the creation of this book.

The Era of Internationalization (1984–1990)

Following the postwar recovery in the 1950s, the cold war, and the inflation-driven recessions of the 1970s and early 1980s, the global economic recovery in 1983–1984 was anticipated by business as another normal business-cycle recovery year. Businesses did what they typically did under the circumstances: took advantage of growth in demand, raised prices to conform with the inflation-driven economics of the past 30 years, and strove to maintain or slightly increase market share in order to survive future market down-cycles.

But the measures didn't work this time. Figure I.1 tells the first part of the story. As the figure suggests, cyclical economic upturns such as those in the early and mid-1970s led to a significant rise in inflation and pricing, and business had come to rely on this. The recovery in 1983–1984, however, did not lead to higher prices; in fact, during the sustained growth from 1983 through today, prices remained relatively flat or dipped throughout the period. Pricing was no longer inflation driven. Corporations had to deal with "real prices" . . . in this case real low prices. Recognition of this state of affairs caused extreme agitation among business executives and a profound shift in strategy, which continued to the end of the 1980s.

By 1984, new economic policies initiated in the United States and the United Kingdom had quietly restructured capital markets in ways that quickly dampened inflationary spikes. At the same time, the emerging countries in Asia, and to some degree in Latin America, had begun an aggressive strategy to export high-quality, low-cost products to support their growing industrial economies. Such policies were often supported by artificially soft currency, very low cost capital, and

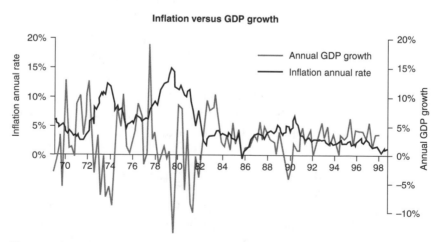

Figure I.1 Price promotion and inflation-driven strategies failed to work, leading to "real prices."

free equity stemming from vertically integrated capital markets and close (that is, closed) financial/industrial relationships. These conditions allowed foreign importers into the United States and Europe to seize growing shares of market, and they also depressed prices.

After corporate leaders had indulged in panicky calls for increased protectionism, exchange rate manipulation, and national industrial planning, the more constructive responses in the developed economies followed three parallel lines.

First, most companies launched international strategies. For example, most U.S. companies were 80 percent focused on their domestic market, 20 percent on the foreign market. By the late 1980s, the balance had shifted to fifty-fifty. For the most part, the shift in market focus occurred through exports and trade policy. However, some companies did begin to copy the Honda model—investing overseas and placing plant and equipment nearer to their ultimate customers in order to slip under protectionist barriers, lower manufacturing costs, and improve supply chain response time to customers.

The key feature of international strategy in the 1980s was that political and trade rules throughout the world were *different* on a country-by-country basis. Protectionist policies, nontariff barriers, exchange controls, tax policies, and rules governing distribution, advertising, employment, safety, and environment differed throughout the world. Corporate strategists attacked a heterogeneous global market on a country-by-country basis, trying to ferret out opportunities among the political risk issues and market variations, and they adopted something resembling a "country of the year" mentality in their strategies. For the most part, they also attempted to expand internationally as cheaply as possible, with the lowest risk, and tended to pursue low-risk, low-reward strategies such as trade, employing local sales representatives, and strategic joint ventures.

The second strategy in response to real prices and loss of market share was to drive down costs and break-even points. While dressed up and packaged as business process reengineering and supply chain management, most of the efforts were, at their core, aggressive cost reduction in order to create leaner companies, to make better use of working capital, and to meet the new pricing requirements of the marketplace. These efforts were largely successful. By the end of the 1980s, a large proportion of major companies was able to throw off a significant amount of cash for capital investment purposes. In addition, because of their policies of leanness they also discovered *found capacity:* they could respond to customer demand faster with lower levels of inventory and higher degrees of reliability and efficiency. In the developed economies, these trends were supported by much more vibrant capital markets benefiting from tax reform in the United States, conservative fiscal policy in most developed economies, and the creation of less regulated capital markets in London, Paris, and Frankfurt.

The third major response to real prices was the beginning of a return to fundamental brand-building and marketing principles. In the inflationary cycle in the 1970s, changes in promotional strategies, products, and packaging tended to be very slow because companies had to burn off existing inventory before shifting to new approaches. Customer understanding suffered as most companies moved to product promotion and pushed marketing strategy. The strongest branded products in the developed economies in the automotive, electronics, and consumer products sectors began to see significant erosion of share to foreign competition and private-label entrants. By the mid 1980s, there was a clear recognition that the brands were no longer strong enough to prevent market share erosion. The reaction took the form of a major reexamination of brand strategy and growth, and it has bloomed in the 1990s into a central emphasis on customer understanding and responsiveness.

The other major forces unleashed during the economic recovery of 1984 led to "real costs." They changed the face of American business during the 1980s, as reflected in Figure I.2.

The long period from 1900 to 1981 was one of zero or negative real interest rates: Since the rate of inflation was generally higher than interest rates, capital was essentially free. Therefore, efficiency in manufacturing and distribution created little value. Inventory had no carrying cost and, during periods of negative real interest rates excess, actually accumulated value. Companies built large warehouses, maintained large work-in-process inventory, and had relatively slow distribution. Suddenly and without warning during the early 1980s, inefficiency began to bite hard. Inventory suddenly had a very high capital cost. Warehousing and large work-in-process drove down Economic Value Added (EVA) and profitability. Not only did

Inflation versus interest rates

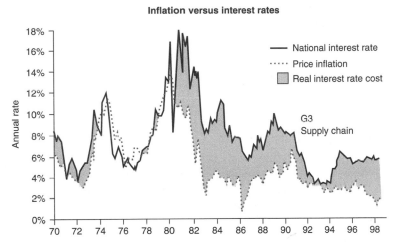

Figure I.2 The 1984 recovery also hit companies with "real costs" ... and focused attention on lean processes and the supply chain.

leaner foreign competitors have the advantages of low-price manufacturing based upon lower labor costs and softer currency, but also many of them pursued lean manufacturing policies that gave them additional cost advantages in this environment. This was especially true in countries like Japan, which maintained artificially low cost-of-capital and cost-of-equity policies. As with real prices, this new phenomenon of real costs created severe confusion and panic among the leaders of the major corporations in the developed economies. They suddenly needed to focus on leanness in their operations and manufacturing processes. Business process reengineering and supply chain management represented exactly the types of operational reforms required during this period.

In addition, real costs put a premium on speed, not only in operations but also in marketing and customer response. Clearly, during a period of declining market share, leaner operations, and reduced inventory, marketers saw an opportunity. They realized that quicker response to customers, promotion development, and product launch cycles, built on a more efficient supply chain, would foster an entirely new model for doing business and a platform on which to rebuild their brands. Real costs combined with real prices to drive companies to reexamine completely issues of growth and brand building, which we now see hotly debated in the 1990s.

- Foreign competition focus on inflation
  - "Real prices"
  - "Real costs"
  - Domestic market share erosion
  - Internationalization
  - Cost reduction

- Heterogeneous global markets
  - Rules different in most countries
  - Piecemeal internationalization—targeting by marginal advantage—country of the year
  - Capital market strengthening (developed economies)
  - Lower costs/leaner companies/more cash and performance
  - Trade focus

Figure I.3   1984–1990: Era of internationalization.

The net result of the period from 1984 to 1990 was much more vigorous global competition based upon leaner and more efficient companies with a better global perspective and higher-quality products sold at lower prices. (See Figure I.3.)

The Era of Global Convergence (1990–1994)

The stage was now fully set for a stunningly rapid transformation of the world economy and the rules of business. During the period from 1990 to 1994, economics and politics went through a profound global change. It is little wonder that the leaders of major companies and countries have had trouble finding their bearings and developing coherent strategies and policies during the 1990s.

Around 1990, leaders of most major market economies simultaneously began to pursue the same strategy:

- *Democratization.* Democratic governments sprouted up worldwide with the end of the cold war. This astounding revolution changed the political face of Latin America, Eastern Europe, and the Soviet Union, and even important parts of Asia shifted to a democratic model in form, if not totally in substance. The view that rapid economic expansion in an increasingly competitive world required more flexible and adaptive forms of government appeared to prevail.

- *Privatization/deregulation.* The strengthening and reform of capital markets that had begun in the developed economies during the 1980s spread to the developing economies, accompanied by an enormous wave of privatization. Most of the rapidly developing countries shifted from economic nationalism and import substitution, coupled with state-controlled enterprises, to the creation of a public capital market with private ownership of the large economic institutions at the core of the reform. Hundreds of billions of dollars of state-owned enterprises were privatized in the period from 1990 to 1994, including most public telecommunications entities, many of the state-owned utilities, state-owned manufacturing and financial institutions, and other significant market sectors. Many countries went, in a period of four years, from having 80 percent of their gross domestic product (GDP) centrally directed by public institutions, to 80 percent of their economy being privately owned and managed. The major reasons for this worldwide sell-off of public institutions were to lower inefficient government spending and public debt, but, more important, to allow local businesses to have the opportunity to become more competitive and to attract inward capital investment to the country.

- *Lower trade and capital barriers.* The lowering of protectionist barriers stimulated a freer flow of goods and services across borders and attracted increasing capital investment to stimulate economic growth. While lowering capital barriers created risk to currencies, most countries judged that the need to attract investment capital outweighed the monetary policy threats.

- *Increased use of computing power.* During the early 1990s, the power of small computers increased dramatically while the cost of computing power dropped precipitously. These changes altered the perspective of governments and businesses toward the use of computers in gathering and understanding vast amounts of information on a global basis, controlling global enterprises and processes, and executing complex transactions quickly and nearly effortlessly.

In a breathtakingly brief period, we moved from a world where the rules in each country on trade and public finance were vastly different, to a world where the rules became the same in most countries. Capital markets strengthened dramatically in developing economies as securities for recently privatized companies were widely traded and citizens could own shares of formerly government-run entities. This shift triggered a wave of entrepreneurship on a global basis unlike anything that had ever previously occurred.

Equally important, large corporations could now fully execute global strategies. They could acquire companies and set up operations in nearly every country in the world. They could move goods and services across borders with far fewer restrictions and difficulties. They could finance enterprises in any currency, in their own or local currencies through local capital markets, and through local ownership they could avoid major foreign exchange rate risk. They could set up global distribution systems, global branding structures, global marketing approaches, and global manufacturing networks. In short, they could become truly global companies.

From an organizational perspective, they could move from country-by-country and region-by-region organizational approaches to fully global organizations based on common products or common market targets. Treasury functions, technology, and financial control could all be driven on a global basis for the first time. Decisions on expansion were no longer defined by low-cost manufacturing or small-market opportunities. Rather, they were made almost exclusively by targeting large-market opportunities, which reduced to 8 or 10 countries out of the 200 or so in the world. Table I.1 indicates the shift in focus to large markets. Countries were ranked on the basis of their gross domestic product and the consumption power of their populations. On a more refined basis, companies focused on countries with urban populations in excess of 30 million people and average per capita consumption power in excess of $5,000 per year. Only a few countries (or combinations of neighboring and closely aligned countries) were appropriate targets from this perspective, and this greatly simplified the strategic issue.

The "country of the year" approach in the 1980s was quickly replaced by a focus and concentration strategy in the 1990s. Experimental joint ventures and alliances, popular in the 1980s, were rapidly converted to aggressive merger and investment strategies in the 1990s. "Look before you leap" strategies of the 1980s were

1997	GDP at Market Prices (U.S.$ in billions)	GDP/Capita	Urban Population (millions)	Urban GDP/Urban Capita	95$ PPP GDP/Capita	95$ PPP Urban GDP/Urban Capita
United States	7,801	29,200	204.9	37,400	27,300	35,000
Japan	4,285	34,100	98.8	42,700	22,300	28,000
Germany	3,450	41,800	71.7	47,600	23,300	26,500
France	1,765	30,200	42.8	40,200	22,600	30,200
United Kingdom	1,277	21,800	52.5	23,900	19,800	21,800
Italy	1,116	19,500	38.0	28,600	19,200	28,200
China	959	800	378.4	2,000	3,300	8,300
Brazil	745	4,600	129.7	5,300	6,200	7,100
Canada	616	20,500	23.2	25,900	23,500	29,700
South Korea	549	12,000	37.9	13,600	14,300	16,200
Spain	528	13,500	30.3	16,900	15,200	19,100
Netherlands	473	30,200	14.0	32,900	20,800	22,700
Russia	447	3,000	112.9	3,700	4,700	5,700
Mexico	393	4,100	72.5	5,100	7,700	9,400
Switzerland	387	54,500	4.4	86,700	26,000	41,400
Australia	381	20,600	15.7	23,600	22,800	26,100
India	378	400	263.5	1,000	2,000	5,200
Argentina	321	9,000	31.6	9,600	9,000	9,600
Belgium	284	27,800	9.9	28,300	20,800	21,100
Sweden	272	30,700	7.4	36,000	22,600	26,500
Austria	268	33,000	5.3	50,100	20,200	30,700

PPP – purchasing power parity

Table I.1 The Convergence Era Triggered a Focus on Markets

replaced by high capital risk strategies in the 1990s to achieve dominance. Major companies began to move quickly during the era of global convergence to become the number one or number two market share player in their sector on a global basis.

A coherent and aggressive global strategy became a necessity for companies and countries alike. Slow-moving countries, especially some of the developed economies in Asia and Europe, which could not make their political structures move quickly enough to adapt to the changing economic environment, experienced serious pressure on their capital markets and structures, disinvestment, lessened competitiveness, rising unemployment, and stagnant growth. Figure I.4 summarizes the box score for this dramatic era of convergence.

- Worldwide change
  - —Democratization
  - —Privatization/deregulation
  - —Lowering trade and capital barriers
  - —Attracting investment
  - —Declining cost of computing power

- Homogeneous global markets
  - —Rules same in most countries
  - —Capital markets strengthening (developing economies)
  - —Integrated global strategies (targeted on markets)
  - —Global structures and network organization (supply chains, marketing, finance, information technology)
  - —Investment and global operations focus
  - —New attention to growth, customer understanding, and brands

- Economic/financial pressure on slow movers in Asia and Europe

Figure I.4   1990–1994: Era of global convergence.

The Era of Global Consolidation (1994–1996)

Before 1990, capital markets still behaved on a sovereign country basis. Central banks, fiscal and monetary policy, exchange controls, protectionism, and related factors represented sufficiently strong barriers that countries maintained a reasonable level of sovereign control over their economies. The dramatic changes between 1990 and 1994 shifted power over capital markets and capital flow to large, private corporate and financial players. Capital began to flow smoothly across borders, based upon the strategic imperatives of companies and industries rather than the economic cycles and policies of countries. Companies wishing to take advantage of the new openness of world markets and the flexibility of financial structures began to make substantial investments on the basis of their corporate strategies and need for dominating markets rather than on the basis of local economic conditions. These changes, of course, combined with network technologies, set the stage for the enormous market disruptions in Asia and elsewhere in 1998. The subsequent wave of change was entirely predictable. As with any market or industry in which restrictive economic rules are relaxed, there was a period of enormous consolidation. The fragmented global economy of the 1980s and before created many small, protected, and inefficient economic players. It was time to clean that up.

In every sector there were the beginnings of what continues to be a wave of massive consolidation. In the automotive industry, 20 to 25 significant nameplate companies grew up in various parts of the world, often under the umbrella of protected markets, governed not only by trade restrictions, but also by safety rules, local standards, and so forth. The high capital intensity in the automotive industry, combined with the lowering of trade barriers, demands a move toward significant consolidation to create global design, distribution, and marketing approaches. It is easy to anticipate that the 20 nameplate automotive firms will consolidate down to 4 or 5 significant global players.

At the end of the 1980s, there were 30 large telecommunications companies operating in various parts of the world, each of which achieved annual profits in excess of a billion dollars. These companies provided similar services, made similar products, and served similar markets. With the lowering of barriers and the privatization initiatives in the early 1990s, it is easy to anticipate the consolidation of these 30 or so players down to 5 or 6 major global players that can compete to provide global telecommunications infrastructure. The difficulty for major telecommunications players is to consolidate while anticipating and taking advantage of convergence with entertainment, education, the leverage of the Internet, computing, and other related industries.

Consumer products companies and retailers have begun consolidating into leading global brands. Brands organize disorderly markets in the consumer products and retail area. The changes in 1990–1994 allow for the creation of global distribution, global branding and marketing, and global retailing approaches. Only two or three leading players will survive in each category. The financial services sector, for its part, needs to follow the trends in other sectors and begin to consolidate for scale and efficiency.

These trends are carrying through to nearly every industry. While scale brings with it many difficulties, effective competition in global markets demands scale and vast resources. Technology, on the other hand, allows management teams to control increasingly vast enterprises.

The box score in Figure I.5 summarizes the changes occurring during this era of global consolidation. As in earlier eras, pressure continues to grow on slow movers in the corporate and political environments who are unable to adapt quickly.

The Era of Global Integration (1996–1998)

The Internet suddenly provided almost infinite knowledge and information at virtually no cost. It allowed the movement to lower-cost computational and knowledge access systems. It advanced global communications geometrically. It transformed the value chains of nearly every industry and is leading to a transformation of most industries into electronics-based information flows, financial transactions, and marketing.

The Internet represents a truly *disruptive* technology. The implications are such that companies need to adjust rapidly and adopt this technology to drive their business processes. Most companies cannot build these processes on the backs of their current business processes. Companies may need to create entirely new corporate and business

---

- Increasingly integrated global capital markets
  - Capital concentrated by sector rather than geography
  - Imperative to be competitive on a global basis
  - Requirement for scale and resources to support global strategy
  - Too many players for an integrated market

- Consolidation of sectors
  - Telecom: $30 \rightarrow 6$
  - Automotive: $20 \rightarrow 5$
  - Consumer products/retail
  - Financial services
  - Health care

- Additional pressure on slow movers in Asia and Europe

Figure I.5   1994–1996: Era of global consolidation.

entities to take advantage of the technology. From this perspective the advantages of size, scale, and *incumbency* or market share are not that they create momentum, but that they provide the financial, human, and intellectual resources to construct entirely new companies on these new technology platforms. Enormous risks and opportunities face the most aggressive and insightful corporate leadership teams.

At the same time, these trends will accelerate the redistribution of global and financial economic power. Inefficient financial and manufacturing systems, built on the backs of inefficient industrial policies, will fail, and fail quickly. Many current situations in Europe and Asia, which have seen slow economic growth, significant disinvestment, and in some cases financial collapse, are examples of these changes.

The Era of Acceleration (1998–2020?)

Large-scale global change at the contemporary rate will not only continue, it will quicken. The logic of acceleration is, as the foregoing discussion should reveal, built into its very engine.

For the most part, this rapid change has served a useful purpose. Markets are becoming more efficient, technology is being applied effectively and, if properly managed, consumers should benefit through a vast variety of choices delivered at highly attractive prices over many easy-to-use channels. On the other hand, there will be dislocations in many large political and industrial sectors not moving quickly enough to adapt. These disruptions need not be intrinsically harmful, although they need to be managed properly. How and whether that will happen is impossible to say.

- Leverage of global Internet and other networks
  - Instant knowledge and financial transfers
  - Dramatically lower cost/broader range of communication

- Collapse of resistant and inflexible markets
  - High value to network/knowledge businesses
  - Convergence of industries and development of new players

Figure I.6 1996–1998: Era of global integration.

In any case, this book is not designed as an exercise in clairvoyance. It is presented as practical analysis, tested experience, and something harder to define—we are calling it *wisdom*—all brought to bear upon concrete problems. In the chapters that follow, we identify, from our own research and from discussions with hundreds of CEOs worldwide, eight large subjects:

Globalization

Growth

Shareholder value

Organization

E-business

Disruptive technology

Innovation

Knowledge management

We think of these subjects as the global business agenda for today and tomorrow. Taken together, they encompass most of the fundamental forces of change in our business environment. Taken separately, they permit an analytic approach to that agenda—which may make it at least slightly less daunting. We address each topic in an introductory section, followed by the commentary of 29 CEOs, writing from their own experience.

1

Globalization amidst Rapid Change

Developing an Aggressive Strategy

The introduction to this book traced the major themes of rapid political, economic, and technological change that have affected business over the past two decades. We argued that globalization is coming even more rapidly than these other types of change, which contribute to it, and that companies need to understand globalization and have the capacity to respond quickly to it.

Examined at any one point in time, the effects of globalization might appear volatile or erratic, but examined over a period of, let's say, 20 years, globalization emerges as far more patterned, consistent, and even inevitable. From a business perspective, the history of the past two decades looks remarkably like the history of integration by the world's market economies and businesses. The contemporary results are dramatic. We have seen mergers of unprecedented scale, like Travelers and Citibank, Olivetti and Telecom Italia, Exxon and Mobil, and Daimler and Chrysler. We have witnessed countries that resist global integration and maintain closed, vertical capital market structures—and suffer badly. They will continue to suffer until they transform their politics and economies. But we have also learned that good intentions are no guarantee of prosperity. Countries committed to liberalizing their economic and business policies—Brazil comes to mind—have been caught in convulsions of the globalizing economy such as the crisis of the summer of 1998, and they suffered painful setbacks.

Figure 1.1 summarizes the political and economic impact of these changes over the past 20 years, tracking trends in global wealth distribution over the period from 1980 to 1999. It suggests the approximate public capital market value of different regions and countries during this period, as well as the net wealth creation resulting from the various corporate and country strategies employed during these years. While there are significant exchange rate issues embedded in these figures, we assume that currency values as well as corporate market values reflect market and economic conditions and that the charts are an approximate representation of the economic impact of global, political, and economic changes since 1980.

In 1985, the emerging internationalization of the 1984–1990 period was beginning to become evident. Market values in Japan had increased, to some degree at the expense of U.S. companies and their U.S. market share.

By 1990, the sustained growth of the U.S. economy, as well as the market value of Japanese companies, had expanded global market

Market capitalization

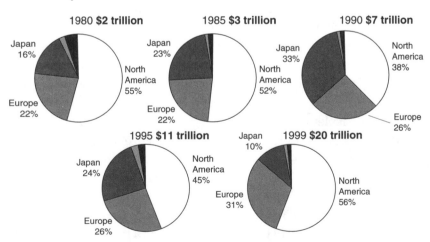

Figure 1.1   The financial impact of the continuing war of globalization.

capitalization to $7 trillion. The success of Japanese companies in entering overseas markets and developing strong global share positions dramatically increased the proportional market capitalization of the Japanese companies to 33 percent and reduced the proportional market capitalization of U.S. companies to 38 percent of the global pie.

By 1995, dramatic shifts in the global economy due to democratization and privatization, as well as the response of U.S. companies in developing global strategies and getting the benefit of reduced trade barriers, began to shift the picture again. Market capitalization continued to rise to $11 trillion and Japan's share began to shrink to 24 percent. The large privatizations in Latin America increased the market cap in that region, although it still represented only a sliver of the worldwide figures. The market cap for North American companies rose to 45 percent of the total, suggesting a substantial rebound during this period of convergence and consolidation.

By 1999, an entirely new picture had emerged. The strong position of U.S. companies and network technologies as well as the relatively sustained expansion of the U.S. economy since 1984 allowed the United States to recapture 56 percent of total global market capitalization. Most dramatically, the severe financial crisis occurring in Asia shrank Japan's share of total global market capitalization to 10 percent and reduced the "other Asia" percentage to 1 percent. Continued privatization and market integration in Europe are reflected in the European expansion of global market capitalization to 31 percent.

While there are many measures of country and corporate success in responding to globalization and global market changes, the amassing of relative proportions of the world's wealth represents one of the most important scorecards. Examining the record, we see a highly consistent expansion of the world's wealth at 12.5 percent per year. The overall beneficiaries have been the countries and companies reacting effectively to the rapidly changing market conditions of globalization and global integration.

There are intriguing implications in this chart. The apparent failure of the vertical capital markets and protected consumer markets of Asia may lead some countries and companies to believe that a change of strategy is appropriate. The low market valuation for many of the companies may make them ideal candidates for joint ventures or mergers, and their need for investment capital may create a new willingness to engage in attractive ventures. Strategists might argue that globalization has simply continued on to the Asian markets and now will begin to open them to direct investment and trade, making Asia a good candidate for business investment and expansion. Figure 1.1 also suggests that investment in Asia should be conditional on significant political movement toward lowering trade and currency barriers and opening the markets up for serious mergers and direct investment. There is a strong incentive for Asian countries to restructure the debt of their major corporations in order to make them good candidates for mergers and acquisitions.

Principles of Global Strategy

Several strategic principles emerge from this discussion. For instance, globalization and global market integration are inevitable, and companies, as well as countries, need an insightful and aggressive global strategy. Global scale will be increasingly important, since trade and business barriers are largely reduced in most of the world, thus creating a more integrated global market where market share needs to be calculated on a global basis. Similarly, communications and information technology increasingly allow management to lead very large global enterprises more effectively. Consolidation trends will continue and the scale of consolidation and corporate convergence will continue to increase.

A key feature of global strategy and business integration will be market focus. Companies must concentrate on the limited number of major market opportunities. Most companies will try to dominate the markets in 10 to 12 countries as the centerpiece of their overall global strategy. There is a 95-5 rule in global business markets—that is, 5 percent of the countries in the world (10 countries) represent 95 percent of the market opportunities in most business sectors, although the specific countries differ for each company and sector.

Market control and concentration of capital are critically important. While in the past many companies have experimented with joint ventures and alliances to limit risk, the vast majority of these have failed because of lack of scale and commitment, misunderstanding the market, or misunderstanding between partners. In moving forward, sufficient capital needs to be focused on a limited number of countries to establish dominant market position. The traditional "look before you leap" strategies of the 1980s are being rapidly replaced by large-scale, high-risk global strategies and consolidations aimed at becoming dominant competitors in particular sectors. To cite just one example, the announcement of the $86 billion Mobil-Exxon merger in mid-1998, sparked in part by weak oil prices, has been followed by a wave of consolidations actual and attempted across the energy industry.

Telecommunications and information technology will move onto a global basis in order to create speed in operation and management decisions, to share information, and to control global enterprises. Correspondingly, global processes will replace national or regional processes in areas such as supply chain and brand management.

There are some important steps toward a successful global strategy. The first is developing a global strategic point of view for the industry. All industries are changing quickly, consolidating, and converging. For any company, it is important to examine each of the major operating units and agree on a sense of where the related industry is going and what will promote successful competition. For example, most public telecommunications companies in the world have been privatized and are being integrated into the networks of private telecoms. Over the next few years, there will be some dramatic consolidation among the large telecommunications companies, although each may be following a different strategy. Some, such as British Telecom with its educational programs in schools, may be pursuing opportunities to drive more content through their networks. Others, such as MCI Worldcom, may see themselves as a platform for emerging e-business and Internet protocols. Others still, like US West, may want to dominate voice communications in the short term and voice/data and other communications in the long term. And some, finally, may see their future in cable and broadband (AT&T).

In the automotive industry, lower barriers within countries and overcapacity are leading to dramatic consolidation. Companies need to decide how they relate to or own their parts networks, as well as the degree to which they need to control distribution and customer sales and service. In the retail industry, companies need to decide whether global integration and global retail branding will organize disorderly retail markets and whether their "go to market" approaches can dominate in a globally integrated market.

Market selection requires rigorous focus. There are more or less 200 different countries/market economies in the world. Approximately 10 of those countries represent over 95 percent of the world's consumer market. Similarly, approximately 10 countries, although not the same ones, represent over 95 percent of the world's materials, intermediates, and industrial parts markets. Less than 5 percent of the countries in the world manage over 95 percent of the world's financial transactions. Success for most major companies involves understanding and achieving dominant market share in the 5 percent of countries that dominate market opportunities in their particular sector. While the other 190 countries play important roles in the world economy and may be important elements of a global strategy, such as regional manufacturing/distribution centers, they are not the central focus of an effective global strategy. The focus has to be: What is the limited set of countries or regionally integrated markets that must be dominated to create the highest value global enterprise?

The 95-5 rule is obvious from Table 1.1. For companies attacking consumer markets, the chart begins to suggest the regions and coun-

1997	GDP at Market Prices (U.S.$, in billions)	GDP/ Capita	Urban Population (millions)	Urban GDP/ Urban Capita	95$ PPP GDP/ Capita	95$ PPP Urban GDP/Urban Capita
United States	7,801	29,200	204.9	37,400	27,300	35,000
Japan	4,285	34,100	98.8	42,700	22,300	28,000
Germany	3,450	41,800	71.7	47,600	23,300	26,500
France	1,765	30,200	42.8	40,200	22,600	30,200
United Kingdom	1,277	21,800	52.5	23,900	19,800	21,800
Italy	1,116	19,500	38.0	28,600	19,200	28,200
China	959	800	378.4	2,000	3,300	8,300
Brazil	745	4,600	129.7	5,300	6,200	7,100
Canada	616	20,500	23.2	25,900	23,500	29,700
South Korea	549	12,000	37.9	13,600	14,300	16,200
Spain	528	13,500	30.3	16,900	15,200	19,100
Netherlands	473	30,200	14.0	32,900	20,800	22,700
Mexico	393	4,100	72.5	5,100	7,700	9,400

PPP = purchasing power parity

Table 1.1 Convergence Triggered a Focus on Markets

tries meriting focus. The chart includes an adjustment useful for global strategy, which companies are increasingly using. The first adjustment is that companies sell products into large urban concentrations, an activity that requires a minimum level of urban consumers (at least 20 to 30 million) and a minimum level of consumer income (at least $2,000 to $3,000 from the point of view of purchasing power parity). The conclusions from this analysis, summarized in Figure 1.2, demonstrate a strategic target frontier of countries with sufficient urban population and sufficient urban income to be attractive markets for major global companies.

For manufacturing markets, where companies are marketing parts, materials, or services to major final assembly manufacturers, the details may be somewhat different, but the result—the need for focus on approximately 10 countries—is the same. As the total GDP figures indicate in Table 1.1, the difference between the largest markets and the next level of markets is exponential, implying that a focus on a large number of small markets never competes with a strategy of focus on a small number of large markets.

To Do: The Management Agenda

The second stage in corporate globalization is to reach consensus among top management on the markets for attack and the handling of several critical issues.

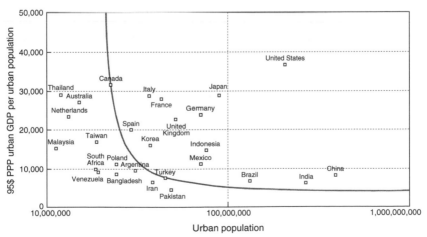

Figure 1.2   Strategic frontier.

Products

The objective is to respect local consumer tastes and at the same time create standardized product platforms. While low-cycle-time manufacturing allows for mass customization and efficient product tailoring for local markets, the integration of global markets has begun a convergence of global tastes so that most large markets are turning toward global brands, styles, and products. Developing products for global markets requires allowing sufficient flexibility to meet a wide variety of consumer preferences while at the same time attempting to limit product complexity, so as to simplify manufacturing inventory management and obsolescence.

Marketing Strategy

Increasingly, urban consumers are aware of global product options and have a variety of channels to desirable products and services. All of the elements of brand management—channel selection, brand identity, fulfillment processes, category management, and frequency drivers—need to be refined into global brand strategies. With more efficient capital markets and the development of regional currencies, consistent pricing management becomes even more important. In short, marketing needs to be developed from a global perspective and customer management systems need to be designed from the perspective of the new global market.

Global Operating Structure

The reduction of trade and currency barriers between countries and regions creates the opportunity to replace country-by-country and regional operating structures with fully integrated global structures. For the most part, manufacturing centers need to be developed close to the ultimate market to support low cycle time and rapid response to shifting customer tastes. Properly distributing manufacturing on a global basis also allows for shortened supply chains and improved management of working capital because of lower inventory and more efficient fulfillment systems. Sourcing and distribution need to be designed on a global basis with the perspective of moving products from manufacturing centers to final assembly points to ultimate markets as quickly and as efficiently as possible. Most international distribution systems were designed during an era of trade and currency restrictions and resemble a patchwork designed to meet protectionist requirements. But with the dramatic lowering of trade barriers, most global sourcing, manufacturing, and distribution systems need to be redesigned to match the market opportunities and the company's vision of the ultimate global system.

Financial Structure

With wide-scale privatization, new capital markets have created entirely new sources of financing. It is useful to consider a tailored financial strategy that allows for local financing, close operations, and sales in order to contain foreign exchange and tax exposure, and to embed the financing strategy into the overall global structure of the enterprise.

Global Business Plan

For most global companies, the business plan needs to emphasize concentration of resources. The objective is not to participate in global markets on a country-by-country basis but to be the dominant player in a sector on a global basis. Significant investment and concentration of resources in the selected 10 or so markets that represent the majority of the revenue and profit opportunities in that sector will produce domination of the sector. The business plan must be designed to achieve rapid market domination in the target countries and to integrate the country operations into the overall global strategy and management structure. Companies today are moving toward very large-scale mergers and acquisitions so that they dominate their sector and have the platform for integrating and controlling the global markets. Such business plans require detailed analysis and planning and a major commitment from corporate leadership and the board of directors to move forward. In the era of globalization, major initiatives are very large and high risk with the objective of market control and high returns. Increasingly, there are very few middle-ground, low-risk opportunities.

Organization Structure

In the past, international strategies have often been built around regional and country organizational structures reflecting the different policies and restrictions of the various countries, as well as the intent to understand and respond to the local markets. They also reflected the complexity of managing large global enterprises and the view that local control of operations was important. For the most part, this view has been replaced by designing companies that match their global product and category markets. Profit and loss statements organized along global product and service lines allow the business to be organized around a common focus on particular products, customers, and product markets. Horizontal global organizations allow for management teams to focus on particular customers and products and improve customer responsiveness. Information and communications technology allows companies to be managed on a global basis in ways that were not possible even five years ago.

Systems

Companies that traditionally install systems on a country-by-country basis, often utilizing technology platforms that did not interface or communicate well, are now developing new global systems to support global customer understanding, product development, marketing, operations (sourcing, manufacturing, and distribution), and financial management and control. While the conversion from country-by-country systems to truly global systems is a complex undertaking, it is essential if global management teams intend to work smoothly as they manage new global enterprises.

The new global economic and technological environment allows for the development and execution of truly global strategies aimed at global market dominance. The need for a global strategy is imperative, and the strategy must be focused on sector dominance to be effective.

These shifts put tremendous pressure on management to understand the dimensions of the global economy and to develop the right strategy. They also require companies to take enormous risks in developing a global plan, engineering the mergers and acquisitions to dominate the sector, and creating the management organizations and systems to generate value from the complex global enterprise.

Niall W.A. FitzGerald
Chairman, Unilever PLC

Value from the Center

The notorious Willie Sutton was famously asked why he robbed banks. "Because that's where the money is," he replied. Why is Unilever a global company? Because that's where the consumers for food and personal care products are—spread all around the world.

Our business must have the stimulus that comes from growth. Over the next decade we are committed to grow at a pace that, until now, was beyond our aspiration. Our business is fundamentally driven by population increases. Over the next 20 years, 3 billion people will be added to the world's population, and they will live almost entirely outside North America and Western Europe. Some 75 percent of the world's additional disposable income is likely to come from these emerging regions. We will be there to help them improve their standard of living with better products that meet their needs for nutrition, refreshment, hygiene, and personal care. Unilever now derives almost 70 percent of revenues from North America and Western Europe, where population growth is largely static. Our growth in these regions will come as we extend our reach across categories and channels and win a greater share of consumers' wallets.

Global and Local—All at Once

Unilever is one of the oldest practitioners of global organization. William Lever, a grocer's son from Bolton, England, pioneered the mass marketing of packaged goods and the concept of the transnational corporation. From the 1890s to the 1920s, he roamed the world setting up subsidiaries in Asia, Africa, and Latin America, giving capital and goals to local managers and then sailing off—returning years later to check on progress. He searched to find the right locations and the best people; he gave his managers clear objectives and then allowed them the room to deliver. So simple. Thus was born a business empire, which today has revenues of £29 billion and 260,000 employees in 100 countries.

Lever authored a conundrum that has faced successive generations of our managers: how to preserve the benefits of the independent local units' intimate contact with local conditions, while extracting the advantages of interdependence from the total corporate entity's scale and scope. Stated differently, yet still paradoxically, our aim is to be a large corporate body with many hundreds of small company souls. That is the way to compete optimally in international markets: simultaneously to have the attributes of a small company—simplicity, speed, flexibility, clarity—and the benefits that arise from size and international spread. Striking the right balance between these two goals has been a long (and always unfinished) learning experience at Unilever.

Although our organization has gone through several mutations in seven decades, it has been our unshakable philosophy that the only way to understand consumer needs and how they might be satisfied is with strong local management teams. At Unilever's 300 operating companies, managers are 90 to 95 percent local, with a sprinkling of expatriates. These expats are not (as is typical with international companies) from a single nation. They come from the world over. An Indian leads Chesebrough-Pond's in the United States. Our top man in Brazil is Italian. A Belgian leads the business in China, and our chairman in Arabia is American. Local managers are critical to achieving intimacy with consumers country by country because, while there are global companies, there is no uniform global consumer. Nor will there ever be, though some may seek to convince you otherwise. Companies that believe only in global brands and homogeneous global markets are likely to get into difficulty. The relatively small number of global brands (McDonald's, Coke, Nike, and a handful of others) should be a warning. Diversity of tastes and individualism are on the rise around the globe, reflecting subtle but enduring differences in local customs and cultures. Accordingly, global companies these days must, more than ever, be responsive to local conditions.

There is no better testament to the intensity with which Unilever pursues globalization than the international distribution of our research effort, which employs about 9,000 people. There are major centers for basic research in the United Kingdom and Holland, and this is natural in light of Unilever's dual nationality and unique dual CEO structure. Yet there are, in addition, major company research facilities in the United States, India, and, latterly, China. We have no fewer than 70 Innovation Centres operating in 20 countries, each one dedicated to product development on a regional basis. No company in the world has such roots in as many local soils.

Until the mid-1960s, the national management of every country where Unilever operated was fully responsible for all operations in that country. There were advisory product groups at the corporate center, but the local manager had the final word on how products were marketed and distributed. Our management has always been acutely aware of the arguments against a greater role for the center, which can be summarized as follows:

- Operating managers know their business better than the center.
- The center may tend to cushion individual businesses so that in time they become risk averse.
- The center's managers waste time and effort seeking mythical synergies between divisions.
- Technology and outsourcing render many of the center's support functions unnecessary.
- As the pace of change increases everywhere, central planning and control become even more ineffectual and are often a hindrance to speed and flexibility at the divisional level.

The Mythical Beast

While these points all had merit in a simpler time when markets were less globalized and competition less intense, the advantages of 100 percent decentralized autonomy have lately weakened. Corporate centers now have greater scope for adding value, thanks to the extraordinary advances of information technology (IT) and communications, the ease of travel, and the integration of national economies into regional groupings like the European Union, NAFTA, and MERCOSUR. These trends require a corporate center that engages in creative dialogue with the autonomous business units and stimulates them to cross traditional business boundaries, expand their conceptions of markets, share ideas and insights, and make new lateral connections. A corporate center can challenge, probe, and demand stretch. The centerless corporation is, or should be, a mythical beast.

Political scientists have long observed that centralized power can lead to bureaucratic procedures that ultimately stifle innovation. Accordingly, our corporate center sets out to be a catalyst, an enabler, providing tools and knowledge that influence local behaviors. The center should be lean but activist; it must have strong people with a light touch, and combine central direction with the stimulation of maximum operating freedoms. It must be self-disciplined, seldom compromising the autonomy of business units but intervening decisively if they move off plan, outside the strategic framework, or away from our business principles.

Unilever's multilocal multinationalism contains competing forces and, occasionally, contradictions. Generations of our managers have self-critically examined how we should be optimally organized so that the separate operating companies and the corporate center contribute maximum value to each other and to the business as a whole. In the mid 1990s, after much soul-searching about our performance, we opted for a radically fresh approach: a series of portfolio changes that reduced product diversification and made our business simpler and more coherent. In addition, we created a more focused organizational structure, better able to execute strategy on a global scale and, hence, better able to cope with change and intensifying competition. With this realignment we achieved a much clearer distinction between corporate strategic leadership (call it portfolio management, if you will) and operational execution. The bedrock of local independent businesses, plugged into their unique environments, remained unaltered. But their lateral interconnectedness or interdependence and their links to the center were strengthened.

No company can achieve significant global scale without an activist corporate center. Our 12 business groups develop regional strategies consistent with, and extending, the overall corporate strategy. The 12 groups retain full responsibility for the growth and profitability of their regions. Aside from commonsense aspects of unity such as common accounts, information systems, statutory functions, and shared services like bulk purchasing for business units, the key responsibility at the center is knowledge acquisition, sharing, and dissemination—from which we obtain the leverage implicit in our scale and scope.

A case in point: Eight years ago we took what was then seen as a highly controversial decision. We moved to open information systems and in a matter of months had over 60,000 PCs networked around the company. We did not spend time discussing the commercial justification. The center recognized that linkage and interactivity were just the technological facilitation that had been lacking. Hitherto, if the manager of a soap factory in Durban had a problem at five o'clock one evening, the best he could do would be to call the center and ask for advice. If his contacts at the center didn't have a solution to recommend, the problem might persist for months while information and advice filtered upward and then downward through the company. By contrast, today that manager logs onto the Unilever "soap network," inputs his problem, and the next morning there will be comments and suggestions from soap factory managers in Bombay, Jakarta, Liverpool, or São Paulo. Sounds eminently sensible—but it couldn't happen without a network, and a culture of trust rather than command and control.

The company's human chain of understanding and interactivity is of immense importance. On paper, Unilever's organization does not convey a great deal of information about how our business really works, which is often through a series of informal networks. Unilever people travel relentlessly and are transferred frequently. Most people in top management, myself included, have worked in a half dozen locations in the company. The result is that we are couriers of knowledge. While the role of the center is, in a sense, to be the gatherer and storehouse of knowledge, actual dissemination gets done mostly by managers moving from job to job and by formal and informal networks. We also encourage our people to visit each other in all corners of the world, often without approval of the center and with disregard for hierarchical niceties.

Knowledge Management in the Global Colossus

In the last two to three years we have put greater emphasis on trying to achieve more effective utilization of our single unique asset, our knowledge. Most large organizations probably manage to use only between 10 and 20 percent of the knowledge embedded in the company and its people. We're anxious to find ways to crank that number up to 50, 60, 70 percent and beyond—as a source of huge competitive advantage. Although this may sound arrogant, it remains true that we have more knowledge of consumers, and of practices that work in very diverse areas worldwide, than do our competitors or for that matter the typical global enterprise. The question is how to access this knowledge within the operating units and make it visible and available to everyone in Unilever—as we must, if we are to meet our growth goals. There is no aspect of our technical or business processes where Unilever does not have an exemplary best practice, somewhere. The trick is to capture this vast reservoir of knowledge and ensure that it is applied everywhere. The challenge is exciting, the payoff extraordinary.

Knowledge sharing has been stimulated by the recent creation of core teams for each of our 12 product categories. Core teams are charged with finding fresh ways to leverage international scale and scope. They ensure that our R&D and our big international brands (like Dove and Lipton) are managed from a global as well as a local perspective. Category core team members come from operations all over the world. Their goal is to blend and balance regional and global needs in the drive for sustained and winning innovation. They also play a key role in brand equity management—increasingly important as we cull peripheral brands and focus resources behind a much smaller stable of power brands.

Core teams are opportunity hunters. They spur the rapid global adoption of new products and processes that have met with great success in one region. In addition, they are catalysts of best practice adoption. One best practice currently being spread around the world is a program called Total Productive Maintenance (TPM), originally a Japanese concept. Under TPM, operators take personal responsibility for production line efficiency and quality. The results have been startling—soap production costs halved in Indonesia, rated capacity doubled in India, highly acclaimed and award-winning team practices in our British food factories.

Here is another concrete example of the leverage obtainable from knowledge sharing. After many decades of struggle and lackluster results, Hindustan Lever has been transformed into an outstanding growth engine. Recently it has doubled in size and profitability every four years and acquired a market value on the Bombay Stock Exchange of over $10 billion. It is acknowledged as one of the best-managed companies in Asia. Our managers there do not think of themselves as working for a subsidiary of a multinational, but as a powerful Indian company that feeds off a global network.

Over a decade ago, Hindustan Lever made a mistake. It failed to recognize an unsatisfied demand for affordable detergent products and instead concentrated on the high-end, middle-class market. Then a local company invaded the market with a low-cost alternative that earned instant success. Hindustan Lever promptly rethought the product, the price point, the marketing strategy, and the whole distribution system, and then introduced its own low-cost brand, Wheel, which won back market share and now outsells the high-end product. Hindustan Lever responded with speed and total determination to develop a complex new business system.

This is not only an Indian story. The eye-opening experience rippled throughout Unilever, upward and outward, and initiated a very different approach to meeting the needs of some of the poorest consumers, who constitute half the world's population and earn less than $200 a month. New products for this market segment have been launched in Brazil and in Africa. They are expected to move ahead rapidly. We will further shift our R&D focus to the vast numbers of our consumers who live in the developing and emerging markets of today, but who will in 2020 drive significant revenue and profit growth.

These days many gurus and policy wonks breathlessly talk about corporate globalization as if it were a great new wonder. The history of Unilever demonstrates that it is an old phenomenon. We've been struggling with, and benefiting from, globalization for several generations. What has changed is the style, tempo, and intensity with which we manage our federation of operating companies. We have moved from laissez-faire to a more activist and integrative approach that fuses strong central direction with maximum business-unit operating freedom. There is no doubt in my mind that this new approach will stimulate growth, employment, and shareholder returns over the coming decade. And after that? Well, the world will have changed again by then, and fresh challenges will spur Unilever to once again remake its organization.

Jacques A. Nasser
President and Chief Executive Officer, Ford Motor Company

Next Frontier of Globalization
Consumer Focus

Few manufacturing industries are more global than the automotive industry, and Ford Motor Company is arguably one of the most evolved global players. Over 30 percent of our sales are outside North America, and we have manufacturing facilities in 26 countries on six continents. Ford has sold cars in Argentina since 1913, in France since 1907, in Australia since 1904. Yet I think it significant that our evolution toward full-blown globalization is still in the early stages. True, we have made huge advances, with greatly improved synergies and teamwork across functions and geographies. The speed with which, in 1997, Ford brought new products to market in South America, India, and China showed our capacity for major simultaneous initiatives worldwide. The following year we demonstrated greater global prowess by launching the Ford Focus, global sales of which will very likely reach the magic threshold of a million units per year—previously achieved by only two company models, the Fiesta and the F-150 truck. Yet I emphasize: We are at the beginning stages of true globalization.

In all likelihood it will take a decade more to create a perfectly seamless global machine at Ford. The scope, scale, and complexities of the enterprise are daunting. One factor driving corporate globalization is, of course, the quest for revenue growth. If a company has a broad geographic footprint, then it can leverage innovations, products, marketing tactics, and all of its talents and creativity across a far bigger market than its domestic base. Another key factor powering globalization in automobiles is world overcapacity. Whether you take the position that overcapacity is chronic or simply a short-term phenomenon, it is putting pressure on prices and margins. It also generates pressure to rationalize production. This has spurred a number of large cross-border alliances, like Ford and Volvo, Daimler and Chrysler, Nissan and Renault, and other combinations will inevitably follow. Within a few years the number of large-scale global producers (those making 5 and 6 million vehicles a year) may well shrink to about half a dozen. A few niche producers in the 100,000-car range will remain.

Six Perspectives for Managing Our Business

In recent years, several automakers have worked toward better global integration of resources. Ford was first out of the box with its Ford 2000 initiative, begun in 1994, which was essentially a $150 billion internal merger of many individual Ford companies around the world. We consolidated international operations into a single, integrated company; simplified core engineering and production to achieve cost reductions; and designed new products around a reduced number of platforms. The tangible and intangible rewards of this effort have been massive—since 1997 we have reduced total costs by more than $5 billion, and for the past two years we have been the world's most profitable automaker. In almost every region of the world we have had significant new product launches in 1998. The cumulative cash earned from several years of record-breaking profits allowed us to purchase Volvo's passenger car business for $6.5 billion, and we still have $20 billion in cash reserves. And so far we have picked only the low fruit from the Ford 2000 tree, in the form of savings from the elimination of duplicate or overlapping facilities. There is much more, on the drawing boards, to be gained from better sharing of components, sharing of platforms, sharing of architectures and technologies, and obtaining the full benefits of global scale.

We take a portfolio approach to managing our global enterprise by looking at the performances of the global company, regions, business units, functions, product lines, and brands. Each cut provides texture that fosters a better understanding of the business (see Table 1.2).

Regional	Global	Functional
Product line	Brand	Business unit
	Consumer	

Table 1.2 Portfolio Approach

Depending on the context, management decides which of the six is the dominant dimension for any particular activity, without neglecting the other five. Take, for example, a business unit such as Jaguar. If I have a marketing problem or a question, I go to the CEO of Jaguar rather than to the marketing experts for the company's brands. The same is true for Hertz: It is an autonomous business unit. Both Jaguar and Hertz are, of course, powerful brands as well as business units, and some issues will be best approached from the brand perspective.

Within our organization, Lincoln has not been as distinct as Jaguar and Hertz as a business unit. I've given the head of Lincoln objectives for strengthening the line, initially from a brand perspective, and with that goes responsibility for revenue growth, profit and loss, market share, and image. In effect, we've created a virtual company and declared, "This is Lincoln—and here are the deliverables for Lincoln."

There is, of course, a distinction between a product and a brand. Mustang is a product line. When I looked at Mustang a few years back, it was losing money. I exploded. I said, "I can't believe this famous brand isn't profitable!"—and I said much more. Today Mustang is profitable because we focused on the product line. We created a different kind of virtual business than that at Lincoln. It even has an internal board of directors—really a cross-functional team dedicated to the product.

We also have the regional dimension. Too much happens too quickly on the ground to be the responsibility of the corporate center: government, taxes, dealers, unions, consumers. All demand a strong, regional, grassroots presence. What, then, does "global" mean at Ford? It means shared strategic focus and shared best practices.

Regarding best practices, we don't expect every business unit to develop best practices. Many best practices emerge somewhere in the functional dimension of our management matrix, and it is our responsibility at the global level to see that they are actually transferred and adopted as widely as need be. Recently, best practices were shared between Jaguar and our plant in Madras, India, which will build a version of the Fiesta. Four engineers and three technicians from India spent 18 months at Jaguar's paint shop to study Jaguar's paint systems and quality methods, which are among the best in the world. This knowledge was taken back to India and incorporated into production of the new Fiesta. This sort of cross-fertilization, which we have been striving for, would have been unthinkable at Ford only a few years ago.

The global dimension includes human resources. If you don't think globally about people, and instead let human resources development occur strictly within the perimeters of the business units or regional units, you end up with a disaster—I know from personal experience. I used to lead Ford Europe, equal to about 25 percent of the company, but I had never met many of the top managers in Detroit. That doesn't happen anymore. In order to build the best team in the industry, we have found ways to bond on a personal level—but globally.

I have described the six dimensions for the most part in isolation from one another, but the truth is that they operate simultaneously. None can be left out of our calculations. Historically, we were very good in the regional dimension and also in the functional dimension. The global dimension didn't exist until recently. We were a good deal weaker in the other dimensions of product line, brand strategy, and business unit. Because the global economy has now opened up, we are giving much more primacy to the business unit and product line, supported by the upper three dimensions in the diagram—regional, global, and functional. We've flipped the chart around to reflect our new practice. When I led Ford Europe a few years back, I would say to myself, When I get time, I must look at product line profits. But somehow that time never became available. This neglect of product line profits was exacerbated by a slow reporting system (since corrected) that made much of the information academic.

No Rules, Be Flexible

Since the landmark 1993 launch of the Mondeo world car, we have learned numerous lessons on the dos and don'ts of globalization. The more we learn, the clearer it becomes that there are no rules, no magic bullets, no one-size-fits-all templates. The key thing is flexibility and adaptability in the supply chain, design, assembly, and customer interface. Consider flexibility in design. Today we can often change the design to suit the needs of a particular geography and adjust the model without a tear-up of the manufacturing, which would have been necessary before. In this respect, common platforms are liberating. They have allowed us to bring to market niche products (i.e., those that sell under 100,000 units a year) which were impossible to justify financially just a few years ago. Many times we looked at reintroducing the Thunderbird, but the numbers were always wrong. Now we are bringing to market a new Thunderbird at an extremely low initial investment because we are using existing processes, facilities, and components. The result will be high value for the consumer, good returns for shareholders, and an exciting, unique product.

I don't wish to sound as if we have all the answers. Some of our approaches are experimental, and on many organizational and management issues we are open-minded. Consider our strategy in Asia. We haven't concentrated our efforts in any one country. We have tended to make what amount to strategic *starts* in several countries. We've tested different models, created joint ventures with local companies and global partners, developed component manufacturing, assembly plants, primary domestic production, and export production. We have sought a varied texture of options with good on-the-ground knowledge. An experienced local partner helps us set a strategy consistent with that country's economy in the longer term. We haven't set out to achieve one comprehensive solution for all of Asia.

The New Ford: Passionate Interaction with the Consumer

By now the reader will have the impression that globalization is a work in progress. Perhaps the greatest global challenge we face is generating a passionate interaction with the consumer. Historically, the big U.S. auto companies have operated by a production and engineering mentality. We grew up believing that the perfect situation is this: Design a wonderful product that people want. Make sure it is defect-free. Ship it to a dealer. The dealer quickly sells it to a customer, and you never hear from the customer again until it is time for another purchase. We were very much nuts-and-bolts and transaction oriented. Everything else was at the outside of the game.

The first part of this sequence remains valid today: We must create desirable products that are defect-free. But the customer-facing part of the sequence is antiquated. We now seek a long-term relationship with the consumer and the family, which means developing a two-way communication process—the more unfiltered, the better. To achieve and sustain that relationship and make it authentic, we must be open and sensitive in many ways we have not been in the past, from understanding actual product requirements to understanding people's aspirations for a cleaner environment.

I believe that Ford is on the threshold of discovering all the elements of the new relationships we seek with the world outside the company walls. We have to break up the logjams—old mind-sets, old ways of doing business. We must continually wrestle against a narrow, inward-facing view. That is one of the reasons we moved Lincoln Mercury from Detroit to trendsetting California. Lincoln Mercury is the first major domestic auto company ever to move its headquarters west of the Mississippi. There is symbolism here: We have left the old stomping grounds, we are physically present in a huge regional market that influences taste and fashion worldwide. Proximity to Hollywood, to great designers and leading-edge innovators in many fields, will be energizing for Lincoln—and it's worth noting that Lincoln was the leading luxury brand in the United States for the first time in 1998.

The companies that win in the twenty-first century will be those that look at the whole business from the customer's perspective. They will drive their businesses by customer preferences and go flat out to develop internal processes attuned to and connected with customers' wants. Introverted viewpoints will be dead ends. Great feats of engineering alone will not cut it. Traditional engineering/manufacturing/sales-dominated companies must mutate into more consumer-focused enterprises.

Our goal is to transform Ford from a solid automotive company to a superior performer as the world's leading *consumer company* for automotive products and services. The global automotive industry is in many respects just what it was in the past—a mass manufacturing business. But today's world is very different from the past in which that business model triumphed. The velocity of change is unprecedented. Thanks to the spread of technology and the advent of the global economy, the global consumer has emerged as the force rewriting the rules of business. It is not the banker, the manufacturer, or the retailer who is rewriting the rules. The global consumer is in charge. Consequently, excellence in manufacturing, engineering, quality, and productivity—important as they are—are not tomorrow's keys to competitive success.

At Ford we must look at ourselves as the consumer sees us. For example, we used to think about costs as *our* costs—supplier costs, manufacturing, warranty, and so on. We must now look at costs as the consumer sees them: repair, service, financing, insurance, residuals, recycling—along with initial purchase price. Understanding the consumer entails more than selling products and providing financing or irresistible value. It requires deep involvement in the consumer's total transportation experience: service, parts, accessories, insurance, and the rest. If you look at market share on that basis, then Ford's share, or the share of any of our rivals, is far smaller than we thought it was, based on traditional measures. The opportunities for growth and new businesses are huge. But so are the challenges. The reinvention of Ford into a consumer-focused company will place new stresses on our technology, our manufacturing efficiencies, our creativity, and our nimbleness.

Yet this strategy is essential if Ford is to fulfill its shareholder value enhancement objectives. Some years ago, shareholder value considerations were not high in the consciousness of many upper and middle managers. We have rectified this situation, in large measure through our Business Leadership Initiative, a program of mentoring and passing on teachable points of view throughout the organization. I have also begun a global weekly e-mail newsletter called *Let's Chat*, which goes to 145,000 people in the company. It is an ongoing, unfiltered dialogue between CEO and employees.

Now that shareholder value thinking is integral to the way we do business, we have turned the spotlight on achieving growth by consumer focus, by striving to delight the end user. What is a consumer company? It is an enterprise that is continually gathering unfiltered consumer insights worldwide. It is an enterprise that strives to:

- Connect with current and potential customers and anticipate their present and future needs.
- Translate consumer needs into a competitive advantage, using fast cycle time and generation of breakthrough products and services.
- Focus on building sustained relationships.

- Effectively manage a portfolio of brands.
- Continually grow shareholder value.

Consider the shareholder valuations of companies with a consumer focus. The median price-to-earnings (P/E) ratio for the Standard & Poor's 500 in late 1998 was about 27, versus 11 for Ford. At our 1998 earnings per share and our present stock price ($55), our price-to-earnings ratio is about 11 and our market capitalization is about $66 billion. If we improve our multiple to 20 (the average for Dow Jones Industrials), our stock price would improve to over $100 a share and our market value would be about $120 billion. With a multiple of 30 (the recent average for S&P 500 companies), our stock price would be $150, with a market value of $180 billion. Since 20 percent of the company's stock is owned by employees, improving our P/E multiple from 11 to that of the average S&P 500 company would mean more than $20 billion to share with our employees and their families. Now that is something to strive for!

Although it is early days, some people outside the company recognize that we have the potential to change our spots. John Casesa, an analyst for Merrill Lynch, has written that a "revolutionary development would be Ford's successful transformation to a genuine consumer-oriented marketing company. . . . This ambition is so grand as to hardly be credible. Nonetheless, Ford is serious about this strategy, and if successfully executed, it could meaningfully improve the company's growth, returns, and consistency of results. Such success would radically change the market's perceptions of Ford and would drive its multiple above the upper limits of the 1980s and 1990s."

Acquiring a Customer Headset

This is the fundamental correlation: Consumer focus = less cyclical risk = growth = higher stock multiple. Unfortunately, our industry has heretofore lacked a good grasp of consumer differences around the world. We need to understand the real differences, the ones that matter at both a rational and an emotional level, and respond to them in the product development process.

Did you get that? Or did it run by too quickly—"emotional"? What we are striving for at Ford is a *deeply felt* perception among Ford managers of customer identities, characteristics, and needs. I want all

Our Research Shows That Top Consumer Companies Share 10 Major Characteristics:

1. *Total customer experience.* Leading consumer companies do not focus just on the product or service but on every point of contact with the consumer. Disney, for example, focuses acutely on both current and future products and services to ensure that each reinforces the Disney magic. Unfiltered customer insight is a key to Disney's success. Our own business unit, Hertz, has a visceral understanding of the needs of the time-starved business traveler and has translated that understanding into the Hertz #1 Club Gold Card and the facilities and services that go with it.

2. *Product "hits."* Or the successful launch of new products that people love but perhaps didn't know they wanted. The focus is on consumers' lifestyles and anticipating their future needs. At Ford, our Truck Vehicle Center (VC) has developed a culture that applies candid feedback received from clinics, focus groups, and other research. The Truck VC focuses on getting to know target customers and then does what it takes to satisfy them. Recent winners are the Expedition and Navigator, which, respectively, redefined one segment and created a new one almost overnight.

3. *Customer loyalty.* Or creating intense, sustained relationships over time. Often, loyalty is built by offering a choice of rewards, which invite the customer to make a personal selection. American Express uses this technique, learns from customer choices, and applies that information to develop future rewards. While other credit cards invest to take customers away from their competitors, American Express invests to build relationships with its present customers.

4. *Retailing and distribution.* The retailer and the consumer company work together to bring mutual benefit to one another. Procter & Gamble, the leading packaged goods firm, and Wal-Mart, the largest retailer, share information to help each other with logistics, category management, and promotions.

5. *Brand process.* Coca-Cola has a process to take mature brands and grow them further. Consistency is achieved through the brand name, advertising, packaging, and even the promotions conducted with bottlers. The process is replicated in new markets and segments. Our Jaguar business

unit has a brand process, characterized by consistent nomenclature, advertising, brochures, and marketing, which has differentiated Jaguar from other brands in Ford's portfolio.

6. *Logistics.* Or creating efficiencies in procurement and distribution to yield the lowest total cost to consumers. FedEx customers may book and monitor cargo to suit their needs. The customer is given more control and logistics are simplified.

7. *Build to demand.* Despite rapid growth, Dell maintains short lead times by marketing to consumers directly and allowing them to configure their own systems. Dell is able to make suggestions via Internet or telephone, and is able to tweak these suggestions on the basis of product availability. Lead times are reduced through communications with suppliers, who are able to keep their inventories in Dell facilities.

8. *Customer knowledge system.* Soliciting, retaining, and drawing insights from the customer base. FedEx surveys its customers several times annually, and the information is shared with its entire organization, not just marketing. The findings are used to improve customer service, promote cross selling, and build competitive advantage.

9. *E-commerce.* Or interacting, distributing, and selling directly online. Microsoft has produced many profitable online subbusinesses. Working with other companies, it has been able to leverage its Microsoft Network to tap into new businesses and create chat rooms to interact directly with customers.

10. *Growth.* 3M reports that 30 percent of its sales are from products developed in the past four years, and two of every three products create all-new categories. 3M boasts a culture of creativity, where 15 percent of every employee's time is dedicated to developing new ideas. Ford's Truck Vehicle Center follows a similar strategy: Dominate by executing new ideas (Expedition and Navigator), and integrate new ideas with existing successes.

Ford people to have a consumer headset (as distinct from mind-set), by which I mean very deep insights into how customers experience our products and services, and how we connect to customers at both the practical and the emotional levels. Ideally, every Ford employee should understand the power of the experience in a company product or service and be able to translate that knowledge back into decision making. We must learn and feel and touch—as individuals. I don't advocate spending more money on conventional market research, far less setting up a consumer affairs functional specialty.

Ford people need to have a visceral understanding of where customers' expectations and aspirations are moving. Market research provides input, to be sure, but in the final analysis we have to listen, taste, and touch, and from these experiences intuitively grow a customer headset. It isn't easy. Many within the company aren't there yet. They need to learn, need to spend more time on the road talking with customers and dealers. We are also inviting more customers to come in and talk to us about their vehicles, their problems, their sales and service experience. Recently I visited aftermarket personalization shops in California, where they "trick up" vehicles. I needed to see what people ask for beyond what they're getting, to understand how these vehicle owners express themselves. There is a communication about feelings, values, and preferences behind all these add-on features, which go unprovided by the traditional manufacturers.

We have developed new techniques for listening to customers and observing their behaviors, including the use of visual simulations that help them tell us what they feel various brands should look like. We are looking at ways of improving distribution, working with our dealers to improve their customer interface (even investing directly in some to create next-generation dealerships), and exploring new distribution channels, not least the Internet.

Transformation in High Gear

The transformation of Ford is in high gear. We must succeed within a few years, not in a decade. Consumers are demanding better value, more choice, and faster product turnaround. They scorn "me too" products and seek more differentiation between manufacturers, and more innovative and distinctive products in the traditional midsize segments. They want a meaningful correlation between the symbolism of brands and product design and characteristics. They want good value over the life of the vehicle. In all these areas we hope to establish a leading edge. This is what our search for a passionate connection to consumers is all about: to give them such value and delight that Ford Motor Company will earn exceptional shareholder rewards.

Sir John Bond
Group Chairman, HSBC Holdings

Banking Is 90 Percent Action, 10 Percent Strategy

If globalization is so ubiquitous, why is it spelled differently depending on where you come from? We hear so much about it that I'm sure many people have come to think that every significant company in every major industry is hell-bent on foreign expansion. That is just not the case.

Many businesses are international; almost none span the entire globe. With more than 220 countries on our planet, and very few businesses with a presence in more than a handful, the word *globalization* may be a misnomer. HSBC may be one of those few. HSBC Bank International Limited, our telephone banking service for expatriates, serves customers in over 190 countries. That compares to 185 countries belonging to the United Nations.

Globalization is a convenient, if ugly, shorthand for a series of complex interacting factors. One commentator recently defined globalization as the integration of finance, markets, nation-states, and technologies to a degree never witnessed before—in a way that is enabling individuals, corporations, and nation-states to reach further, faster, deeper, and cheaper than ever before.

Globalization means different things at different times to different people. To a banker the emphasis may be on the international movement of capital; for an educator it may be about long-distance learning through new delivery channels; for governments it may be about challenges to national sovereignty. The one thing almost every commentator does agree on is that globalization is here to stay. Whatever globalization consists of, we can expect more of it.

The conventional wisdom about the internationalization of financial services ignores the fact that for many years banks have backed away from foreign ventures, the latest large-scale retreat having occurred in Southeast Asia. Historically, many of the investments made by British, Continental, and Japanese banks to penetrate the

highly competitive U.S. market, for example, have ended up in igno-
minious retreat. The reason for these misadventures (often destroyers
of shareholder value) has nearly always been the same: a failure of the
entrants to a national or regional market to achieve a viable domestic
base of business within a reasonable time. They didn't appreciate the
exacting risk/reward ratios of their geographic extensions of domain.

HSBC is very aware of these risks. Our group has endured as an
international entity for over 130 years, while increasing shareholder
value more than 20 percent annually, compounded over the last 30
years.

From birth, HSBC was international. It was founded in 1865 in
Hong Kong, then a backwater far from the orbit of world money centers, by Scots, along with Parsees, Norwegians, Germans, and Americans on its board. Its initial territorial expansion followed trade
routes to the north, south, and west. In the course of our history, we
have survived some pretty turbulent times. However, we have
endured to create a network of more than 5,000 offices in 79 countries and territories.

This background, which has shaped our character, is very different from that of most other major banks on the world scene, such as
Citigroup or Deutsche Bank. Much more typical of international
banks is that they have sallied forth in the last few decades from very
powerful domestic bases.

A Strong Balance Sheet, an Eye for Opportunity

One key to our success has been something not today as fashionable
as it once was, and that is a strong balance sheet. In discussions on
globalization, rarely does one hear people speak of the importance of
a conservative financial position. Yet because we were founded on
Scottish banking principles and because of our history, we have been
unswerving in this regard and today operate with considerably less
leverage than most of our major competitors. We lend about 50 percent of one of the most conservative balance sheets in our industry,
while some of our rivals lend as much as 75 percent of theirs.

Without a conservative balance sheet, a bank cannot long endure
the choppy seas of the world's financial oceans. Viewed in long-term
perspective, international finance has grown enormously, despite
occasional cyclical declines in regional or banking markets that can

temporarily affect the market capitalization of high-quality institutions. This is when we step in and make strategic acquisitions, preferably without paying premium prices.

Because we have an eye for opportunity when turbulence provides it, we have prospered at a time when others are weak or struggling. At such times, our financial conservatism attracts deposits away from less sound institutions, and we look for acquisition opportunities. When the market is buffeting our competitors, then is the time to be bold. In 1965 we bought Hang Seng Bank in Hong Kong when it was experiencing a difficult period; similarly, Marine Midland in the United States in 1980 and the Midland Bank in 1992 when they were facing problems. In 1997 we purchased Banco Bamerindus in Brazil, one of the largest commercial banks in the country, again at a time when it was experiencing serious difficulties.

Our acquisitions were not merely opportunistic. In each case our decision was based on the belief that here was a good consumer franchise that we could nurture. Where there is a sound fit with our business, we are not afraid to look at good banks.

We use our selective acquisition strategy to grow because of the significant costs of building franchises de novo. It would be impossible today to re-create the client-based branch infrastructure of a Midland Bank: The effort would run out of money many years before a profit was in sight.

We constantly screen acquisition possibilities. Our strategic proclivities are well known to the investment banks, yet they frequently try to interest us in acquisitions where we simply fail to see value. We have been besieged with propositions to buy this or that bank in the United States or in Europe, typically at large multiples. If we did buy these offerings, it would be a ridiculously expensive way to acquire share in overbanked markets, where the only way to expand the client base is at the expense of a competitor.

Contrast this with the situation in an emerging market, such as Brazil, where it is possible to buy a franchise at below net asset value. This in a country where only about a quarter of the population has a bank account, so the prospects for organic growth are excellent. There is also very favorable pricing there: Middle-class Brazilians are pleased to have a bank account and pay $10 a month for one. There is no way you could get someone in the United Kingdom or the United States to pay that.

One of the prime advantages of our international reach and scope is that the economic impact of our strategies has a ripple effect around the globe. For example, major new product development efforts can readily be migrated across borders and their costs amortized over a larger base than most of our competitors command. What's more, there is a benefit to operating in countries with varying stages of maturity in banking services. Know-how developed in one place can be exported to another. First Direct, our pioneering U.K. telephone banking operation, contributed significantly to later HSBC telephone banking initiatives in the United States and Asia.

If franchise creation in banking is difficult, so too is product innovation. Ours is a very transparent industry with a high degree of homogeneity. If you design a brand new banking product that's a roaring success, you might gain a lead time of six months before somebody copies it. If you come up with an internal process innovation—do something with imaging technology, say—the lead might be as long as 18 months before someone on your staff quits, goes to another bank, and introduces the innovation there. The lasting competitive strength in financial services is having a performance- and action-oriented corporate character, or culture, as some like to call it.

Our financial results have justified our strategy. We are one of the largest financial services organizations in the world and one of the most geographically diversified—a constant source of strength. In 1998, for instance, HSBC suffered the consequences of the Asian financial crisis, which required the largest provisions in our history. Yet in spite of these adverse conditions, we managed to produce a return on shareholders' funds of 15.5 percent and pay a dividend up 11 percent from 1997. In our view, this vindicates our strategy of geographic diversification, and the consequent diversity of risk.

90 Percent Action, 10 Percent Strategy

Banking is not rocket science. The underlying principles of success are simple. They are (1) focus on clients, (2) good credit quality (so that your loan loss experience is better than the competitors'), and (3) tight control over expenses. Banking is about doing: It is 90 percent action and 10 percent strategy. Tried-and-true teamwork is essential to running an international business, which, by definition, has more complexity than a domestic one. That is the key to competitive advantage. One of our outstanding characteristics is good teamwork and coordination. We have tremendous talent but, deliberately, very few management stars on the payroll.

Half of our profit is made while I sleep. So I had better know that there are people on the other side of the world who are doing things the HSBC way. If we are to provide our shareholders with something more than a portfolio of banks, there cannot be a loose federation or a do-as-you-please holding company philosophy. We are constantly working to extract cross-border benefit, thereby making the whole worth more than the sum of its parts.

One keystone of our teamwork is that we try to give people lifetime careers, which, I recognize, may be a little old-fashioned these days. But we've found no better basis for team building. As quid pro quo for job security, we pay our middle and senior executives sensibly but not excessively, meanwhile offering them a climate of fair reward, a progressive and varied career, and a good pension. Little wonder that there is a canard that HSBC stands for "Home of Scottish Bank Clerks." Jokes aside, the key to good teamwork is a stable and predictable work environment. We are not, however, reluctant to reach for new blood and recruit on the outside.

Expense Discipline: A Matter of Culture

To succeed in the international arena, a company must have competitive fitness across all business functions. We are fanatics about expense discipline: Not only is it good for shareholders, but it permits us to tolerate price wars wherever they might flare up. I'm not bashful about telling people that I know exactly the amount of the electric bill for our headquarters building. When I leave my office, however briefly, I turn off the lights. Since the onset of the Asian financial crisis we have twice tightened the rules for first-class eligibility on our executives' flights abroad. In New York our people don't stay at five-star hotels, they go to middle-of-the-range ones in downtown Manhattan.

So ingrained is this character trait that we make heroes of people who think up expense reduction ideas. The bottom-line benefits are considerable. A U.K. competitor, which is both smaller and predominantly domestic, spends twice as much on travel and entertainment as we do, even though we are operating on every continent. Our total operating cost as a ratio of revenues is probably the lowest of any large international bank. Accordingly, we are prepared for the huge productivity war brewing in banking. Every advance in information and communications technology and in financial deregulation puts pressure on our revenues by reducing customers' float. Ultimately, success will belong to the lowest-cost producer.

We have obtained fantastic productivity from our homegrown information technology (IT) system. Unlike many banks, we do not buy core IT systems from external providers and we outsource as little as possible. We preserve our systems independence because we believe that it attracts the best people into our IT area—those who like pioneering and original work, not the frustrating game of tying together acquired software packages.

As an international bank we have the ability to exploit the comparative advantage of different locations for IT development. We operate four software and systems development centers: in Vancouver, Buffalo, Sheffield, and Hong Kong. Because of our overall control of IT architectures and applications, there is unusual uniformity of systems throughout the bank; the same screens are available everywhere in the world that we operate a terminal (excepting recent acquisitions, which still have some of their legacy systems).

Rebranding on a Global Basis

A bank so steeped in history stands in some danger of being a little complacent. But we're not backward-looking. When the situation calls for it, we deviate from past patterns and can be creative in our strategies and tactics. A case in point is the global rebranding exercise launched in late 1998 and executed throughout 1999. All our wholly owned commercial banking subsidiaries now carry the HSBC name along with our red and white hexagon logo.

Why the change? A consistent acquirer inevitably ends up with a tapestry of regional and national brands of varying effectiveness. A few years back we operated under about 300 different names scattered around the globe. Recent structural changes in the banking market made us question the multilocal approach to branding. Merely local brands no longer have the old magic, especially in developed economies.

Symbols and artifacts with a pan-global cachet have become very powerful, from foodstuffs to high-fashion wear. When we analyzed the chief drivers of value within our franchises, it turned out that a very large part of our retail profits is generated by a comparatively small segment of customers. To paraphrase Pareto's law, 20 percent of our customers yielded some 80 percent of the bottom line. Moreover, that 20 percent contained customers who are now highly international and geographically mobile.

Our bank managers in the developed world repeatedly found customers returning from foreign journeys complaining that we didn't have local service when actually we did, albeit disguised by another name. The opportunity to satisfy that customer, and to cement loyalty, was being lost. Among institutional customers in trade finance and wholesale and investment banking, there was a similar story: When making customer contacts, these people wasted time explaining to clients the details of our global network and its complex of names.

People get attached to names and symbols. Midland Bank was a fixture on thousands of U.K. High Streets; the same was true for Marine Midland in the upstate region of New York state. But venerability and/or familiarity should not be confused with brand strength. Our research in the United Kingdom showed that First Direct, our telephone bank, actually had a stronger brand than its Midland parent. First Direct is 10 years old and Midland's name goes back to 1836. This is worth pondering: In less than a decade we created a brand with greater perceived value than a name that has been around for 150 years. The message is clear: Customers are discerning about the sources of value. They think pragmatically. "What have you done for me lately" is critical.

It is our aim that the HSBC brand express differentiation in the depth and quality of our services. In tune with our character, this branding exercise is being done on a very low cost basis. As the *Economist* dryly reported, "HSBC has eschewed the services of expensive image consultants. It is spending a mere $50 million, and whatever it can filch from local banks' marketing budgets, on launching its new name—barely enough for new notepaper—to alert 30 million customers to the change." (The $50 million excludes advertising.)

Global branding is in its infancy in the commercial banking field. Ten and twenty years hence it will be as common as in automobiles today. The institutions boasting dominant brands then will be those that caught the brand-making wave early and that offer the four Ss—service, scale, scope, and synergy. Although the day is a long way off, I think that the leading brands will be able to charge slightly higher prices because of their power to represent value to the customer.

To sum up, the foundations of our success at HSBC are a strong balance sheet, good expense control, a team culture, and the beginnings of a great global brand. We are aware of the perils and opportunities of operating internationally. Globalization is perhaps the last great frontier for business—but frontier life, remember, is exacting and exciting.

Bertrand P. Collomb

Chairman and Chief Executive Officer, Lafarge Group

Organizing and Managing for Global Success

There are clearly many forces involved in the creation of multinational companies and the environment in which they thrive, the global marketplace. Trade, capital, and technology flows today are all at unprecedented high levels. In the background, many unlikely corporations are forming themselves into global entities and, as they do so, changing the economics of previously indigenous activities.

Lafarge is one of the leading diversified global construction materials companies. Its business mix includes cement (35 percent of total sales), concrete and aggregates (32 percent), gypsum products (7 percent), specialty products (11 percent), and roofing products (15 percent). The Lafarge construction markets are local, and that gives the global business its complexity but also its great opportunities for innovation.

If you go back 20 years, the cement and building materials industry seemed rooted forever in the local soil. I mean that literally, since production is dependent on local mined inputs and the finished products are of such weight and low unit value that they cannot—like computers, autos, and pharmaceuticals, for example—be shipped far and wide. Nor can they be given the attributes of a global brand. If there ever was an industry that seemed entrenched in the hands of local capital, this, surely, was it.

Yet today a growing, albeit still small, portion of the output of this multilocal industry is produced by a handful of global producers—one of which is our own firm, Lafarge. And there continue to be many cross-border acquisitions in any one year, some of them running to big numbers. How did this transformation come about, and what is the economic logic behind it? The answers to this question, I think, tell us a great deal about what is, in effect, the most consistent shaper of globalization. Trade and capital flows surge and ebb across the globe, but the inner logic of globalization, as I've experienced it, is steady and constant, vibrant in good times and bad.

I think it has taught us some subtle points on how to organize and manage a global company.

Acquisition and Integration Know-How

In essence, a corporation is a body of know-how and a culture. In my industry there has been an enormous increase in the depth and range of that know-how in the past decade. And it is increasingly finding new fields to conquer—some of these (and this is significant) in the already industrialized parts of the world. A few years ago, Lafarge bought a cement plant in Alpina, Michigan, operated by a local outfit that had other assets we liked. Now Michigan is not an underdeveloped country, so you might expect that most of its units of production of almost anything manufactured would be at or near world standard. Not so. The plant was so bad that we initially offered them one dollar for an option to buy it. Management decided to close the plant, and for the next three to four months we weren't sure whether it was worth that dollar. Finally we did buy it and brought in a new team of managers from our own ranks. With practically no new investment, they lowered production costs by 25 percent. Then, with an outlay of about a third of what a new cement plant would cost, we dropped costs of production by another 25 percent.

These benefits sprang from the core of Lafarge: a grasp of optimal forms of organization and how to disseminate them. This particular plant had previously been operated along traditional shop-by-shop lines, in which work is highly compartmentalized. In this case, a man in the grinding shop had never seen the kiln because it was in another building. We changed all that—by orchestrating a lot of little things for which there is no patent, but which cumulatively decide who wins and who loses.

"Low-tech" industries such as cement illustrate some of the purest forms of competition between companies. No player has a big edge from process technology, or from sources of capital or labor. Anyone with a checkbook can call up any one of three or four global suppliers of cement plants, who will deliver a turnkey, state-of-the-art unit in just a few years. Differences in margins and rates of return between companies are largely the outcome of management skills and organization.

Lafarge's confidence in these skills has been rising in recent years and finding expression in an aggressive acquisition strategy and an always improving know-how concerning how to integrate and get the best out of a merger. But it was not always so. Many years ago, Lafarge of Canada became the largest shareholder in the much larger Canada Cement. On paper it was a great transaction, but implementation was complicated because local management felt that there were specifically Canadian circumstances that justified unique procedures. It took some time to apply our know-how to fully integrate the acquisition.

This pattern of strong local autonomy led to relatively slow integration. Another big acquisition followed in the United States, where we bought General Portland. Investigation showed that managers of these facilities had expected the acquirer to demonstrate strategic intent and apply some of its systems and methods. When these were not forthcoming, local managers concluded that the people at headquarters didn't know anything more about the cement business than they did, and they went on their merry way. Subsequently, when Paris wanted to intervene, guess what: They resisted.

At this point it became clear that there is a short window of opportunity in every acquisition, and that if we were to be a really effective global company we had to exploit it: We had to calm the anxiety and insecurity in the management of the acquired company and reassure them with our decisiveness.

Our global organization is now designed to exchange valuable knowledge and act quickly. We have developed a 50-page manual, which spells out what we do in the first and second phases of an acquisition, and we have used it to integrate recent acquisitions in the United Kingdom, Poland, the Philippines, and Jordan. It is not a book of rules that amount to headquarters cracking the whip. It is an open-ended framework that allows for adaptation to local situations. In 1998, we acquired the U.K.-based Redland PLC, which had extensive global assets totaling almost $4 billion—and the integration took roughly six months.

Integration of merged entities is a critical skill in today's environment. Without it a company is likely to stagnate. It is also very difficult to do well, as can be seen by the many academic studies of poor merger and acquisition outcomes, the majority of which end up in failure. And this, of course, means that those who beat the odds are likely to forge ahead and achieve dominant industry positions. Taking an existing plant situated in a market context, operated by people who may not be ideal, then raising that plant to high standards is a very specific skill, which requires subtle and complex responses. There are no ready-made solutions. We have put our method in the pages of a manual, but solutions based on it are still custom-made. The acquirer gains a kiln with particular characteristics, and a mill that has other characteristics, and raw material sources that will differ in quality and kind from others. All this has to be integrated into a solution with minimum investment and maximum value creation. This is know-how we at Lafarge have clearly developed, and it is one of the main engines of our growth, targeted conservatively at doubling revenues in 10 years.

Authentic Multiculturalism

Another powerful tool is the authentic multiculturalism that we practice. Many companies are global in outlook up to the point where the forces of globalization make personal demands on top managers— when they have to acquire fluency in a foreign language, when they have to get inside a national culture and not just be a bystander. Circumstances forced Lafarge into a rapid evolution of multicultural attitudes. Having achieved a rich 35 percent market share in France in the 1960s, the company sought growth abroad. By the mid-1970s it had achieved 40 percent of sales outside France and the die was cast; we were international. Henceforth, our growing ability to accommodate all kinds of corporate and national cultures, as we make acquisitions around the world, began to be a powerful differentiator against more parochial institutions.

By law, our board meetings must be conducted in French, but our international advisory board uses English. Our executive committee meetings are in English *and* French—recently, nearly always in English because there is a new member whose French is rusty. Of the eight executive vice presidents, four are not French. That is only the tip of the iceberg of a pervasive multicultural outlook that is part of our culture, and which we portage to every location where we operate. An acquirer of a company in a foreign country has the option of accepting the extant local corporate culture or, alternatively, of overlaying a transcending corporate culture. We've gone the latter route and place very strong emphasis on respect for the individual and social cohesion. Our people don't work simply because there is a contract, but for something larger.

The factor of social cohesion does not usually feature in management consultants' or security analysts' estimates of competitive ability. But I believe it does influence economic outcomes over the long term. I recently attended a "town hall" meeting at a facility we had recently taken over in China. One of the foremen stood up and volunteered a comment—a pretty unusual act in itself. The comment could be paraphrased as follows: Since Lafarge took over we work harder than before, but we have more clarity about why and what the fruits of our effort are, and we like that.

A Mature Industry—Yet Subject to Unpredictable Scenarios

I believe that a humanistic base will become increasingly important in coming decades. Even an industry as mature as ours, whose main product is over a 100 years old, faces the possibility of serious discontinuities. Aside from the continuing consolidation of the industry, there is a high probability of unpredictable scenarios, of players tangential or adjacent to our industry perhaps coming at it from unexpected angles—although whether this is a likely threat, or even what form it might take, is not at all clear.

Even in such a mature business we cannot claim to know everything about the factors of competitive success in the years ahead. For instance, there is no guarantee that the relatively low rate of technological change will persist. This is why we are investing in research with a view to finding new ways of manufacturing and new products. There are two aspects to this effort: first, better measurement tools that analyze and control the messy process of mixing raw materials that, because they are mined, are never exactly the same. This used to be done empirically, but with better sensing instruments and computers, we are able to do this much more efficaciously. Second, we are looking at new materials and mixes of materials that include chemical additives. We have, for instance, a joint research project with Rhône-Poulenc and Bouygues that could yield a material with more flexion resistance than steel. This would be a tremendous breakthrough. But even if the material comes up to our expectations, there will then be the formidable problems of getting it accepted and widely used. Innovations in building materials do not race across the world like a new motherboard, or a new ethical drug discovery, or even a hot concept like sports utility vehicles. Construction practices and regulations differ widely from country to country, and in most countries there is built-in resistance to change.

On the other hand, our variety of complex local markets, with differing physical and regulatory conditions, forces innovation and creative solutions. In an important way, this gives a large global player like Lafarge an additional competitive advantage. Only a globally organized and managed corporation has the clout and the economic staying power to significantly spur the adoption of innovation. And this alone, without even considering many other factors, creates value and justifies its continuing existence.

CHAPTER 2

Growth

Reinvention Is the Key

In recent years, business managers have focused more on efficiency than on growth. Many CEOs of the 1980s and early 1990s strove to improve operating and asset efficiencies, to great and good effect. But we believe that the rules of the game are now changing. Reengineering processes in order to meet customer needs is no longer enough. Product innovation is essential but insufficient in itself. As efficiency becomes the basis for survival but not necessarily for prosperity, the future will confer its greatest rewards on growth and on those who reinvent the business itself—the model, its scope, its competencies.

Our work with clients and analysis of markets suggest that growth energizes those firms and management groups that create outstanding shareholder value. The top shareholder performers in the past decade delivered double-digit revenue growth rates. They were not pledged to growth at any cost, to growth without consideration of asset intensity, and certainly not to growth through acquisitions that pumped revenue without creating value. However, there were shining examples of growth through new products and services, through new strategic models, new supporting tactics, new technologies, and new organizational architectures, all of which created value for customers and led to both higher revenue and margins.

To prepare this chapter, we have examined the growth records of the value creation leaders, researched their approaches, and in three cases interviewed their chief executives. What follows then is based both on fact and on dialogue with some of the principal architects of successful corporate growth. It also offers views we have reached about the winning growth firms of the future.

The Importance of Growth

To understand the importance of growth, we examined its impact on shareholder value. We started with the value creation record of Fortune 500 companies over the 10-year period from 1987 to 1997. Only 168 companies on the earlier list were still around a decade later. We divided the 168 firms into four quartiles based on their total shareholder return (TSR) rankings. The results, shown in Table 2.1, strongly support the importance of double-digit top-line growth to value creation. The top quartile grew shareholder return over 25 percent per year, behind revenue increases of 10.1 percent. The bottom quartile grew shareholder return 5.7 percent annually, with revenue increases of 6 percent a year. The strong correlation ($r^2 = 0.92$) across the quartiles suggests that shareholder value is indeed strongly driven by revenue growth.

	Quartile 1	Quartile 2	Quartile 3	Quartile 4	Total
Average revenue CAGR	10.1%	8.6%	6.2%	6.0%	7.7%
Average annualized TSR	25.6%	18.3%	14.3%	5.7%	16.0%

CAGR = compound annual growth rate

Table 2.1 Double-Digit Revenue Growth Drives Top-Quartile Shareholder Return

Interestingly, when we eliminate the averaging effect of the quartiles and plot revenue growth against shareholder return growth for each individual firm, the correlation coefficient drops to 0.36 (Figure 2.1). What does this mean? On *average*, revenue growth is strongly correlated to value growth, but individual firms can grow without creating value. In fact we found some that grew revenue and destroyed shareholder value. Clearly, growth can enhance value but does not inevitably do so. Assessing and managing the costs of creating that growth are as important as creating it.

Our analysis led us to conclude that top-line growth is a significant and sustainable engine of shareholder returns. Double-digit revenue growth rates in particular are associated with strong value creation. Strong revenue growth stems from innovative product and service offerings that create distinctive value for customers and allow companies to capture higher margins as well as higher growth. These offerings in turn require innovative business systems. Growth is not, however, a stand-alone objective. Firms must seek to penetrate and manage the costs of growth.

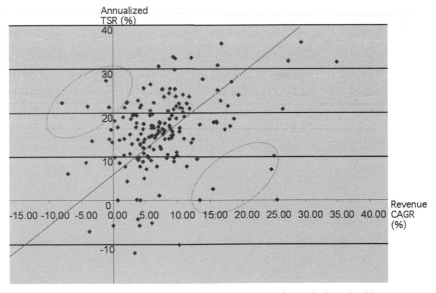

Figure 2.1 Correlation between revenue growth and shareholder return for individual firms.

Effective Approaches to Growth

Innovate Products to Drive Differentiation and Margins

High-growth firms commit to product innovation to create competitive differentiation and sustain margins. Chief Executive Alfred M. Zeien has predicted that 50 percent of Gillette's sales will soon come from products introduced within the past five years, up from 41 percent in 1996 and twice the level of innovation at the average consumer products company. By putting its power behind the most innovative products, Gillette has also been able to enhance margins by justifying high prices to its customers. Gillette is counting on the recently introduced Oral-B Cross Action toothbrush, priced at $4.99, almost a 50 percent premium to the usual price of $2.50. Even more interesting is that Gillette tested the product at a price of $3.99 and found little difference in potential. Consumers were willing to pay for the innovation.

In the pharmaceutical industry, incumbent firms need to invest in innovative drugs just to survive. The expiration of patents on a few key drugs, which generate billions of dollars in revenue, can seriously damage business because generic substitutes erode sales rapidly. Between 2000 and 2005, Merck, the pharmaceutical giant, will see patents expire on a handful of key drugs that represent $5 billion in U.S. sales.

Sweat the Pricing

Obsessed with units and volume, firms too often ignore the potential of price customization to drive revenue and value. American Airlines did not. It changed the rules of the airline industry by using value pricing for revenue growth. Through sophisticated yield-management modeling and enabling software, AA tracked ticket demand right up to takeoff and determined how much it should charge travelers at any point in the booking cycle, based on projected demand for the remaining seats. American Airlines estimates that its yield-management system boosts annual revenue by as much as $200 million (*The Wall Street Journal,* November 3, 1997, A1). The industry has followed, but the advantage was real for several years.

Change the Rules, Then Do It Again

Most software firms now give away their product free, to establish standards and reap "network effects." Scott McNeally and Vinod Khosla of Sun Microsystems were pioneer practitioners in 1982. Sun keenly needed to win a bid to become the in-house technology provider for Computervision. Even though it was sure that it possessed the best knowledge concerning how to deliver the right technology for Computervision, Sun lost the assignment. Khosla couldn't take no for an answer. He changed the rules of the game and made his company the industry standard by offering his technology for free.

Now Red Hat is changing the rules again, by *charging* for previously free software. Red Hat has decided to package the Linux operating software system, which is available free on the Internet, and offer Linux support services for a fee of $50. Now that there is a price on the market for Red Hat's broker services, consumers are forced to place values on their time and on their need for a functioning Internet system. The days of doubt about consumers' willingness to pay for Internet services are fading. While Red Hat's success is undetermined, competitors like Microsoft, IBM, and Oracle are taking notice, and Intel has decided to invest.

Experiment with Customer Segments

Many firms fuel their growth in a competitive marketplace by redefining their markets and applying customer segmentation. Companies that can identify untapped growth and profit potential in new customer segments and quickly reconfigure their business systems are able to realize the potential growth.

The automotive business had long been an underperformer at AlliedSignal, and Wall Street analysts were surprised that the company's no-nonsense CEO Larry Bossidy kept it for more than two years, in light of his GE-like mantra that each division must either generate an 11 percent return or be divested. What did Bossidy have in mind? He knew that the key to turning around this division was to move the business from being an original equipment manufacturer (OEM) supplier to the penny-pinching automobile manufacturers to being a vendor of replacement parts, a business in which the margin is double that of the OEM sector. The auto parts group is currently 65 percent aftermarket, and Bossidy wants to see that percentage grow to 80 percent by the year 2000. To make the shift, he has been on a shopping spree to buy firms in the aftermarket business and has started to reconfigure the group's distribution network to support the new customer segment (see *Forbes*, April 20, 1998).

Exploit the Potential of Each Segment and Customer

Growth firms act on the belief that market penetration battles are won store by store and customer by customer. Growth firms are aggressive users of micro-marketing data–mining tools to identify their existing customer segments. Fingerhut, for example, has been able to accelerate revenue growth by tracking information such as demographics, customer buying and payment histories, product preferences, and even birthdays and anniversaries, for over 30 million customer households. Data mining has enabled the firm to deepen its knowledge about its existing customer base, and to broaden its customer base in combination with other online resources.

Firms can also achieve higher growth by exploiting the frequency of customer usage and the range of products marketed to them. Investment and retail banks use cross-selling to increase customer product usage by tracking personal information through stockbrokers' databases to identify a customer's upcoming needs from other areas of the bank. Household International, the consumer finance giant, plans a similar strategy. The company's customers in the home equity business, mostly lower-middle-income households, can expect sales pitches from salespeople trying to push the company's credit cards. The company has good reason to believe that its deep understanding of this customer group will help it market another product to them (*Forbes*, November 2, 1998).

Internet companies such as Yahoo!, iVillage.com, and ESPN are trying to increase each customer's usage by offering a broader scope of products and branding their sites as "specialty portals."

Reinvent Distribution or Service Delivery Channel

Avon ladies have been selling cosmetics door-to-door for 112 years. Despite past success, the sales scheme had become antiquated and its image stale. The Avon Company repositioned itself to market to young professionals through new distribution channels. In 1998, the company began a test rollout of freestanding retail mall kiosks in 40 U.S. cities to attract new customers. Two-thirds of customers who shopped at the Atlanta kiosk were first-time buyers. In addition to kiosks, the company has also started selling products over the Internet.

In many emerging markets, the lack of established distribution networks and infrastructure often necessitates innovative approaches. Warner-Lambert has more than 30,000 street vendors selling its Chiclets brand of chewing gum in Colombia. And the company has discovered that, for rural areas throughout Latin America, van rancheros are the best distribution channels (on new strategies in emerging markets, see Arnold and Quelch in *Sloan Management Review*, October 1, 1998).

Exploit Global Potential

Managing globalization requires firms to fashion sophisticated mental maps of the dynamics of market development, as well as of patterns for exploiting them. Mature globalizers use these maps to provide a strategic investment framework that helps them judge the nature and level of resources to deploy against markets at different stages of evolution. Use of the maps tends to avoid overinvestment and value destruction. They also function as a means of identifying the level of product adaptation to support in individual markets. As firms move to thinking of the world as the marketplace for their product portfolio, this ability to balance cost and complexity against returns will become vital to creating and sustaining value throughout the global organization.

GE has a so-called smart-bomb strategy to drive the company's international expansion, especially in its high-growth appliances sector in Asia. Executives examine each of the country markets microscopically and customize a mix of products, brands, manufacturing, marketing, and retail approaches to wring the best performance from each. By a rigorous process, they evaluate long-term growth potential, the competitive situation, and the availability of skilled labor. Finally, the investment has to meet GE's lofty hurdle rate: 20 to 25 percent return on investment. In 1996, GE appliances division operating earnings rose to 11.8 percent of the division's $6.4 billion in sales, as compared to the industry average of only 5.7 percent (*Fortune*, July 21, 1997).

Firms with a one-way information flow, from home headquarters to country distribution, need a two-way conversation that communicates lessons learned at local country levels and across supply chains. High-growth firms have already developed these mechanisms in key business areas. They actively seek feedback on customer needs and new products, build it into the innovation process, and then reapply the lessons elsewhere. Procter & Gamble has learned a great deal in Japan about diapers, sanitary pad technology, and related marketing approaches that it has reapplied in the United States. Successful companies will refine this ability to roll out global programs even as they constrain central bureaucracies and allow individual markets the space to adapt, innovate, and originate winners.

Companies that seek growth in international markets should also understand political and partnering risks, and be prepared to stay the course. Market entries are expensive not only in money but also in time and learning, and consistency is key to sustaining long-term growth and value creation. We have witnessed investors in Latin America who were quick to divest when the market turned in the 1980s. Upon market recovery, firms trying to reenter quickly discovered that they had to do so at much higher prices and had lost significant goodwill. Although the depth of the Asian crisis remains strongly imprinted on our minds, investing when times are good and running when times are bad may be a thing of the past.

This line of argument suggests more complex organizational forms. Some years ago, firms tended to adopt either a *multinational* or a *global* pattern. While neither followed a set formula, both models provided guidance on how to organize. In the former, linkages across markets are moderate, and both the costs and returns are driven more by local than by global factors. In the latter, economics are largely global and information sharing across markets is largely one way. Products and programs are standardized; customization, minimal.

In the evolving world, we believe that mature multiproduct firms will adopt more diverse models. Consistency of aspirations, standards, and information will require greater global consistency across product lines. Speed and the management of complexity will require organizations dedicated to product lines across the globe, not just at the center. Common customers will demand coordination across product lines and organizations. Managing this triage of geography, product, and account will require the development of new organizational forms and mechanisms. We believe that the global reorganizations around product groups announced by ABB and Procter & Gamble in 1998 represented early moves to respond to these forces, and that they represent the trend.

Reinvest in Brands

Growth leaders recognize that they will not always have demonstrable technology edges, and that brands are their ultimate asset. They maintain brands and invest in them through good times and bad. In the 1980s and early 1990s, even as many brands succumbed to promotional pressures, the leaders still maintained brand-building investments. In the late 1990s, not just consumer goods giants such as Coca-Cola and Procter & Gamble were concerned about their brands. Brands had become increasingly important in high tech and many other industries. Bill Gates tapped a 26-year Procter & Gamble veteran to help develop a better brand identity for Microsoft. General Motors jumped on the "brand wagon," hiring heavyweights from packaged consumer goods industries to polish its car brands. The highly successful Saturn division is to a large extent a successful branding story, capitalizing on the newly established brand equity of "a different kind of car and a different kind of company." Intel's "Intel Inside" campaign and, later, its Pentium brand have given the company tremendous differentiation in an industry where conventional wisdom used to hold that "a chip is a chip."

A brand is a promise, an assurance that the products with that particular brand and logo will deliver what consumers have come to expect. The average computer buyer is willing to pay for the "Intel Inside" label on a computer because it promises quality. The successes of Yahoo! and Amazon.com are great brand stories in the new Internet age. Amazon's Jeff Bezos said, "As important as brands are in the real world, they are even more important in the virtual one, because, online, people have so few visual cues. If I'm walking down a street and spot a large bookstore, I don't even need to notice the name to have a pretty good idea of what the experience will be like.

But on-line, all Web sites look pretty much the same. Is it a 40,000-square-foot Web site or a 2,000-square-foot Web site? Without a clear sense of the brand, I might never log on" (*The Wall Street Journal,* April 3, 1998, A19).

Research has demonstrated that stock return is strongly correlated to changes in brand equity. Although brand building might negatively affect short-term profits, it will drive shareholder value and matters immensely to long-term health and growth. To sustain long-term growth, brands must deliver real value. This explains why leading companies invest aggressively in research and development. They innovate continually in order to remain on the cutting edge in product design, as well as in advertising and promotion. Gillette insists that 40 percent of sales will be derived from new products every five years—which requires 20 new products per year.

Procter & Gamble invests aggressively in advertising and promotion to keep its brands contemporary and visible. The company supported the launches of Secret and Sure, new personal care products, with the big advertising and promotion budgets typical of this consumer goods giant. In addition to spending $20 million on print and TV advertising for Secret, and another $18 million on print and TV for Sure, P&G also fielded more than 22 million samples of the two brands (*Advertising Age,* May 19, 1997, 14). Overall, Procter & Gamble is the second-largest advertiser in the nation. Based on consumer insights, the P&G brand teams develop brand concepts and copy strategies based on the single most important benefit consumers want from the product. The product is improved time and again, while the brand concept and copy strategy are carefully monitored to ensure consistency. After years of brand-building efforts, each of the company's brands represents in consumers' minds a certain benefit. The brand nearly becomes synonymous with that specific consumer need and benefit. The mechanism that delivers this result is not just a one-time effort at consistency, but a process within a highly dedicated organization.

Supporting Reinvention

High-growth firms support their innovations by committing significant sums to R&D. Only in this way can they sustain their competitive edge. Gillette devotes 2.2 percent of its annual sales, or over $200 million, to R&D—roughly twice the average for consumer products companies (*Business Week*, January 19, 1998, 70). For the recent rollout of its Oral-B Cross Action toothbrush, Gillette spent six years in preparation and significant sums on R&D. Procter & Gamble has an annual R&D expenditure of $1.5 billion (4 percent of sales), higher on a percentage basis than Gillette's overall average, although lower than the commitment Gillette made to a single, promising turnaround product in the company's recent history.

In technology, "best to market" is often preferable to "first to market." Apple's Newton was four years ahead in handheld organizer development, but it did not satisfy customer needs because it failed to recognize handwriting. Palm Pilot promised conservatively but delivered real if not spectacular advances against important needs. The reward for the parent, 3Com: a $300 million product in one year from a standing start. A rather less well known fact is that 3Com spent over 10 percent of sales on R&D in its last fiscal year.

Rework the Processes for Speed

General Electric popularized strategic planning and then radically refocused it. Jack Welch changed GE's revered strategic planning process to prepare it for the fast-moving business environment of the 1990s. The incumbent systems didn't allow for the speed of decision making needed today. As Welch put it, "Divisions, strategic business units, groups, sectors, all were designed to make meticulous, calculated decisions and move them smoothly forward and upward. This system produced highly polished work. It was right for the 1970s, a growing handicap in the 1980s, and it would have been a ticket to the boneyard in the 1990s. So we got rid of it, along with a lot of reports, meetings, and the endless paper that flowed like lava from the upper levels of the company. When we did this, we began to see people— who for years had spent half their time serving the system and the other half fighting it—suddenly come to life, making decisions in minutes, face-to-face, on matters that would have once produced months of staff gyrations and forests of paper. But this transformation, this rebirth, was largely confined to upper management. In the 1990's we want to see it engulf and galvanize the entire company" (*Harvard Business School*, April 12, 1994, 8).

What Jack Welch learned within his own business is echoed by some leading strategic thinkers. In this new world of constant change, strategy can no longer be the end product of annual planning sessions; it has to be a dynamic *process* to sense changes in the environment and drive changes within the company that enable it to adapt quickly. Instead of striving for a conceptually elegant strategy, the winning company learns to generate strategy on a real-time basis. (On this topic, see, for example, Gary Hamel in *Sloan Management Review*, January 1, 1998.)

Use Technology to Enable

High-growth firms measure the value of technology by its capacity to help them meet specific objectives and enhance implementation of their strategy. American Airlines achieved a much higher capacity utilization than its competition through its application and control of the SABRE reservation system. Wal-Mart dramatically increased its inventory turns by establishing electronic data interchange (EDI) links with a large number of vendors. It is also very likely no coincidence that P&G's implementation of an enterprise-wide SAP system was shortly followed by the move to global product divisions based on enhanced business visibility.

Technology has also helped up-and-coming companies to circumvent entry barriers by setting up alternative service delivery channels. Amazon.com applied the latest electronic commerce technology to compete with traditional booksellers, based on its favorable cost structure and high-quality service. The latest technology also changed the delivery model of several institutions of higher education by enabling them to expand their programs and customer segments through distance-learning programs in the cyberworld. A student in Jakarta or Nairobi can have a real-time discussion with a professor and student peers around the world. As distance-learning leaders exploit emerging technologies, they may make it necessary to rethink a number of traditional university models. Likewise, banks that lead in electronic retail home banking will revolutionize the retail banking industry. Wells Fargo, the largest provider of Internet banking, is using new technology that provides real-time links to credit bureaus and databases with checking account histories. This enables customers to apply for home equity loans over the Internet and obtain a three-second decision on a loan specifically structured for them. Wells Fargo vice chairman Terri Dial has said flatly: "You either invest in the technology or get out of that line of business" (*Fortune*, September 28, 1998).

Technology has also helped companies make quantum leaps in the area of sales force management. Avon recently demonstrated how the company could improve sales force productivity by using Tactician, a newly developed computer-mapping program that can track sales representatives' records and sales penetration by country, state, county, city, and even specific street. Managers can click on an icon to look at an individual sales rep's sales level and reference it against internal benchmarks as well as market specifics such as the population and ethnicity of the rep's region. These data improve measurement of sales force performance and uncover markets with high growth potential (*The Wall Street Journal*, September 21, 1998).

Use Alliances to Advance Strategy

Too often, acquisitions are a substitute for coherent growth. Growth leaders use acquisitions to absorb technology, build distribution, and gain access. They have a distinctive ability to exploit the acquired or partnered assets, and a sensible plan for doing so.

AlliedSignal—which entered into a transforming megamerger of its own—formed a strategic alliance with Caterpillar in anticipation of future acquisitions. Caterpillar developed information systems and modeling techniques to forecast on a real-time basis customers' demands for product availability in the aerospace industry. The two companies are studying how best to link their information service networks. By early 2000, AlliedSignal and Cat Logistics expect each partner to start operating the new distribution system in parallel. Once the two companies are satisfied that the system is performing up to expectations, they will ramp it up on a larger scale. In addition, this absorption of technology and systems will allow them to provide customers a still larger volume of aftermarket products—already the source of more than $6.2 billion in annual revenues to AlliedSignal Aerospace.

Microsoft is known for obtaining new technologies and capabilities through acquisition and assimilating them quickly, thereby gaining the competitive advantage of quicker rollouts and setting market standards. In 1987, the company acquired Forethought, the applications software company that created PowerPoint and FileMaker Plus. In 1996, tiny Vermeer Technologies Inc. was bought by Microsoft. At the time, its FrontPage software for creating web sites had sold a grand total of 275 copies in four months. In 1997, sales of FrontPage 97, the newest version of the software now carrying Microsoft's logo, were expected to run into the hundreds of thousands.

High-growth firms also use mergers and acquisitions to invest in human capital and therefore expand capability. In 1993, Jack Welch decreed that GE's high-tech businesses were to "stay on the leading edge" through acquisitions and large R&D investments, and services were to grow "by adding outstanding people who create new ventures and by making contiguous acquisitions" (see "Jack Welch: General Electric's Revolutionary," *Harvard Business Case,* April 12, 1994). Firms need to have both a mission and a method for the discovery of the right people, those who can lay the foundation for future acquisitions. Microsoft has mastered this skill—and it has more cash than all other high-tech venture capitalists combined. Capable of attracting rising talent, it has been acting like a venture capitalist by prowling in Silicon Valley and other centers of the new knowledge economy in search of emerging technologies and outstanding programmers.

High-growth firms use alliances to build distribution. Consider The Knot (www.theknot.com), which has become the leading online wedding resource and gift registry. It strengthened this position through strategic alliances with America Online and Intuit. America Online will feature The Knot as the in-depth wedding planning tool in its Weddings area—and AOL's membership of some 13 million surely includes plenty of engaged couples. As Intuit's Quicken.com moves into AOL's Life Events Channel, The Knot will also become the exclusive wedding content and services provider, and share in distribution through other Quicken gateways.

Alliances also gain access to new markets. Welch has reshaped GE through more than 600 acquisitions and a forceful push abroad into emerging markets. AlliedSignal has broadened its distribution channels into Thailand, Singapore, Malaysia, and the Philippines by teaming up with Ultro Technologies. It has also expanded in the

United States through an arrangement with Eastern Components, which exemplifies AlliedSignal's determination to remain competitive in the race to capture global computer and electronics market share.

Understand and Manage the Costs of Growth

Growth carries costs and in many instances these costs exceed the benefits that growth generates. The value-creating growth firms know how to tell the difference. Product-specific costs and investments such as new product development, marketing, and new facilities are well understood. The subtler costs of process and organizational complexity are often not. Often these costs are difficult to isolate, creep up slowly, and trace to separate sources, departments, and executives. Nonetheless, they are real and they destroy value. Understanding and managing them is vital to avoid the downside of growth.

Product proliferation in the interest of finer segmentation is a case in point. Grocery manufacturers introduce 17,000 new products a year, against the average supermarket's stock of 30,000 items. The result: barely differentiated products, waste in marketing, complexity at the factory, more changeovers, lower plant utilization, lower asset efficiency, and high costs. While a number of manufacturers recently announced initiatives to prune their lineups, the leaders have been doing so quietly since 1992. Prior to 1998, Avon ladies in 135 countries peddled some 500 brands of cosmetics, fragrances, and toiletries, many unique to specific countries. Marketing was handled by 18 agencies. By year-end, there was only one agency left and half of the company's business was contributed by 11 global brands (*Forbes*, January 11, 1999).

Corporations experience similar problems and lose focus when they diversify across too many businesses. Even acquisitions in the same industry often bulk up size but not value. Most acquiring managements articulate scale and scope arguments to justify the acquisitions, but integration is a difficult task and few CEOs have credible records of realizing the anticipated synergies. We are skeptical that several of the gigantic mergers announced recently will realize enough value to pay back the premiums.

Household International, the consumer finance giant, refused to grow for growth's sake. In the words of CEO Bill Aldinger, "I'd love to be a glamorous growth stock, but not at the cost of falling on my face. I won't do dumb growth" (*Forbes,* November 2, 1998).

After acquiring Beneficial Corporation, his ultimatum was an 18 percent after-tax return on equity for each of the 10 subsidiaries—or they would be sold. Out went a commercial real estate arm, a stock brokerage, and an insurance group. The company finally stripped down to two lines of business: credit card and home equity loans. The result? Per-share earnings have jumped more than 20 percent annually and the stock price has more than doubled.

Conclusion

Beneath the research, the interviews, and the numerous examples reside some plain and rather homely truths. First, there is no single path to growth that produces significant rewards for shareholders, no magic formula. The variety of approaches to growth that we have discussed demonstrate that different companies, industries, and regions require different solutions. One firm can learn from another, but copying is probably of limited use. Globalization may be integrating the world economy, but it is leaving a great deal of complexity and individuality in place. Second, it is obvious that a successful beginning does not ensure endless success. Vision demands revision. No strategy is sacred. Some are interesting—but often for a limited time.

Finally, growth will not come painlessly and effortlessly. Growth requires change—sometimes constant change—and that is always difficult and usually expensive. Senior management committed to growth will have to explain to people at every level why this change is in the interest of the firm and its employees, what benefits will accrue to whom and when, and how the process will work. In other words, growth requires not merely an appreciation of complexity and a commitment to persistent revision, it also demands leadership and powers of persuasion, perhaps the most important weapons in the modern CEO's arsenal.

Michael S. Dell

Chairman and Chief Executive Officer, Dell Computer Corporation

Creating and Managing Hypergrowth

Hypergrowth is generally defined as consistent year-to-year sales and profit increases of at least 30 percent. At Dell Computer Corporation we have been living with this level of growth, and higher levels, for some years. For those companies that are now facing, or will soon face, the challenges and opportunities that hypergrowth brings, I want to discuss here some of the solutions we have developed at Dell to meet the management challenges of hypergrowth.

Dell's Path to Hypergrowth

At Dell we have achieved approximately 54 percent compounded sales growth since fiscal year 1992. During that period, there was only one year when sales grew at less than 30 percent, and that was due to measures we took deliberately to restrain growth that year.

How did this rapid growth occur? Not through acquisitions. Dell's growth has been internally generated. And not because the information technology industry offers certain growth—there have been many successes but even more failures.

The formula for many companies in the IT sector is *sustainable product advantages*. Intel's microprocessors and Microsoft's personal computer operating systems and applications are examples of sustainable product advantages. For Dell, the formula is different: A new business system that relies on direct customer relationships has been the key to our continued success. We call this system Dell's Direct Model. But the Direct Model would not have generated hypergrowth without our people's drive for excellence and constant focus on innovation.

Our most significant innovations have been in expanding our model and evolving it from the direct mail business we founded in 1984. In the early years, our vision was to use the then-mundane direct mail business as a springboard to something very exceptional. The powerful customer linkages that were embedded in the way we did business could be deployed to go far beyond mere order taking. They could be tools for satisfying computing needs well in excess of any known meaning of the phrase "customer satisfaction."

One of the early innovations at Dell that strengthened customer relationships was in the area of service. We introduced the industry's first money-back guarantees, toll-free technical support, and next-day on-site service.

In those early days, we sold predominantly to individual buyers. But as we continued to develop the capabilities of our model, we applied them to the much more complex and demanding corporate PC market. Today, we sell about two-thirds of our computers to companies and governmental customers, and we are continually improving the closeness and depth of our customer relationships.

Another area of innovation has been in manufacturing. By taking significant chunks of time and costs out of computer assembly, we operate with less than six days of inventory and have given new meaning to the phrase "just-in-time inventory management."

We are also saving our customers significant amounts of time and money by selling to them over the World Wide Web. Internet sales now generate for us a daily average of $30 million in revenues. These sales yield higher operating margins than voice-to-voice or face-to-face links because operating costs are lower. It also costs our customers less to place an order with us over the Internet. With both sides thus motivated, we anticipate that our Internet sales will continue their significant contribution to hypergrowth and someday may account for half of our total revenues.

Sorting Out the Wisdom about Hypergrowth

Two items of conventional wisdom about hypergrowth companies are that they are out of control or very nearly out of control and that, even in brilliantly managed companies, hypergrowth will not last because of the inevitable company life cycle—vigorous youth, slowing maturity, and ultimate death.

The first view is based on the premise that if you are lucky enough to experience hypergrowth, you will be unlucky enough to lose control of it. Contrary to this thinking, and to the bankruptcy statistic of "bad controls" as a primary cause of entrepreneurial failure, if a young growth company sufficiently believes in its future, it will invest in management skills and controls that can sustain high performance over many decades.

As to the second view, the greatest corporations worldwide, some with a century or more of continuous activity, have all had to renew themselves. Hypergrowth may not be sustainable over decades of corporate activity, but it is one of the best foundations for decades of impressive and reliably managed growth.

Let's look at some of the macro factors involved in the management of growth. Failure to attain growth is often due to poor market fundamentals. Under that scenario, all industry participants are penalized to some degree. Yet statistics show that corporate rates of growth differ dramatically within any industry. They also show that it's possible to generate high levels of growth in near-static industries such as oil and steel. In the IT industry, growth and survival rates vary dramatically. Dozens of highflyers have failed or accepted very secondary status. Others are doing remarkably well.

Hypergrowth is driven by internal speed and urgency, by the need to preempt competitors swiftly and to exploit opportunities. Each new opportunity, when first recognized, has many unknowns embedded in it. For this reason, managers should accept mistakes philosophically and rapidly learn from them.

Over the years at Dell, we have moved from last place to the industry's front rank in some areas. We made mistakes in inventory, treasury management, and product development, then fixed them so thoroughly that we sped past our competition. In the early 1990s, the company earned dubious notoriety when we brought to market a notebook and then withdrew it as soon as we realized that it didn't meet our customers' standards or our own. We then earned fame when, after more than a year on the sidelines, we returned to market with a top-selling notebook.

Comparatively speaking, hypergrowth companies lack a past of sacred strategies or long-established practices and procedures. This enables them to improvise as they go. Hypergrowth companies are quintessential learn-by-doing organizations. Their survival depends on swift adaptation. Because resources and people are stretched, they may not have excessive formal or structured systems in place. Without these extra layers, hypergrowth companies place fewer limits on their people's intellectual creativity and ability to implement new ideas. As a result, their people work smarter.

Hypergrowth cannot be sustained for long by operating in an emergency mode. Fire fighting, crisis managing, and letting all tasks and issues assume equal urgency and importance are not examples of improvisation. Improvising in a hypergrowth environment is to take nothing for granted. Improvising is using the intellectual capital of the company to respond swiftly and certainly to exploit competitive opportunities and capitalize on the strengths of the company.

The picture may keep changing and always must be monitored and managed. Hypergrowth demands discipline up and down the line. In many respects, Dell's excess of revenue opportunities requires us to be diligent as we evaluate, sequence, and prioritize our opportunities, and invest in the most promising ones.

Customer Loyalty Drives Hypergrowth

What most often propels hypergrowth in today's economy are superior interactions and relations with customers. Dramatic changes in supplier/customer relationships have led to the creation of trillions of dollars of value that didn't exist a generation ago.

Manufacturers used to do some market research and then develop products that roughly met customer needs. But customers in some industries weren't satisfied. They wanted more than participation in a focus group or filling out a wants-and-needs questionnaire. In the scientific equipment industry, customers have long played a very active role in product design. Sometimes they actually built prototypes that would then be handed over to their suppliers for commercialization—an early sign that customers wanted to be more active in shaping and defining what they bought. Thus was sown the seed of mass customization.

Although serving the customer is hardly a revolutionary idea, the intensity with which the idea must be pursued in today's environment is new. Let me give an example. Initially, Dell defined product quality by and large in terms of hardware failure rates. We gradually learned to broaden that definition to include the delivery of solutions that meet or exceed customer expectations. We introduced, in effect, two additional concepts: delivery and expectation. Focusing on delivery means that we critique and improve every stage of the delivery path. Focusing on customer expectations means that we look at every issue surrounding the experience of purchasing from us.

The cornerstone of Dell's hypergrowth comes from the many ways we have found to be intimate with customers throughout their experience with us. Our growth is predicated on the relentless pursuit and elaboration of this idea; it is exemplified in everything we do from new product design to final shipment. In the pursuit of customer loyalty, we have repeatedly segmented and resegmented our business around the behavior of customers. The "K through 12" customer set in the educational market is just one example. This customer set buys very differently than do colleges and universities. The "K through 12" customer set has different product service needs and responds to different kinds of marketing. As a result, we developed a dedicated business unit to serve these customers and tailor our offerings around their unique needs.

Caveat Benchmarker

Hypergrowth is rare. In any one industry there is typically only one company with hypergrowth. In most industries there is no great difference between one company and another. Their practices, people, and outlooks are remarkably alike. Hypergrowth suggests that a company is an original. It suggests that the company has an uncommon competitive advantage. For Dell, that uncommon advantage is our direct business system and the quality of customer experience it fosters.

The uniqueness of hypergrowth companies should make them beware of standard benchmarking. It can cost them their edge and intensity. In the 1980s, our industry was recording 30 percent sales growth. Dell was doing better than that. We could have said to ourselves, Wow, look at how much better we're doing than they are! That would have been shortsighted. It could have blinded us to the massive and still untapped potential in our future.

In many typical benchmarking areas, our industry ranks somewhere between "not great" and "terrible." For example, one of the most important performance standards in our industry is the cost of product warranties. In truth, it is far too high for all participants in our industry. A significant improvement in Dell's warranty cost could drive our customers to unheard-of levels of loyalty. That is why we disregard any industry norms and strive hard to do better by our own internal standards of service.

In contrast, we eagerly participate in benchmark studies outside of the computer industry. We need to understand the experience of others, just as the Dell management team has, from time to time, been enriched by hires of seasoned pros from inside and outside the industry. In some areas, we simply didn't have the talent in-house and recognized it. Publicly we often project a winner's confidence, but underneath we are humble about the need to learn and adopt best practices in everything we do.

Freedoms and Constraints of Hypergrowth

Hypergrowth offers both unusual freedoms and unusual constraints. Under the heading of freedoms, management can slow the pace of growth if the company becomes overheated and error prone. Another freedom is the luxury to sidestep many internal conflicts. For example, if the executive team cannot achieve reasonable consensus on a large capital project abroad, they can pursue one of the many other opportunities available and revisit the issue in conflict later.

The constraints of hypergrowth companies typically are twofold: (1) insufficient working and investment capital—not a problem for Dell in recent years, and (2) the recruitment, training, and deployment of people on a scale that most companies never experience. Currently, over one-half of the Dell workforce has been on the payroll for less than two years.

This constant influx of new faces, new names, and new voices above, alongside, and below our seasoned middle managers forces us to project a simple and coherent culture that everyone can understand and support. It requires a reward-based compensation scheme that everyone finds appropriate and challenging. The company functions better with an operating style based on a high level of individual performance and stretch goals, not just in financial terms but in all aspects of operations. Our culture encourages communicating these values and goals effectively and continuously.

A Goal List for Hypergrowth Companies

No list of attributes of hypergrowth can be complete. The process is so dynamic that it defies easy generalization. Here are some of the goals that we strive to reach at Dell. We believe that every one of them contributes to our hypergrowth.

- *Scalability.* Our systems and facilities have unusual flexibility and scalability, due in part to the number of worldwide facilities—nine, with four under construction. Each facility is constructed on modular principles. This high concentration provides many benefits in both production and distribution. It also greatly eases information sharing and communication, which are the chief lubricants of growth.

- *Consistent execution.* We continue to hone our skills at execution. Flawless execution across the value chain is critical to our hypergrowth, and good systems are essential to support it. You do not maintain hypergrowth for long without doing a lot of little things right.

- *A sense of destiny.* Hypergrowth readily fosters an evangelical culture, a zeal and pride that come from exceptional results. Call it a sense of destiny. Regardless of age, most of our people are the type to believe in a cause, not just collect a paycheck.

- *Constant learning.* We have good crisis management and learning skills. The speed at which the company moves and the newness of systems and people will create bottlenecks and the occasional stumble. A company with hypergrowth inevitably stumbles. What's important is to keep a cool head, learn from the stumble, and never make the same mistake twice.

- *Productive fear.* We strive to be risk averse wherever possible and have made enormous strides with inventory risk, receivables risk, and opportunity risk. Our current expansion into China and Brazil, for instance, was backed by very prudent risk assessments. Fear underlies a lot of our thinking when it comes to risk evaluation and strategic decision making. We welcome that sense of fear and use it as a guide in an industry that is always in a state of rapid change. We are not striving to earn every last dollar of growth or to capitalize on every opportunity; that is dangerous. We aim for reasonable growth that we can sustain without massive problems. At Dell, we are in hypergrowth, but we haven't lost our heads and we don't intend to.

Some Final Thoughts

What can hypergrowth-seeking businesses learn from the Dell experience? The roots of our success lie in continually analyzing what we are doing and drawing out the correct inferences and interpretations from the environment, without falling victim to what I call "analysis paralysis." Easy to say, hard to accomplish.

We have been guided by consistently good interpretations of where markets are heading and what customers need, and by a compulsion to question and deconstruct conventional wisdom. These aptitudes transformed us from a direct mail company to the pioneer of a way of doing business that is becoming dominant in our industry. Our analysis has occasionally misfired. Some years ago we mistakenly entered the retail market, but we quickly recognized our error and walked away. Watching all those unsold computers on the shelves at retailers resulted in more confidence than ever in the power of our direct business model.

We are gluttons for gathering and studying industry data and doing competitive intelligence and technology assessment. We've also sharpened our intuitive sense of the tempo and direction of industry change. Everyone in Dell upper management is expected to have a hands-on feel for the latest nuance in our markets, via surfing the Internet and talking to current and potential customers, suppliers, and employees. Management's analytic power must be proportional to the company's capacity to react to the new and the unexpected. That is why we have built an infrastructure that can respond swiftly to changes in the environment or in company direction. In contrast, many of our competitors do not lack for good insights, but they are hobbled by internal infrastructure in trying to implement them. This obstacle can be seen in the difficulties many of them experience in trying to adopt the direct business model. But we can't assume their floundering will go on forever. We need to maintain a healthy sense of fear and continue to focus on innovations that enrich our customers' experience. Only in this way will we continue to achieve hypergrowth.

Stephen R. Hardis
Chairman and Chief Executive Officer, Eaton Corporation

Growth
The Engine of Global Leadership

Events in the 1980s taught America's industrial companies some difficult lessons. Eaton and its peers learned the importance of practicing the fundamentals—quality, productivity, service. How could we have lost sight of things so obvious? History provides at least part of the answer: The United States went through a postwar period in which we enjoyed very high growth and for a long time virtually no global competition. Particularly in the 1960s, the stock market rose exuberantly and the appearance of growth became a substitute for fundamental growth. We saw the emergence of conglomerates that didn't have an economic rationale. They were just pyramiding stock values. Many companies did model changes as opposed to fundamental product development, and many companies steadily lost productivity.

The wake-up call came primarily from overseas competition, best exemplified by the Japanese. They quickly gained scale, and they were very good at the fundamentals such as quality, service, reliability of design, and unit cost of production. They caught American industry out of balance and relatively flaccid. That story was told on campuses and in the economic press throughout the 1980s.

In retrospect, Eaton responded remarkably well to a competitive situation that had changed radically. We recognized the competitive threats very early in the 1980s. We cut expenses, limited spending to projects with quick payoffs, and concentrated on defending our markets and profit margins. We demanded all the facts—which is virtually an impossibility—before making any decisions. We did not feel comfortable enough to invest any significant amounts on uncertain future growth because we weren't sure we could afford these costs as we tried to bring our expense structure into better alignment with those of our global competitors. We successfully defended our markets and our margins, but, unfortunately, we did not adequately grow our businesses.

And while we continued to play defense, the emergence of a truly global market was placing an ever greater premium on growth. A global market implies that you go from local to country to regional to global competition, and the number of suppliers rises geometrically. In addition, today's extraordinary communications capabilities make it possible for buyers to get bids from suppliers all over the world. The resulting deflationary effect shows up in two ways. First, it affects the actual prices you can charge. Second, the customer is able to shift the cost of doing business to his or her supplier by relying on supplier research capabilities, requiring just-in-time shipments, and demanding near-perfect quality. The only way a supplier can generate an adequate return—with more and more entrants coming into the market and the fixed costs of doing business trending up—is through economies of scale. You cannot grow fast enough to get the required scale in your own domestic market, so you have to find it by going global. That gives companies the economies of scale to absorb the higher fixed costs and to generate a reasonable return, even when pricing is under pressure.

In the global markets of today, the companies that are not clear winners, or don't have a reasonable chance of becoming a clear winner, will eventually become part of the food chain for the winners. Many niche players that used to be able to make a nice living alongside the leaders are being marginalized. The automotive industry is a prime example: The OEMs are dramatically reducing the number of suppliers, and those remaining must provide the technology, manufacturing capabilities, global infrastructure, and information technology enhancements their customers require. If you can't do all of these things, you won't be invited to be on the design team. That means you won't be able to effectively bid. You'll never see the opportunity. Today, global leadership is necessary not just for higher profits, it is required for survival. Growth is the engine of global leadership.

A Strategy for Sustainable Growth

In the mid-1990s, we looked at a variety of global scenarios for our main product lines—electrical power distribution and control equipment, truck drivetrain systems, automotive engine components, hydraulic products, ion implanters, and a wide variety of controls. These powerful franchises presented us with an astonishing number of growth opportunities, and we began to develop a realistic, credible strategy for global leadership in each of our major businesses. Going forward, we knew we had to increase R&D spending dramatically, we had to invest heavily to move our strong North American franchises into countries rapidly industrializing, and we had to be alert to new acquisition opportunities. In each of these cases, we knew there was always the possibility of failure. Evaluating the risks involved was at the heart of our strategy. I think a lot of companies are fuzzy-minded about risk. People use the term *strategy* mistakenly when they mean a series of tactics or a set of aspirations. You don't really have a strategy unless it incorporates risk assessment and an understanding of alternatives. We concluded that global leadership was such an imperative that we had to accept higher risks and make the required investments.

We felt that sustainable growth required that each business be an industry leader, be capable of at least 10 percent earnings growth through the economic cycle, and generate returns 300 to 500 basis points above the cost of capital. We divested businesses that did not meet these criteria. These included operations providing about one-fifth of our total sales, including appliance controls, the automotive leaf spring business, and defense electronics. In one unusual transaction, we did an asset swap with Dana Corp., in which we traded our founding product, truck axles (and brakes), for a faster-growing and more technologically relevant truck clutch business that strengthened our leadership position in truck transmissions. Of course, divestitures penalize sales volumes in the short term, and often they negatively affect earnings per share. But in the long run, we expected these moves to help us create an enterprise capable of sound and more sustainable earnings growth and one that deserves a higher market valuation. The divestitures also had another effect: They sent a strong signal to investors and our own employees that we were serious about our growth strategy.

Sustained high growth among U.S. industrial companies has been rare. The term *industrial* normally applies to companies that serve mature end markets with relatively low growth. In real terms, 3 percent growth has been about the norm. At Eaton, our question was, how do we get sustained 10 percent growth in this kind of environment? The answer, of course, is by outperforming the end markets. Eaton's strategy to outgrow its end markets incorporates the following key elements:

1. Use the discretionary cash we generate to finance acquisitions that will further strengthen our leadership posture and enhance long-term earnings growth.

2. Take our major products into the critical emerging markets of countries undergoing rapid industrialization.

3. Use the technological strengths developed to protect our existing franchises from global competitors to build significant incremental new earnings sources.

4. Rethink every fundamental activity within Eaton in order to achieve best practices when benchmarked against the best global competitors.

5. Enrich our tradition of management strength by developing new talent and by encouraging a more venturesome corporate culture.

A major part of rethinking our activities was to restructure basic expenses. All of our units committed to at least 4 percent per year productivity improvement. Beyond that, we had to reengineer and restructure our financial and information technology capabilities to lower overall costs. We also enlisted our suppliers' help to find ways to reduce costs. Between 1994 and 1997, we took $100 million out of our cost structure, and between 1997 and the year 2000, we need to take out an additional $150 million (beyond our ongoing 4 percent annual productivity goals). These savings help offset our growth investments as we wait for those investments to produce positive returns.

Acquisitions have played a major role in our growth strategy. Smaller, focused acquisitions have strengthened existing businesses. Often, these types of acquisitions bring a particular product line or market channel or geographic presence. They don't lever Eaton's total growth materially, but they do strengthen the ability of individual businesses to achieve their growth and leadership goals. Larger acquisitions provide leverage for Eaton in total. The Westinghouse Distribution and Control Business Unit, which we bought in 1994, had $1.1 billion in sales. Aeroquip-Vickers, a leader in mobile and industrial hydraulics, which we bought in April 1999, had $2.2 billion in sales. These acquisitions also help offset the negative effects of divestitures on our growth targets.

I think a company always has to be willing to look at acquisitions but should be in a position to meet its growth objectives without acquisitions so that it can be very selective. We tend to be very disciplined in pricing acquisitions, and that's made it difficult to find attractive candidates. Over time, we would like to reduce our dependence on acquisitions in order to achieve our 10 percent earnings growth target, but it will take some time for us to gain momentum in terms of new product development and a positive return from our global start-ups.

Eaton's worldwide customer base, involving sales to more than 115 countries, and worldwide manufacturing operations—44 percent outside the United States—make Eaton a partner of choice in developing countries moving rapidly to industrialize their economies. As part of the growth strategy, Eaton targeted five countries as key developing markets—China, India, Korea, Brazil, and Mexico—all of which have significant long-term growth potential for Eaton's products far surpassing those of the developed countries of Europe and North America. We substantially expanded our business in Brazil by acquiring a Brazilian supplier of medium duty transmission components. That operation is now the linchpin of our medium-duty truck transmission business worldwide. Eaton has also made large investments in China (truck transmissions, engine valves, hydraulic components, electrical equipment), in South Korea (automotive controls, differentials, and semiconductor equipment), and in Poland (engine valves, truck transmissions, and automotive controls). Not all of our moves in these developing markets will pay off, but I'm confident that in total they will ultimately improve our returns.

The Power of Innovation

The real long-term key to Eaton's growth strategy is innovation. We determined that new products should eventually contribute more than half of our total growth. The old Eaton was very skilled at using innovation and technology to defend existing product positions, to extend product lives, to satisfy customer demands for applications engineering, and to establish differentiation from rivals' products.

Fundamental new product development, however, was lagging. Accordingly, our whole approach to innovation had to be revised to boost the throughput of product innovations. One area of particular emphasis was to fully exploit the potential for "smart" or "intelligent" products. The company had already developed smart heavy-duty transmissions and vehicle steering systems, smart circuit breakers and power tool controls, but greater emphasis and more development were needed to extend and exploit this capability.

The amount of money we invest in R&D has risen from about 2 percent of sales in the early 1990s to 5 percent in 1998, and it undoubtedly will go higher. One of the sticking points in business is that just spending money does not ensure that you're going to develop successful new products. But the corollary is that it's highly unlikely that you will develop new products if you don't spend the money. To better manage the innovation process, we have imposed new analytic and accountability disciplines consisting of exit criteria for faltering projects and demanding time-to-market and time-to-profit schedules. We also have a very strict investment criterion governing any capital outlay for new products: They must earn at least 500 basis points above the cost of capital. We are trying to better leverage our total innovation capabilities by encouraging cooperation among our units.

We're now looking at shorter product lives and a much more rapid rate of innovation. These require being able to move in parallel, being more nimble, acting quickly even when all the data aren't available, being able to change course quickly. We have a lot to learn from technology companies, and we have to conquer the learning curve if we're going to achieve our growth objectives. By the year 2001, we anticipate that products introduced in the 1995–2000 period will contribute about 35 percent of sales. Given the slow pace at which many of our transitional customers can adopt even the most attractive innovations and incorporate them into the design of their end products, this 35 percent number is a reaching target. One way we're getting more impact from our R&D outlays is by rewarding home runs, that is, seeding research programs that have the potential of generating $50 million or more in sales in five years.

We've already gained some attractive new products from our expanded R&D effort:

- The unique Eaton-VORAD radar-based collision warning system for heavy-duty trucks and buses

- The Fleet Advisor System, which provides the world's best technology for improved communications and logistics control within truck fleets

- A new family of engine superchargers, including those for small displacement engines, which are in demand from global automotive OEMs

- An advanced power center capable of communicating with personal computers and other devices to provide energy management, lighting and electrical load control, and electronic submetering

- New semiconductor equipment offerings capable of handling 300-mm wafers.

Growth initiatives also had a positive effect on our customers, who, in many cases, are beginning to think of us as the place to go for tomorrow's solutions. Customer confidence has been evident as we've repeatedly been invited to be part of customer teams involved in new product development.

Eaton *Is* a Technology Company

Most people make a very sharp distinction between technology companies and industrial enterprises such as Eaton. If the principal measure were the degree of difficulty involved in solving the customers' requirements through technology, Eaton would have a very legitimate claim to be viewed as a sophisticated technology enterprise. But most people think of technology companies as those that address high-growth, end market opportunities, created through new technologies that offer fundamentally new functions and the promise of major productivity enhancements—technology applications that literally create new demand. Unfortunately, by this measure, most of Eaton's businesses are not technology companies.

What we have come to understand, though, is that the distinction between technology companies and industrial enterprises is too hard-edged and extreme. This should not be a black or white choice. Eaton and its peers do, indeed, have the opportunity to accelerate their growth by adding important functionality to almost all of their products. We do not make microprocessors, but our components must be designed so that they have the ability to relate to logic devices and control systems. In many of our products, software design is becoming at least as critical as hardware design. We can help our customers offer *their* customers unique, more complete solutions to their needs and, thereby, create opportunities for Eaton's growth. We now understand that our goal must be to be seen in each of the markets in which we compete as *the* supplier best qualified to offer solutions to tomorrow's requirements.

Assessing Our Progress

When we rolled out our growth strategy at the end of 1995, we probably didn't understand all that we were taking on. We knew it would be difficult. Changing the management culture from avoiding risk to embracing risk continues to be the most serious challenge. It goes to the heart of the way each of us thinks, and that's difficult to change. We've made solid progress toward achieving our growth objectives, but we're not happy with our rate of progress. As this book goes to press, we're behind schedule due to a number of factors, including the Asian economic crisis and the severe global downturn in 1998 in demand for semiconductor manufacturing equipment, a market in which we're a world leader. Our 1998 sales declined due to the divestitures, but we expected to make up substantial ground in 1999 with the acquisition of Aeroquip-Vickers. It will require a significant effort on our part, successful execution of a great number of major initiatives, and a healthy economic scenario, but I still believe we have a chance to achieve the growth metrics we laid out in 1995.

Although I can't be certain we will achieve our publicly stated goals, I have absolute certitude that there was no choice but to redirect Eaton to become a company capable of higher levels of sustainable growth. I believe any enterprise that does not offer its owners, employees, and customers a genuine opportunity for growth, will, by definition, begin to lose competitive position. If a company is not advancing, it is in some form of retreat. Over time, it will inevitably fail to be an outstanding enterprise. Even if we don't achieve our growth objectives, I think we've accomplished a great deal in addressing our internal management practices, our attitudes, and our culture, and we've planted seeds that will germinate and lift future returns.

In the final analysis, Eaton has to compete for the world's best talent against all the other companies in the world. That's the real challenge. We have powerful product franchises and excellent distribution systems, but the real pacing factor is talent. In order to attract the best talent, we have to offer an exciting future, one where people are not only rewarded financially, but can be emotionally gratified. That means working for a winner, and that's only possible if the enterprise grows. I'm absolutely certain we're headed in the right direction.

Charles R. Shoemate
Chairman and Chief Executive Officer, Bestfoods

Satisfying a Global Appetite

You can teach a college course about the benefits of one uniform market—and then turn around and teach it on why you need to be close to the consumer. It's really a question of how to balance global/local needs. We have a tremendous benefit at Bestfoods in that, early in our history, our people established local infrastructures around the world. Since the 1920s, when we pioneered new business in Latin America, we have continually extended our geographic reach. Today, Bestfoods has businesses in more than 60 countries. Our intimacy with the local consumer is an absolute competitive advantage—and the good news for us is that this is extremely difficult for our competitors to build quickly.

For Bestfoods, the key to everything we do is aggressive growth of our three core businesses: savory products, primarily under the Knorr brand; dressings, primarily under the Hellmann's brand; and catering, or food service, where we see major opportunities for leveraging our brands. We are driving all of these businesses via new products and geographic expansion, including acquisitions. Our strategy is to go proactively into geographies when we make the judgment that the timing is right—meaning, among other things, that the population has the economic capability to buy.

Building Our Core Businesses

We like to see McDonald's go into China because they take mayonnaise into the local cuisine, and that offers an opportunity for rapid growth. But most of our products are at the cultural core of local eating habits and are adapted to the tastes of local consumers. Eating is intimate; we enter into traditions, preferences, and lifestyles. Among the many lessons we've learned in our long history of international expansion is this one: In developing new markets, you need to get in early and offer affordable products in tune with local culinary habits.

Take bouillon, for example. You may not think bouillon is a very exciting product—until you understand its effectiveness as an entry vehicle into emerging markets. Bouillon is affordable for nearly every
consumer. It has applications in every cuisine in the world. New consumers don't just buy our bouillon, they buy into our brand, and as
the emerging economy develops, they move up the ladder into our
soups, sauces, and other products.

Two brand names tell much of the Bestfoods story: Knorr, the
chief brand of our $3 billion savory products portfolio, and Hell-
mann's, the lead brand of our $1.9 billion global dressings business.
Soups, bouillons, and meal makers under Knorr and related brands
hold first- or second-place market positions in 75 percent of their
dozens of markets around the world. In sauces, Knorr and related
brands are first or second in more than 50 percent of their markets.
Our dressings products, chiefly under the Hellmann's brand, hold
first or second position in close to 70 percent of their 42 markets. Better yet, the current performance of these brands is easily matched by
their potential for further vigorous growth in our established markets and, even more important, in emerging economies. Our fast-
growing food service business also markets our leading brands—a
linkage that distinguishes our food service business from those of
most other companies.

Acquiring Strategically

Acquisitions are a key element of our strategy for growth. At Bestfoods,
all of our acquisitions must have strategic as well as immediate financial value. We have made more than 50 acquisitions in the last 10 years,
which have accounted for about half of our top-line growth in the last
five years. In addition, nearly all had a positive impact on profits in
their first year. Pot Noodle, one of the five, has added tremendously to
our savory expertise, reflected in our cup product activities around the
world. Some of our acquisitions are important for adding critical scale.
For example, our purchase of the Starlux business in Spain added $160
million in sales, tripling the size of our Spanish affiliate. Starlux is a
model acquisition—close to our core businesses, reasonably large, and
significantly enhancing to the existing business in terms of product
offerings, manufacturing, and distribution.

We can work a slight variation on our core acquisition strategy. We call it our "Manila" alternative for acquisitions outside of our traditional expertise. The term *Manila* refers to a large acquisition we made in the Philippines, which included an array of leading core and noncore products. More recently, we purchased a business in Israel, which included leading products in noncore areas such as cereal and chocolate. Both of these acquisitions positioned us in a new economy as a strong local manufacturer.

We also do an occasional experiment. For example, we acquired Thomas Morel, a frozen food catering business in the United Kingdom that serves pubs with ready-made frozen meals. The business is small, but it brings with it a product line of microwaveable meals that we can leverage into other markets. However, we can count on one hand the number of such deals in the past 8 or 10 years, and they have all been small.

Two basic kinds of benefits can be achieved through acquisition. The first are what I call the hard synergies. They are thoroughly identifiable: savings in manufacturing, distribution, or sales. But beyond the point of integration these don't add substantial growth except in the longer term. And that leads me to the softer synergies: the systematic, strategic use of the brand that you gain with the acquisition—in another venue, across another geography, across another set of products.

A Willingness to Take Intelligent Risks

Bestfoods derives 65 percent of its earnings from markets outside of the United States and more than 25 percent from emerging markets, including Latin America, Asia, Africa, the Middle East, and Central and Eastern Europe. Not long ago, I was introduced at an industry conference by a Wall Street analyst who said, "It's rare when 25 percent exposure in emerging markets is viewed as a positive." It's true that much of our activity has been in regions and countries considered too risky by many of our peers, but these are precisely the areas that provide above-average growth opportunities for the future.

Our powerful brands, affordable products, and experienced local management give us the advantage in roller-coaster environments.

The best economic hedge you can have is local management who know the situation. The skills of our local management, honed over 40 years, enable us to restrain declines in sales and to preserve our profitability in the face of economic downturns. What we've learned over the years is, first, that we must maintain profitability—and sometimes that means raising prices! We may lose a bit of market share, but we gain strength to grow and prosper over the longer term. Beyond that, we don't pass up opportunities to invest in the region. But we don't do these things at huge prices.

Building on Our Core Strengths

We have always prided ourselves on our decentralized worldwide organization. It has given us unusual flexibility, kept us in close touch with the dynamics of local markets and eating habits, and built into our business the skills and instincts of the entrepreneur. Local managers have always been key decision makers, and they always will be. But we also recognize new opportunities when we see them. The global marketplace has changed in ways I don't need to describe. In a world of opening borders, instantaneous communications, and a common European currency, our best opportunities lie in bigger projects with bigger results, accomplished faster and with the most efficient deployment of resources.

Our central issue is how to capture the regional efficiencies required without destroying our intimacy with the consumer. Our approach is to achieve more integration via a global interchange within Bestfoods that transfers our learnings, technologies, and expertise around the world. We do this in a number of ways. One is through a mobile management group. We have Europeans working in the United States, and Americans and Europeans in Asia; we have Latin Americans trained in Europe and the United States. The other way is through our worldwide task forces and workshops. For example, we currently have three international strategic business teams, one for each of our three worldwide core businesses. The teams meet frequently via videoconference and in person to coordinate approaches and activities worldwide. We rely very much on this stepped-up, cross-border learning.

We also operate the Senior Management Development Program. We bring 25 of our high-potential managers together for a two-week period to go through a whole range of topics—from corporate culture to guiding Wall Street's expectations. We purposely mix the functions, layers, and nationalities of the group to assemble diverse viewpoints. A recent group ranged from staff managers in compensation and communications to country managers from Romania and Indonesia. We have been at this for 12 years now, starting with our most senior managers and working our way down. By the time we reached our third year, the program had become a change agent for us. Our younger people dared us to do things we wouldn't otherwise do. The diversity in these groups continues to enhance our performance.

Bestfoods has always included people of many different nationalities. But by diversity we mean more than that. We also mean the inclusion of people who don't look like the norm or think like the norm, people whose experience has been different from the norm. Diversity stimulates innovation, creativity, and faster problem solving—all drivers of superior growth.

Innovation

Innovation is extremely important for our future—not just innovation in theoretical terms, but innovation based on specific understanding and anticipation of consumption trends and consumer behavior in a variety of environments, from the United States and Europe to Latin America, Eastern Europe, and China. We already have a reasonably good innovation rate, defined as the percentage of sales generated by products introduced during the past three years. Comparing 1998 to 1995, when we began this measure, the innovation rate in our core businesses grew 20 percent to 10 percent of sales.

Our European business, especially, has a strong record of product innovation, mostly in our Knorr product lines. Nowadays many of our new European products have pan-European impact. Knorr culinary cubes, now marketed in 17 countries, are a prime example. Faster preparation is another area of increased innovation. If you look at the average cooking time of a Knorr soup product, it may have been 15 minutes 10 years ago; it's down to an average of 8 minutes now. Our most dramatic success in this segment is Knorr Hot Mug instant soups in Poland. We sold more than 260 million units in the first two years, contributing significantly to the Knorr brand's growth in that country.

Satisfying a Global Appetite

Our strategy evolves, but we're not changing the basic ingredients. The key remains aggressive growth in our three core businesses via product innovation, geographic expansion and acquisitions, and leveraging our capabilities through world-class execution as close as possible to local markets.

We have identified the next 10 emerging markets where we are likely to build businesses. For each we have created a surrogate general manager who takes the point of view of the country—what other products to bring into the market, when to go to a dedicated distributor, when to start thinking about putting a sales manager in place.

In addition to these 10 emerging markets, there are about a dozen sizeable markets in Asia, Africa, the Middle East, and Central and Eastern Europe where we are engaged in varying levels of developmental activity. Activities in these markets will range from stepping up exports to establishing full-fledged operations.

The best international food operators have the ability to set the tempo of their growth to what the market can absorb. Scale is important, but only as long as it has focus. At the end of the day, building brand scale is the most important success factor in our business. Every company has its own growth DNA. Ours is a consuming passion: *satisfying a global appetite.*

CHAPTER 3

Shareholder Value

Refocusing on Meaning over Measures

Over the past two decades, the triumph of free market economics and the proliferation of technology to support the free flow of information have created a powerful global capital market. A number of factors will intensify competition in worldwide markets and increase the pressures on CEOs to strengthen shareholder value. Investors will gain access to more information, and they will become more familiar with value concepts. The execution of transactions will become even easier. Deregulation in certain industries such as telecommunications and utilities will continue to erode the protection that some corporations have enjoyed in the past. As Europe moves to a single currency, investors will be better able to compare performance across borders. While there is uncertainty about the speed of change, there is no question about the direction of change. The shareholder value movement is here to stay, and participation is mandatory.

Investors in this environment are losing any remaining tolerance for the unproductive use of capital. Ira Millstein, a professor at Yale Law School, articulates this trend in comments on the recent Asian economic crisis: "Nobody was watching management; they were growing for the sake of growth *with no concern for shareholder value.* Capital is global ... if you can raise capital without emphasizing shareholder value, go ahead and try it, and God bless you." As a result of these global trends, shareholder value has captured center stage in the financial community and business media, and has become a staple in communications to investors. The issue before corporate leaders is, then, how to organize mandatory participation in the shareholder value movement. Our answer is, in short: Link corporate strategy directly to value.

The Scope of the Problem

Chief executive officers have long understood that capital is not free. In response, a large number of them have adopted a shareholder value mantra in their mission statements and strategy documents. However, for many the search for value ended glumly with continued generation of below-average returns. In fact, a study of 32 companies that announced a commitment to shareholder value in 1994 revealed that nearly 60 percent of them underperformed their industry peers and almost 70 percent underperformed the Standard & Poor's (S&P) 500 index.

The companies' underperformance is attributed to their adoption of partial solutions to the challenges of managing for value. For most, it meant choosing an internal measure or group of measures that closely correlate with external returns, then providing compensation schemes to enforce the value focus. This approach led to the creation of a new language of increasingly meaningless corporate finance acronyms. For example, evaluating business unit managers on EVA (economic value added) does not empower them to make better decisions because they have little impact on the key forces behind EVA. The results are confusion and frustration.

The key to value creation is not new measurements. It remains where it has always been: in making the right choices and ensuring that they are implemented. Companies need to take a holistic approach to the challenge of creating value and to transform their organizations so that actions and decisions at every level reinforce

the goal of value maximization. To achieve this ambition, five qu___
tions must be addressed:

- What does it mean to create value for investors?
- What business strategies will drive value creation?
- How do we translate these strategies into operational activities?
- How do we ensure that these activities take place as planned and have the desired effect?
- How do we reinforce the required commitment to value creation by making it part of the corporate culture?

Our approach to addressing these questions is to apply an embracing set of principles for value management that companies can apply. We define *value management* as follows: the process by which the firm actively plans, manages, and reinforces the economic contribution of the business.

These principles shift the emphasis from context-free value measures; they integrate strategic, financial, and operational planning. Four mutually supporting elements must be addressed to achieve the desired results in business performance (see Figure 3.1). In the remainder of this chapter, we describe how companies can use this framework and transform their organizations into engines of value creation.

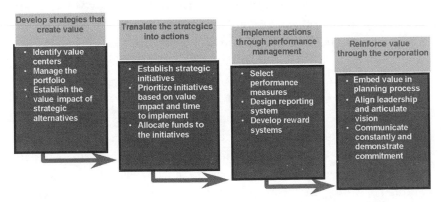

Figure 3.1 Value management framework.

The Value Management Framework

Peter F. Drucker provided the following definition for *value:* "Until a business returns a profit that is greater than its cost of capital, it operates at a loss. Never mind that it pays taxes as if it had a genuine profit. The enterprise still returns less to the economy than it devours in resources. It does not cover its full costs unless the reported profit exceeds the cost of capital. Until then, it does not create wealth; it destroys it" ("The Information Executives Truly Need," *Harvard Business Review,* January-February 1995). "Profit" here is economic, as opposed to accounting profit, and is defined as the operating profit of a company minus a capital charge that represents the opportunity cost of capital invested by the business. The value of a company is equal to its invested capital plus the present value of future expected economic profits. Therefore, a company creates shareholder value only if it generates returns on invested capital (ROIC) in excess of its weighted average cost of capital (WACC).

Strategies That Create Value

Our approach to strategy development is based on two premises. First, there is an intrinsic link between strategy and finance, despite the fact that many companies allow these two domains to operate independently. Second, strategy is about choice. Companies consciously choose which of their current markets to invest in, where they will compete now and in the future, and how they will develop and maintain positions of advantage. These premises, coupled with our understanding of value creation, lead to our definition of strategy: *Strategy is the collective set of corporate choices to gain and hold positions generating returns on invested capital in excess of the cost of capital.*

To generate such returns, a company needs to participate in markets that offer high economic returns and/or in markets where the company can develop and sustain competitive advantages. Michael Porter introduced these concepts in the early 1980s through several definitive works on strategy and competitive positioning. While many companies embrace these concepts, the link to value is assessed qualitatively or at high levels. Our approach incorporates quantitative value assessment as part of the company's strategic selections at multiple organizational levels where strategy and competition differ.

Companies that consistently make decisions based on these two characteristics realize higher value creation than their peers. In an analysis of 416 companies over a five-year period beginning in September 1993, companies participating in highly attractive industries* or competitively advantaged in their industry† realized total shareholder returns (TSR) significantly better than those of the average company. Further, companies with both competitive advantage and competing in highly attractive industries had even higher average five-year TSRs. Interestingly, we also found that even within industries in which the average competitor had a negative ROIC-WACC spread, those companies with competitive advantage still did a reasonable job of enhancing shareholder value. These companies had a five-year TSR of over 11 percent, just below the average of 13 percent. (See Figure 3.2.)

To realize superior value creation consistently, companies need to be highly analytical and discerning about the strategic choices they make and place value maximization as the overriding objective that drives decisions. Companies that do not follow this discipline risk destroying large amounts of value. Dow Jones's is a perfect example. In 1990, signaling a change from its core business of financial media, it chose to enter the financial information services market by purchasing a company called Telerate for $1.6 billion. Between 1990 and 1996, Telerate consistently lost market share to competitors' more technologically advanced products. In 1996, Dow Jones operating income took a huge dive and the company's market value fell to $2.6 billion from $5.4 billion 10 years earlier. Some members of the Dow Jones family began to argue for selling Telerate and cutting the company's losses. The company chose instead to spend $650 million to overhaul Telerate, but the investment was too little, too late. By Jan-

---

* We defined "highly attractive industries" as those in which the average ROIC-WACC spread was above 2 percent over the past five years.
† We defined "competitively advantaged" companies as those whose ROIC-WACC spreads were at least 3 percent better than those of the average competitor in the industry.

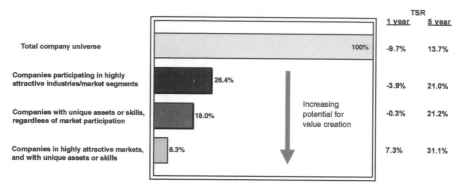

Figure 3.2 Potential for value creation.

uary 1998, Dow Jones announced that it was dramatically scaling back the planned investment in Telerate. Finally, in March, the company sold Telerate for $98 million.

Creating Value in Three Ways

Companies can avoid such value destruction by adhering to three value-creating concepts. First, successful companies realize that markets exist that may not have a standard industry definition. As a result, these firms extend their analysis from industry or business unit to the true economics and competitive dynamics surrounding specific products, customers, or combinations of them. This persistence enables them to choose with some precision where and how to compete. We advocate disaggregating a business into value centers— economic units subject to distinct strategic conditions that can be managed independently for value—and undertaking the associated strategic and financial analysis at this level. Value center definitions may deviate from the company organizational structure, but applying analytical rigor at the level of the value center enables an enhanced definition of a market's attractiveness or competitive advantage.

Companies content to identify attractive market spaces at a higher level may fail to understand the details of a particular market. As a result, value-destroying positions may go unchecked while value-creating spaces remain unexploited. For example, CarCo, as we will call a major automotive corporation, is organized by manufacturing platforms—small passenger cars, sport utility vehicles, large passenger cars, and trucks. Each of these organizational units hides a mixed grouping of value-creating and value-destroying markets. A value center view disaggregates the business along two dimensions—the passenger area (small, medium, large) and the primary customer need (luxury, sport, transport, off road, heavy cargo)—and determines the specific economics of each. CarCo could thus make more value-creating choices for its business.

Second, to extract value throughout the market life cycle, successful companies define value centers with their potential ROIC-WACC spreads. The resulting portfolio view of the value potential of each business has several benefits. It identifies current sources of value and prompts management to generate creative alternatives regarding future value-creating ambitions; it offers explicit guidelines for the efficient allocation of resources; and it brings the need for divestment into sharp focus. This perspective also forces companies to define the objectives of every value center. In so doing, they understand the life cycle stage of a particular value center and how the competitive landscape may be changing. Successful companies manage value centers as a portfolio of assets with the objective of deriving the most value from them over their life cycles.

Say that CarCo participates in the midsize sport utility vehicle market, currently an attractive market segment from an ROIC-WACC perspective. Yet CarCo realizes spreads that are lower than the industry average. CarCo then decides where the value center is in terms of life cycle, asks whether it should aggressively pursue improving its position, focus on niches, or plan an exit strategy. A positive ROIC-WACC today may forestall making this sort of analysis. But how long are such results sustainable, and how much does the corporation stand to lose if appropriate action is not taken?

Finally, successful companies will select the strategic option based on value-maximizing impact. They assess their differentiation capabilities by identifying the various attributes that are important to customers and assess positioning relative to competitors to determine strengths and weaknesses. They improve certain attributes, then assess the value impact and quantify the impact of each attribute on the key drivers of value.

ChemCo, the name we will give a large chemical manufacturer, used this approach to analyze and select strategic options. It started by determining the various customer attributes and their prioritization (cost, quality, safety, innovation), then assessed its ranking relative to competitors along each of these attributes. ChemCo's conclusions demonstrated strong product quality but weak innovation, both of which were important to customers. ChemCo can now decide whether to improve product quality and exploit its current advantage or improve its poor innovation. In order to decide between the alternatives, ChemCo determined the value of each strategy by projecting its expected impact on customer behavior, hence on key value drivers and the overall value of the business. This thorough analysis revealed that focusing on improving product innovation would have the greatest impact on the value of the business.

Translating Strategies into Action

Even with a winning strategy, a company will create value only if it is able to translate the strategy into action by addressing the issues of prioritizing, funding, and monitoring the progress of strategic initiatives. Prioritizing investment decisions requires three criteria: value impact, time to implementation, and probability of success. Analytical rigor through the prioritization stage makes funding decisions more objective as it decreases the entitlement mentality* embedded in traditional funding processes. As investment occurs, monitoring value creation is a critical component of continued strategic choice.

The value map illustrated in Figure 3.3 assesses returns realized in proportion to investments made. Assessing a business through the use of a *staircase* leads to greater understanding of where resource deployment may be changed to increase value. A manufacturing company with two divisions and a capital base equally divided between these divisions employed this analysis and arrived at a decision to sell the underperforming segment of the business. Within 48 hours of the sale announcement, the company's stock nearly doubled. It then employed the proceeds to strengthen its overperforming division through several acquisitions.

Companies continue to make investment decisions driven by measures other than value creation. In 1994, Warren Buffett noted

---

* The entitlement mentality is a result of allocating resources employing a rationing approach between business units or departments and being limited by a fixed budget notion that is driven by available funds.

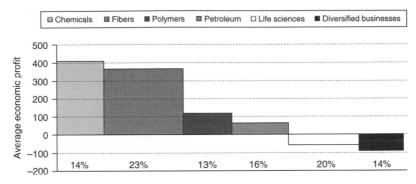

Figure 3.3 Average invested capital (1994–1997).

that "when managers are making capital allocation decisions . . . it's vital that they act in ways that increase per-share intrinsic value, and avoid moves that decrease it. This principle may seem obvious but we constantly see it violated. And, when miscalculations occur, shareholders are hurt." To further illustrate this point, consider a hospital management group that ran 100 hospitals, some of which it owned. This group employed return on net assets (RONA) as the sole criterion for investment in strategic initiatives. But the oldest hospitals were generating the highest RONA, thanks to their asset base, and were therefore the favored sites for additional investments. The result was aging hospitals with high-tech equipment, which was in turn underutilized. In addition, these favored hospitals were mostly in areas with a nonpaying customer base; even when used, they were not generating revenues.

Implementation through Performance Management

Performance management is the bridge between value measurement and strategy on one side and the operational level on the other. A value-based performance management framework provides a company with measures that combine lead (predictive) and lag (result) indicators, and identifies the linkages between the different measures. Value measures have traditionally been translated to financial targets that are historically focused and reflect current issues to be addressed immediately. Leading-edge companies understand that financial outcomes tend to be preceded by indicators about customer perceptions in the marketplace. This perspective results from individuals' working in concert to achieve a specific target in the company's operations, processes, and service capabilities, and building their performance management framework to include measures covering all these aspects.

Pure value measures are meaningless and confusing at the business operations level. To quote a divisional manager, "The CFO is really hooked on this shareholder value thing. Out here in operations, it means nothing. It simply hasn't been translated into terms we can relate to. We haven't got a clue how to put it in action." Translating these measures to such immediately applicable terms can be achieved by developing value driver trees (see Figure 3.4), which decompose shareholder value drivers and targets to meaningful frontline targets. Value driver trees enable the selection of appropriate operational measures and the establishment of targets at multiple levels where individuals have control.

Throughout the 1970s, Xerox leased copy machines and earned revenue on every copy made. Sales and profits from leases and supporting items (paper, toner) were growing, yet customers were disgruntled by frequent breakdowns and malfunctions. In an effort to enhance financial results, Xerox began to allow direct purchase of the machines and set up a repair service as a separate profit center—rather than focus on improving quality. All financial indicators (sales, profitability, return on investment) seemed positive. Yet customers were still dissatisfied; when competing machines produced comparable copies and did not malfunction, Xerox lost both market share and

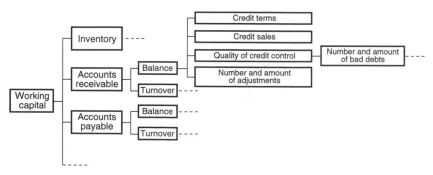

Figure 3.4   Working capital value driver tree.

value. Xerox was forced to make a new commitment to customer service and quality in the 1980s.

Reinforcing Value

Two elements that reinforce value throughout the corporation are compensation and culture. Dr. William H. Joyce, CEO of Union Carbide, has said, "A program that has downsides in it when I don't perform is a good thing. Betting your money just like shareholders is a thing that balances the risk equation between management and investors." Laudable though these sentiments are, research for 1995–1997 shows that CEO salary increases and compensation outstripped increases in shareholder returns.

A value-based compensation scheme has three characteristics: It addresses all organizational levels, establishes metrics appropriate for each individual's responsibility level, and determines targets that demand superior performance. For example, tying a CEO's compensation solely to market shareholder returns is insufficient as it overlooks competitive aspects. An improved scheme would compare the returns and link them to a market or peer performance index.

Companies targeting the creation of a value-maximizing culture need to address two challenges. First, since culture is neither explicit nor tangible, executives need to take steps to define it in preparation for change. Second, since culture arises out of the business and market circumstances in which the company operates, it is deeply embedded and almost certainly has elements of resistance to change, which will be magnified only in uncertain environments. A key premise of changing culture is to prove that yesterday's success resulting from existing beliefs and behaviors will be challenged tomorrow as a result of those beliefs and behaviors.

Companies can successfully change their culture through each stage of the value management framework by recognizing the key levers for change and defining tangible actions to take along the way. At the strategic level, senior leadership alignment around the value-maximizing objective ensures that the organization will fund initiatives with the highest value impact. As initiatives are funded, leadership commitment to overcoming the entitlement mind-set and eliminating unprofitable growth signals a key change in both belief and behavior. When performance and compensation schemes are developed, leadership's explanation to employees of the linkages between targets and value-creation objectives reinforces dedication to value and prepares employees for experiencing change.

The Future for Value Management

Linking strategy to value will require a great deal of information. This need will force companies to overhaul their internal management information systems. Companies need financial and nonfinancial data, historical and predictive measures, internal and external information in order to understand the interplay between their strategy and the business environment. They also need to keep track of competitors, customers, suppliers, new entrants to the marketplace, potential substitute products, and so forth. In the Internet age, information is available in overwhelming quantities, although the quality and organization of the data are often poor. In the future, companies will have information systems capable of identifying, filtering, and analyzing the vast amounts of available data to make them relevant to decision-making needs. More and more companies will adopt systems that enable them to analyze instantaneously the impact of alternative scenarios on value drivers. These systems will be capable of integrating strategic, financial, and operational information in a way that supports all management processes. Ultimately, these information systems should create transparency across the enterprise so that all decision makers can directly link actions to value.

Investors will demand improved reporting from companies. Companies will need to report value-based information, both financial and strategic, as opposed to traditional accounting measures such as earnings per share (EPS). Investors will command an improved understanding of both the company's historical performance and its prospects for the future.

Finally, and most important, some companies will learn, at the expense of others, to thrive in this shareholder-driven world. We believe that these value champions will have embraced the holistic approach described in this chapter. They will reap the rewards of aligning their organizations behind a value-maximizing agenda.

John F. Antioco
Chairman and Chief Executive Officer, Blockbuster Inc.

Changing the Rules
A Path to Shareholder Value

Two years ago, Blockbuster launched a sweeping and fundamental transformation of its industry, the first in the 20-year life of the U.S. video rental business. We did not do this from a position of great strength but in semidesperation. The result: a revolutionary reshaping of our supply chain, which changed the economics of the business much to the benefit of ourselves and of our customers. My guess is that other companies will examine the details of this story, and in time we'll see something similar in other industries. As in our case, the opportunity for changing the rules of the game may be hard to recognize, but it's possible to win big.

I was the third Blockbuster CEO in 18 months. The corporate landscape was not a pretty sight at Blockbuster in mid-1997. Sales, profits, and customer counts were declining. In a misguided attempt to diversify product offerings, most of the 6,000 stores were selling T-shirts, music, candy, and comics—unsuccessfully. The marketing of these products and of video rentals was out of sync. Another weakness: Blockbuster had lost a fair amount of institutional memory about a month before I arrived. Some 70 percent of the management team had declined to relocate with corporate headquarters from Fort Lauderdale, Florida, to Dallas, Texas. The company's chief assets were the strength of its brand plus its market share of roughly 23 percent, both of which were slipping. On Wall Street, however, some analysts who followed Viacom, our parent, valued Blockbuster at little more than zero, chiefly because of precipitous declines in cash flow. The scuttlebutt was that, in buying Blockbuster two years previously, Viacom International Chairman Sumner Redstone had made the biggest mistake in a lifetime of stellar deal making.

A Flawed Supply Chain

Certainly, the bearish analysts were right about one thing: The video rental business had been sliding for a year or more. The bloom was off the rose. Consumers were disaffected. My personal consumer habits as a video renter reflected those of many in the population. The repeated disappointment of going to the video store on a Friday night and finding nothing worthwhile finally got to me. I gave up trying. Here was a retail industry incapable of satisfying the demand for new movie titles and turning away people with, "Sorry, try again later." The average customer had to visit a typical Blockbuster location no fewer than five consecutive times to get the movie he or she wanted. About a fifth of all visitors walked out without buying anything. Frustrated retailers tried to work around frustrated customers by advertising to bring in first-time renters to replace those who had either done without new titles or opted for home entertainment via satellite TV.

This discontent was embedded in the industry supply chain. For two decades, the movie producers sold rental videos at an average (by 1998) of $65 per copy, with negligible volume discounts. Neither chains nor mom-and-pop outlets could afford to stock copies of hit releases in sufficient depth to satisfy the demand. Attempts had been made to use our market share as a bargaining chip with the studios—we needed price cuts to afford more copy depth. However, the studios were not obliging. Since nobody knew how to break the mold of industry custom, the stalemate continued and profits sank.

The immediate fixes at Blockbuster were not difficult. We junked the nonvideo products and focused on video rental alone, while cutting costs by constraining store expansion. But the structural problem remained. We were trapped inside a failed economic model with a huge gap between choked supply and unsatisfied demand. Blockbuster was careening downhill in transactions, customer count, and almost every other measure of performance—but these realities made it easier for us to decide that the only remedy lay in a sweeping overall change in practices.

The odds of success were improved by two factors. First, despite declining video industry numbers, people genuinely like watching movies at home. Sales of VCRs were at all-time highs in 1997 and again in 1998, and consumers consistently rated video rental as one of their favorite leisure-time activities. Their only unhappiness was not being able to rent the movies of their choice.

The second reason behind our chance to change the rules that had always governed the game was that home video sales represent the lion's share of Hollywood's domestic profits, far more than revenues from theatrical showings, pay-per-view, network television, or any other movie-watching venue. It was in the studios' best interest to help fix the video rental category. But it was up to Blockbuster to show the studios that the category *could be* fixed and that we knew how to do it—at least for our company.

Testing Our Concept against Market Realities

In late 1997, we undertook a test in six markets. We financed our own copy-depth programs to prove that customers would respond positively when enough new-release movies were in stock to satisfy peak weekend demand. We aggressively advertised the availability of the hottest movie titles and promoted other consumer-friendly changes we had put in place. We boldly told consumers that Blockbuster was dedicated to making sure that they would "Go Home Happy."

We began to see results almost immediately. More customers were coming in more often, renting more movies per transaction, and walking out of our stores more satisfied. Additionally, we began to see a decline in the number of customers who split their business between a competitor and ourselves.

At once we approached a number of the studios with our results and suggested revenue-sharing programs in which Blockbuster would pay 80 to 90 percent less per copy, buy much larger quantities, and split the revenues generated by the rental of the tapes. Revenue sharing was by no means new. Movie houses already used it, and some studios had revenue-sharing arrangements with third-party distributors that supplied small retailers.

The studios responded to our test results and revenue-sharing proposal in a variety of ways. Some cautiously. Others much more optimistically and beyond our expectations. By the end of the first quarter of 1998, we were bringing in some 25 percent of our new-release movies through revenue-sharing arrangements. Midway through the year, that percentage crept up to about 50 percent, and by the third quarter—less than a year after our test—almost all of the new movies in our stores were acquired under revenue-sharing agreements. We were able to increase our copy depth of new movies by 150 percent and simultaneously increase the number of new movie titles available at our stores by 61 percent.

There were risks at the beginning, and risks as we continued this structural revamping. Would the roughly 40-60 revenue split between the studios and ourselves actually allow us to maintain decent profit margins? Would projected store traffic and revenue gains in fact materialize? Retailer's instinct told me that this was the right track—that we didn't have to sit around and deliberate or call in consultants. But I give Viacom credit for granting me a free hand and accepting the risks. Several times over, I rehearsed my arguments with Viacom senior management; they prodded and probed and asked, "Are you sure this is the right thing?" On the outside, I displayed complete confidence. In truth, nobody could be totally confident of a plan that was such a break with the past.

In 27 years in retailing, I have never seen such a response. By the end of the third quarter of 1998, only six months after restructuring our supply chain, our transaction numbers were up about 20 percent, and 23 percent by year-end. Membership in the course of the year rose by 10 percent. In just over six months, we had changed a business model that had existed for 20 years. Our market share soared from 23 to 27 percent by the end of 1998—and should continue to grow in the years ahead.

Other Strategies Were Needed

Needless to say, revenue sharing alone is not a cure-all. Of necessity, we brought a number of other strategies to bear. We changed from a national price structure to one based on local competitive situations. We lowered the prices of cataloged items in order to compete more effectively. Revenue sharing helped us guarantee the availability of many new releases—but if copies were out of stock, we made the attractive offer that the customer could rent the movie later at no cost. In another important shift, our $133.2 million annual domestic advertising campaign moved out of category identification ("Make it a Blockbuster Night") to affirm customer satisfaction as our number one goal ("Go Home Happy"). And we were able to promote specific titles—a distinct change from the past—because now we actually had the titles in stock and could tell customers about them.

Some independent video retailers felt the earth tremble underfoot. They protested that similar revenue-sharing agreements were unavailable to them. We had absolutely no exclusive deals, we replied, and no most-favored-nation clauses with the studios. We had done nothing, either by contract or by any other means, to prevent studios from signing even better deals with retailers big and small. And as more of our rivals did just that, the protest fizzled.

People started to take notice. *The Hollywood Reporter* for June 1, 1998, wrote: "Blockbuster's move to revenue sharing could even help the entire video industry by changing the rules of the game." A competitor in Illinois was quoted in the press as follows: "They're driving customers into their stores. For the first time in the history of home video, they're meeting customer demand." Blockbuster's recovery "has had a halo effect for the rental industry in total," said Mitch Koch, chief of North American operations for Buena Vista Home Entertainment.

Beneath the Stream of Events

That is our narrative. Now let's go beneath the stream of events and do some analysis. Obviously, there were some fundamentals in our favor—chiefly the fact that we were the biggest retailer in the sector. Consumers identified us with the category and, thanks to our size, we were able to persuade suppliers to listen to a radical new idea.

I believe in keeping things simple—most truths in business are simple. Any consumer proposition can be summed up as: Find out what they want and give it to them. Although the degree of pent-up demand in video rental before revenue sharing has few parallels, it is an instance of a common phenomenon: misalignment of interests and perceptions between suppliers and customers. What revenue sharing did, in essence, was to align the interests of studios, rental retailers, and the end customer better than before. The structure under which the studios tried to induce Blockbuster to buy as many copies as possible at as high a price as possible was the wrong structure. Today, the studios' marketing interests coincide with ours. The sale isn't over when a studio gets the initial purchase order for 10,000 copies of this or that movie. Nowadays the dialogue between us starts more like this: "What is the potential of the film, and what is the best way to take it to market?"

The vitality of the category helped our strategy—for example, a string of hit movies in 1998, compared to disappointing 1997 releases. Changing the rules is tougher when demand is declining or prices are falling sharply. Only if good industry fundamentals exist will the many players in the supply chain assume the risks of changing the economic model. In our case, there was a widespread perception that the category was good, that most people like the value proposition of a movie rental.

Changing the rules of the game starts with the insight that the game isn't working, but it *could* and *should* work. The complete pattern of positive change may not yet be clear. But you begin worrying at small illogicalities, mismatches of economic interests, areas of irrational conflict, and that sort of thing. You bring all your experience and shrewdness to bear on analyzing the structure of economic power in an industry, the rationale behind it, the weak points in it. You plug away at these discrete issues, always asking *why* is this the practice and *why not* something different? And at some point the light dawns—the possibility of a new model emerges in your mind. After that, it needs only good negotiating skills and powers of persuasion to convert the vision into reality.

Harry M. Jansen Kraemer, Jr.
President and Chief Executive Officer, Baxter International Inc.

Building Value the Baxter Way

Is shareholder value a growing movement with long-term positive impact or just another passing fad? Certainly, the value-building concept is sound, since shareholders must be satisfied that they have made the best of many possible alternative investments. The problem, as I see it, is that too many CEOs take too narrow a view of how best to build and sustain shareholder value. Some place all their efforts in strategy. Others focus exclusively on the economics. And what about other factors affecting both strategy and the numbers? These also cannot be ignored. Shareholders are important, but can any CEO satisfy shareholders while ignoring the other stakeholders in the enterprise: employees and customers? The CEO who will be most effective in building value over the long term will perceive and act on the direct link between strategy and economics, and on the relationship among the company's people, its customers, and, ultimately, its shareholders.

Building Value at Baxter

As CEO, my approach to building value at Baxter is really quite simple and can be summarized by the following formula:

$$\text{Strategic goals} + \text{economic goals} + \text{people} + \text{customers} = \text{shareholder value}$$

Let's start with strategic goals. At any given moment, I must have before me a clear set of goals, the accomplishment of which will have a direct, positive impact on shareholder value. At Baxter, these goals center on global expansion through strategic acquisitions and leadership in technological innovation. But strategy is not enough. Each strategic investment decision must be firmly grounded in solid economics. What are the cash flow implications? What are the trade-offs? Is the action under consideration the best use of our resources, both human and financial?

Any investment decision—even one that makes both strategic *and* economic sense—is dead in the water without the right people to implement it. That's why we have, and I strive to maintain, a team that is second to none among global health care companies. Our people understand what affects our stock price, and, most important, they are focused on serving our customers and patients better than any competitor.

This customer focus is critical; without customers, nothing else matters. The key task for all Baxter people is to build and sustain positive customer relationships. They understand that customer satisfaction is our most sustainable competitive advantage; it's what distinguishes us in the marketplace. And our products are the basis of that satisfaction. Each of our customers must at all times be completely satisfied with our products, for today's satisfaction is the best guarantee of future sales.

Where, then, do the shareholders fit in? As CEO, if I have the best people focused on building and sustaining solid customer relationships, I will also have all the ingredients I need financially to improve the stock price.

Strategic Acquisitions That Build Value

Strategic acquisitions are one prong of Baxter's value-building strategy. Studies have shown that most acquisitions destroy rather than build the value of the acquiring company. Fortunately, at Baxter we are able to succeed where so many others fail. We view acquisitions in the same manner as any other value-building investment. With acquisitions, as with other value-building strategies, success depends in large measure on binding the strategic factors to the economics of the deal.

Whenever an acquisition opportunity presents itself, it's usually the strategic aspects of the deal that fire people up—particularly those in the executive suite. I don't exempt myself from this reaction. When a potential acquisition offers us the opportunity to build on our product lines, achieve economies of scale, or further penetrate strategically important markets, I am as excited as anyone else. Not feeling that excitement, in my view, is a major red flag. But a CEO should never let that excitement blind him or her to the fact that the economics of the deal have to be equally exciting, or it won't work. Dealing realistically with the economics requires focus and discipline, but doing so is the only way to ensure that the acquisition will create rather than destroy value.

When I consider a strategically appropriate acquisition, I stay focused on one overriding principle: acquiring the company for *less* than it is worth. I ask myself and my management team: What do I have to believe in order to be convinced to pay X amount of dollars for a company? What combination of projected growth rates, margins, expenses, taxes, and investments do we need to achieve before we commit to the deal? Because one thing is certain: If the company cannot be acquired for less than its future discounted cash flows, including synergy savings, it will destroy value, regardless of how strategically right the acquisition may appear to be.

In evaluating an acquisition, giving disproportionate weight to either strategy or economics is one way to destroy value. Another is to delay rapid integration of the acquired entity into the acquiring company. Parties to a deal typically view the consummation of a desirable acquisition as the successful conclusion of a major and complex value-building effort. But even as the celebration party commences, the value clock starts ticking and value begins to erode. The reasons for this are clear. More shares are now outstanding and, depending on the return they earn, meaningful dilution could occur. Or the significant outlay of cash needed to complete the deal may be generating exorbitant amounts of interest expense. For these and other reasons, quick integration of the acquired company is absolutely crucial to its making a significant contribution to value.

The need to integrate quickly seems obvious, yet delaying integration is more the rule than the exception. There are many good reasons for this. The acquiring company is often sensitive to the anxieties and uncertainties of the acquired company's employees and slowly moves to alleviate them. This seems the right thing to do, both from a value and a people perspective. But clearly, from the value side, as I've illustrated, slowly will not do. What about from the people side? In my view, there are two things that human beings dislike most: uncertainty and change. Experiencing either one causes great discomfort. Experiencing both simultaneously is intolerable. Up-front answers to questions regarding employment, roles, and the time frame in which change will occur mitigate this discomfort. With these answers in hand, employees can make a decision: either opt in or opt out. The sooner that happens, the better. The longer you wait, the more value you destroy.

The Unique Challenge of Building Value in a "Portfolio" Company

Over the years, Baxter has evolved into what may be termed a portfolio company—that is, a company that consists of a number of separate but related businesses. Each of our four businesses is in some way concerned with technologies related to the blood and circulatory system. While there are distinct advantages to this type of company, one of them is *not* the ease with which value is created. Consider the issues from a CEO's perspective. In order to ensure the highest shareholder value, the CEO must look at opportunities, risks, returns, and trade-offs across the entire portfolio simultaneously and then rank these areas against each other for each business and for all the businesses. He or she must then prioritize likely investment opportunities, select those most promising in terms of alignment with strategy and realistic economics, and then assign appropriate financial and human resources. Adding to the complexity are the inevitable conflicts that arise among the business unit leaders, who, after all, are fiercely protective of their respective businesses.

This last issue is the most critical part of the value equation in a portfolio company, and it is the CEO's greatest challenge. Put another way, how does the CEO of such a company get senior managers who are deeply committed to the success of their respective business units focused on the overall value of the company? How does one get them to think strategically and economically about both goals simultaneously? This conundrum has been the bane of CEOs since the dawn of multibusiness corporate structures. Many solutions have been tried, and most have failed. At Baxter we knew that a unique approach was necessary to the long-term perpetuation of our value-building focus. We wound up breaking new ground.

Refocusing the Incentive Structure

As a portfolio company, Baxter is not unique. In addition to fostering a kind of tunnel vision on the part of business unit leaders, such a structure encourages a disconnect between these leaders and senior corporate executives. That distance generates the false perception that only the senior corporate executives are in a position to evaluate objectively the strategic and economic appropriateness of investment opportunities across the portfolio, and to prioritize these opportunities and allocate resources. The challenge then becomes how to change this perception, or, in other words, how to focus the business unit leaders not only on their own businesses, but also on the good of the entire company.

To illustrate the point, let's sit in on a hypothetical planning meeting at Baxter. Attending are myself, our chief financial officer, and the heads of our four business units. The leader of our cardiovascular unit has just concluded that he could use additional capacity—to the tune of $30 million—for heart valves. He also concludes, based on his analysis, that the investment will yield a 40 percent return. Naturally, he is convinced that his heart valve project represents an outstanding investment opportunity that is right, strategically and economically, for his business. But he also knows, or at least believes, that decisions impacting the overall company lie not in his hands but in the hands of the CEO. Therefore, while he is extremely enthusiastic, he is also somewhat disengaged. After all, he has presented his best case. I'll either accept it or reject it. But he is not as disengaged as the other three business heads, who, understandably, have their own projects to propose, projects that will affect the performance of their respective business units. Their indifference to the project pitched by the head of cardiovascular does not reflect ill will toward him, but in their minds there is only so much they can worry about beyond their own businesses.

For a company that consists of related businesses, this represents a less than optimal situation. While their businesses are different, each of these individuals has a broad and deep overall understanding of the health care industry and of relationships among the different kinds of businesses within it. Imagine the power of the collective thinking that is *not* being brought to bear upon the achievement of Baxter's overall value objectives, because the company's structure forces the business unit leaders to take a narrow view that does not look further than their respective niches.

To solve this dilemma, we first took a hard look at traditional approaches. What, we asked, would be the result of bonuses based on overall company—rather than individual business unit—results? We concluded that while such a plan might serve to refocus people away from their individual businesses and onto the company as a whole, this desirable change might ironically also cause the individual businesses to suffer and eventually defeat the larger goal. Conversely, we concluded, incentivizing on an individual basis would simply fuel the existing problem and have a negative impact on overall results. How, then, to find the proverbial happy medium?

Next, we speculated that the answer might lie in focusing on what we were really trying to do: increase the stock price. To that end, we looked at how closely we could tie incentives to the stock price, without perpetuating problems similar to those raised by the bonus plan. Stock options seemed a good idea, but the plan lacked a downside. In other words, if the stock price went up, everyone would be happy. But if it went down, nobody would really suffer beyond the abstract loss of an unrealized gain.

The Solution: A Stake That Matters

Finally, we concluded that if we wanted our top managers to focus consistently on the overall value of the company, we would have to create a situation in which they operated not only as heads of individual business units, but as collective owners of Baxter. In short, they needed to own a significant portion of Baxter stock, a portion large enough so that changes in the stock price would have a meaningful impact, positive or negative, on their financial well-being.

Therefore, we offered the top 70 people in the company a shared investment plan. Under the plan, each individual secured a personal loan of $2 million and invested the money in Baxter stock. If the plan was to work, the managers would really have to feel the pressure of the obligation, so the loans were arranged through an outside bank, not through the company. Of course, it was not our intention to subject our top managers to unacceptable risk. Therefore, Baxter helped in two ways. First, the company guaranteed the loans (as a recourse of last resort), thereby securing an extremely favorable interest rate. Second, we arranged for the loans to be for 100 percent of the stock purchase price.

How has this new plan affected the thinking of our top managers? Let's return to our hypothetical meeting. Now, when the head of our cardiovascular unit proposes a $30 million capital project for heart valves, everyone—not just the champion of the project—engages. After all, with their income potential and ability to service a $2 million loan tied directly to Baxter's stock price, each manager is very focused not only on his or her individual business, but also on the overall value of the company. The managers are no longer content to leave capital allocation decisions solely in the hands of the CEO. The "it's your decision" attitude that characterized this meeting before the shared incentive plan was in place has changed to "it's our decision." Everyone is now focused on overall as well as business-unit strategy and economics, and on the project prioritization and resource allocation process. All decisions are now benchmarked against the key value drivers that influence Baxter stock. The notion that somehow the cash will be there is transformed into a keen interest in where the cash is coming from and where, alternatively, it might go. Suddenly, the most efficient sharing of resources among the business units becomes important. Miraculously, the prevailing attitude becomes, "We're all working for the same company. We're all in this together."

Institutional Investors: Influencing Value

Baxter's stock price is, of course, most directly moved by the efforts of Baxter people. The shared investment plan has certainly maximized those efforts. But investor gains are also affected by outside forces, such as the market's understanding of the value created by a company. While many factors shape this understanding, chief among them are the purchasing decisions of institutional investors.

Some CEOs feel unduly influenced by the expectations of institutional investors. Management sometimes feels pressured into taking actions that might satisfy those expectations but, at the same time, might not be in the best long-term interest of the company. Personally, I consider institutional investors tremendously helpful. They may pose tough questions, but they're usually right. And they give me the opportunity to strengthen, as well display, the kind of discipline to which the market responds favorably.

In my view, the key element underlying a positive relationship with institutional investors is the credibility of the CEO and the management team, a credibility established by articulating a well-defined strategy and demonstrating the economic discipline necessary to implement it. Simply put, if our actions are consistently in harmony with our words, if they result in outcomes we have predicted, and if what we say and do makes sense logically, strategically, and economically, then we can have enormous influence in the stock purchasing decisions of institutional investors and a reasonably significant impact on the company's value.

Another hypothetical scenario will serve as an example. Let's say that I have publicly articulated my expectations about Baxter's earnings for the short and long term, and that my projections make strategic and economic sense. I have emphasized that we are looking at both the short and long term, and that earnings projections are based at least in part on our intention to put more money into research and development and capital expenditures.

Let's also say that despite the soundness of my forecast, institutional investors ask me a question like the following: "Harry, to the extent that foreign exchange will improve, could your short-term earnings be higher?" Let me rephrase the question to reveal its subtext. What the institutional investors are really asking is, "Harry, despite the fact that you've established and will meet certain expectations about short-term earnings, will you now revise those expectations upward in light of a possible change in circumstances?"

From my perspective, buckling under to that kind of pressure would be a mistake. To do so might make the institutional investors happy for the moment, but over the long term it would damage my credibility and hurt the company. Instead, I would reinforce my earlier statement and, by rejecting a short-term gain in favor of accomplishing our long-term vision, demonstrate the discipline that is the basis of our ongoing credibility. That credibility is far more important to Baxter's long-term value than any incremental stock increase that would result from my being pressured into doing something contrary to our stated intentions—particularly when those intentions are solidly grounded in a credible strategic and economic plan.

To summarize, the CEO must manage the expectations of institutional investors and not allow these expectations to get ahead of where the company is going. If the CEO has the discipline to do this and do it consistently, he or she will earn the enduring respect of institutional investors, a respect necessary to building and maintaining value over the long term.

Shareholder Value: U.S. Obsession or Global Imperative?

Another powerful external factor influencing shareholder value is global competition. This influence is of a subtler nature. Baxter is a global company competing in global markets, and global expansion is a key component of our strategy. In fact, a significant portion of our sales comes from outside the United States. Therefore, it is important to consider how non-U.S. attitudes toward shareholder value impact the share price of global companies, like Baxter, based in the United States.

Some maintain that shareholder value creation as a key company priority is an American obsession not shared by companies based outside of the United States. There is some truth to this assertion, although resistance to the idea is stronger in Asia than, for example, in Western Europe or even Latin America. Rather than shareholder value, many Japanese companies focus on providing high-quality products and on building prestige and brand recognition. These alternate priorities affect the share price of U.S. companies competing globally to the extent that they alter the competitive landscape. Baxter's foreign managers sometimes state that Baxter's focus on shareholder value places the company at a competitive disadvantage in certain foreign markets. They claim that while Baxter is committed to providing shareholders with, say, a 15 percent return, many foreign-based companies need only generate a 3 or 4 percent return to satisfy their owners, in many cases banks and/or foundations.

This argument raises two questions. As a U.S.-based company competing in global markets, is Baxter misguided in maintaining its focus on shareholder value? Worse: Is that focus placing the company at a competitive disadvantage? The answer to both questions is no, and the reason lies in the future direction of the global economy. Global markets and capital flows are becoming more and more pervasive. Ultimately, all companies will be competing globally for capital. As companies abroad find themselves held more and more by global funds, and find themselves sensitive to global capital flows, the competitive scenario will change. Such companies will experience that if they are not generating high rates of return equivalent to those produced by value-focused U.S. companies, they will be the ones unable to compete.

Looking to the Future

Building shareholder value is an enduring commitment at Baxter. Will we be doing anything differently to drive value growth over the next two or three years? I don't think so. The fundamentals with which I began this section—*Strategic goals + economic goals + people + customers = shareholder value*—have thus far stood and I believe will continue to stand the test of time.

Therefore, our value-building strategy for the foreseeable future will be a simple one. We will continue to build and maintain the best team. We will strive to satisfy customers and patients better than any of our competitors. We will foster and continually refresh a culture at Baxter in which value is the dominant motivator. And we will maintain the discipline necessary to implement the strategic and economic policies that result in steadily increasing value for our shareholders.

Sir Brian Pitman
Chairman, Lloyds TSB Group

Building Shareholder Value with Strategists—
Lots of Them

Shareholder value has got a good press in recent years. Any reader of newspapers or annual reports would hardly be blamed for thinking that just about every top management team in the country is 100 percent dedicated to this goal. They would be wrong. I think that the mixed results of these proclaimed strategies suggest that many managers are not yet fully committed to the fundamentals of shareholder value creation. Too often managements offer lip service to the concept but lack sufficient conviction and single-mindedness. They fail to recognize that shareholder value must be the sole intellectual discipline that guides all decision making in an enterprise. Easy to say, but in practice hard to do. Other considerations so easily creep into management thought processes and deflect from the goal of shareholder value maximization or act at cross-purposes to it.

There are many companies whose real criterion for success is something other than shareholder value maximization: for instance, to be number one in size. A bigger size is usually accompanied by a bigger salary, a bigger office, a bigger car. In the past, there was no denying the fascination of size in banking, an industry that suffers from a strong herd instinct. For decades, the performance chart that fascinated most bankers was size of assets. Yet the largest banks, measured by size of assets, are not necessarily the most profitable, often because they carry product lines or apply technologies where they cannot do a distinctive, let alone unique, job.

Another popular catchword has been the quest for greater market share—the given rationale for a great many corporate mergers these days. Examples abound of companies with large shares that lag smaller rivals in profitability. Chasing market share frequently ends in tears. Another beacon that some companies steer by is globalization: seeking to cover the world with their corporate escutcheons. The objective of achieving global market leadership has enormous appeal to many managers. Yet there is ample evidence that many companies that have attempted to have leadership in markets and products all over the world have produced very poor returns.

The managers pursuing these approaches do not, of course, entirely disregard shareholder value. They say that the successful outcome of their pet strategy will, it stands to reason, contribute value—only to be surprised when so frequently it does not. Their mistake is more than just lack of analytic rigor: It is, rather, the failure to make shareholder value a sine qua non, an absolute, the purpose of all strategic reflection and intent. This blunt fact was not immediately clear to us at Lloyds Bank when we first explored this topic two decades ago. It seemed to us then that if we were very good managers, shareholder value creation would flow out of the things we did. It took a while to realize that we were putting the cart before the horse, that we had to make shareholder value the prime mover. Our deliberations and decisions had to proceed first from the goal of shareholder value enhancement.

We now use the template of shareholder value as a method for raising management performance rather than the other way round, i.e., raising performance with expectations that it will yield greater shareholder value. The order of priority, the sequencing, putting shareholder value first, turns out to be critical.

Our criterion for every strategy is whether or not it creates wealth. It is a criterion that often leads to a company limiting its field to areas where it can obtain market leadership (in niches or otherwise) or areas where it can foresee achieving significant operating advantages over the competition. Weak market positions destroy rather than create value. There are businesses where the market as a whole is not particularly attractive, but the market leaders still earn high returns.

Another source of value creation is, of course, superior cost control—particularly in banking, where competition is likely to create an irreversible decline in margins in many products. Conventional banks with their high cost structures are finding themselves at a disadvantage against competitors who have much lower distribution and delivery costs. Only the most productive companies are going to win.

Let us suppose that a company's top management team has asked itself its definition of success—although, in fact, I think few really do seriously debate this issue in depth. Let us further suppose that it picks shareholder value as the key benchmark. What then? Obviously, the first step is to analyze the existing portfolio of activities and dispose of those that do not earn some good return over the cost of capital. Second, it has to seek competitive advantage through distinctive strategies or operations. When managers come to me with a proposition, my invariable response is, please tell me what we will do that is different from the competition? Difference is the key to high rates of return.

Economic theory would suggest that in the commodity sectors of banking high rates of return are next to impossible to achieve. As far as classic loan syndications are concerned, I would agree. But there are other wholesale banking activities from which we at Lloyds Bank can create value. For instance, we are the leading shareholder registrar in the U.K.; we are also the leading leasing company in the U.K. In those areas of financial services where we cannot find differentiation in the product offering, we strive for differentiation as the lowest cost producer. The advantage of being the lowest cost producer is that you widen your options. For example, you can manage for market position or for profitability—whichever will create more value over the longer term.

Differentiation is the Holy Grail for our entire management team. Every product manager and every market manager is charged with developing three strategies for creating more value. We don't accept that our current strategies are necessarily the best ones, so we keep pressing for more—not only in number, but in clarity, in logic, in market understanding. We believe that there is always a different and better strategy just around the corner—it's just that we haven't thought of it yet. This exercise stretches and focuses our minds. Over time, you end up developing a body of managers who are really good strategic thinkers, and this capability becomes a competitive advantage that is hard to match.

Strategy is a capability you can help people to develop. It is a mental discipline that our managers acquire through dialogue and interchange. They proffer what appear to them to be wonderful strategies and then are forced to answer some very tough analytic questions from the managers above them about the logic, the risks, the value creation embedded in their proposals. The role of the corporate center is to make sure that very high standards of strategy development take place throughout the organization. If you give people the opportunity to learn how to develop different strategies, they become much more committed to the one they have developed themselves than if it were imposed from above. That is why we devolve strategy development. Our task at the center is to help those managers develop approaches that meet our highest standards for value creation. The cleverer you get at formulation, the better, too, you become at execution.

We don't ask for three strategies to make things tough for our managers, but because strategic thinking is an important source of creativity. We further believe that setting the value-creation bar very high will spur innovation, which is our lifeblood. Three strategies ensure that we always have new ideas bubbling up, thus constantly increasing our strategic options. Strategic reviews are normally an annual event, but our managers also respond to structural or regulatory changes in their markets with new strategies when required. Because we live in a rapidly changing world, constant adaptation is necessary.

When Lloyds Bank first investigated the precepts of shareholder value creation, many of our critics argued that it was just another evanescent management fad, a hyped-up panacea that would be gone in a decade's time. Others argued that it would ineluctably lead to a short-term focus and failure to build the business. At that time very few British companies were using cost of equity as a benchmark. We made several transatlantic trips to the various corporate Meccas of shareholder value, where top managers in several companies were amazingly open, candid, and encouraging. Three things I remember from those visits:

- The claim that, over time, the competitive gap between adherents of shareholder value and nonadherents increased

- The cool confidence with which these believers in shareholder value creation forecast dramatic surges in future value

- Their certainty that top value creators are not only superior at attracting capital, they also excel at satisfying customers and in maximizing the potential of their employees.

So we decided to set the goal of doubling shareholder value every three years—and this was a defining moment, as they say nowadays.

It was an audacious target. Some of our managers thought it utterly quixotic. Audacity was critical: Only such a goal would be capable of generating the kind of radical change we needed. A doubling every seven years would not have done that.

At first it proved difficult to get the principles of value creation into the heart of our managers' decision making: They failed to grasp the basic principles and unconsciously incorporated criteria that were not value creating. Their resistance sprang also from the fact that only about half of our portfolio of businesses had a rate of return exceeding the cost of capital. Those that did not, their defenders argued, were turnaround situations. They soon would earn a return above the cost of capital. So we looked at these would-be shining stars of the future and said, "Fine, five years hence you will be earning the cost of capital. Let us now discount the cash flows of the intervening five years and see if they do or do not have a positive net present value." That was an eye-opener, and helped us develop discipline.

One seminal event in the early days was a weekend management conference. The discussion focused on likely decisions for an imaginary company that had taken over Lloyds Bank. We worked on this outside-in perspective and came up with a long list of actions, including divestitures, which would increase value. The weekend began as a merely academic exercise. But when we clearly saw the unfolding of the potential values, we decided to adopt these decisions and do to ourselves what a new owner would have done.

I don't deny that it was painful surgery and that a lot of our people were unhappy at the breakup of the status quo. Shareholder value in some people's minds has become quite wrongly associated only with restructuring and consequent large-scale redundancies—in short, with some lessening of the benefits of corporations to society as a whole. This criticism evaporates when we count up the huge increments of value that have been created at companies like ours. Over 50,000 employees and pensioners who have shares in the company have done very well. Those who put £1,000 into the company 15 years ago would find it worth today, with dividend reinvestment, about £60,000. Many of our employees have made more money on these shares than they ever could have saved from a salary. When you have employees earning £20,000 per annum holding shares in the company worth £200,000, the culture of managing for value gets powerful reinforcement.

It is important to demonstrate to everyone that value creation is not just good for the shareholders, but good for the staff, good for customers, and good for the country. Today we are selling more products to more people than ever before. And we are also one of the biggest charitable givers in the U.K. Donations by the Lloyds TSB Foundations in 1999 were some £27 million, mainly to help disabled and disadvantaged people play a fuller role in society.

Another common accusation against shareholder value is that it is so obsessed with short-term results that it frustrates innovation and is obsessed with cost cutting. Not so. We view it in terms of building value for the long term, and we are constantly innovating for the long haul. We are equally skilled, I hope, at taking bold, visionary initiatives. Lloyds Bank, for instance, has invested heavily in online banking, which is not likely to be very profitable any time soon. We also know how to take risks. Currently we are the only U.K. bank with a program to put bank branches in supermarkets. True, some of the supermarkets are trying to go into banking on their own. But we are betting that our brand, customer service, and the quality of our offerings will be competitively decisive in this market. We might turn out to be wrong—though so far it's going well—but we don't live in a risk-free world. We must have the courage of our convictions and our strategies. If we succeed in this project, it will be difficult for our banking competitors to catch up with us.

A growing number of companies benchmark themselves against their competitors to measure their performance as value creators. If world-class means anything, it means world-class performance in value generation. For almost two decades we have doubled the value of the company's shares every three years, but we are not resting on our laurels. Today we are actually more prepared for change and in a better position to beat the competition than at any time in the past—thanks to those many strategists in an organization that is constantly abuzz with new ideas and fresh viewpoints. One of the messages I frequently deliver to our people is this: There are only two things that will stop us from continuing our world-class performance in value creation—either a lack of ideas or a lack of courage. At present, we lack neither.

Organization

The Pathways of Organizational Transformation

Imagine that the legendary Alfred Sloan of General Motors, originator of the decentralized corporation in the 1920s, were to return to Earth to inquire about the current state of organization theory. He would be bombarded with revolutionary concepts and buzzwords such as *boundaryless, centerless, virtual, horizontal, postmodern, federated, molecular, networked, cellular, individualized, self-organizing,* to name but a few. And he would be told by the champions of these concepts that their mission was to topple the hierarchical structure that Sloan had pioneered (the *strategy-structure-systems,* or 3S, model), and that arguably contributed to the wealth creation of large corporations for many decades.

If Sloan were to go on to investigate the real-world rate of adoption of these trendy ideologies, he would find that most corporations had given them a respectful hearing, but that relatively few had so far put them into practice. The gurus of organizational revolution are at the barricades, no doubt about it, but when they look over their shoulders, they find that the crowd is hanging back.

Yet their critique has served well. It has exposed the weaknesses and drawbacks of older organizational architectures and practices, chief of which is a tolerance for, even a preference for, sluggish responses to change. The radicals tirelessly argue that the classic centralized, hierarchical form is simply inadequate to cope with major exogenous forces: intensifying global competition, the momentum of information technologies, the rise of partnerships and alliances. Most managers don't deny that this is so. Yet the majority seem reluctant to jettison the 3S model. Instead they adopt attributes of the new networked organization or the new learning organization, without adopting the whole. They want to move slowly toward the risks of large-scale adoption.

On his tour of the contemporary scene, Alfred Sloan would observe one major change in organizational theory. Today it is widely accepted that an organization is not, as frequently portrayed in the past, simply a machine for imposing appropriate authority and circulating information to appropriate parties. It is more. There is something like the spirit of an organization, there is an energy level, there are behaviors. If the Sloanian organization chart were akin to an anatomical drawing of a skeleton, a contemporary view would focus on flesh and nerves. And the chart would be in three dimensions to render the complexity of networks.

The organizational concept that Sloan pioneered at GM, which also took root in DuPont, Standard Oil, and Sears, was a model of order, a pyramid of ascending boxes and connective reporting lines from level to level. Basically, it was a set of relays that permitted knowledge and data to flow up and down closely defined channels. It was primarily an administrative mechanism to help large companies cope with multidivisioned complexity. The quest for flexibility, or entrepreneurship, was no part of Sloan's agenda.

Organizations today are far less geometric. They are, in fact, often messy and inconsistent. Hierarchy coexists with antihierarchical features. Managers on the firing line aren't concerned with ideal Platonic forms but with the materials at hand. They eclectically adopt some of the attributes of networks or of horizontal organization and graft them onto the existing frame. They use some aspect of the virtual organization in one place and elsewhere tighten hierarchical control, perhaps by imposing shared treasury services on global business units.

As Peter Drucker sagely observes, "There is no such thing as the one right organization. There are only organizations, each of which has distinct strengths, distinct limitations and specific applications." In his view, organizations are heterodox. They emerge out of competitive perceptions and circumstances. Consider two highly successful companies, one with a high degree of hierarchy, the other apparently with almost none. The first is the U.K.'s Rentokil Initial, a global company providing environmental, health care, and property protection services. Tightly run by CEO Clive Thompson, there are no fewer than eight levels of hierarchy between himself and the company's service operatives. In Denmark, there is Oticon, a small and innovative manufacturer of hearing aids, which boasts a paperless office and whose president, Lars Kolind, has "replaced departments with a chaotic network of continuously changing project teams." Kolind has also said that "to keep a company alive, one of the jobs of top management is to keep it disorganized." Somewhere between these two poles is Andy Grove, the founder of Intel, who has said, "Let the chaos reign, then rein in the chaos."

Companies within the same industry can take very different organizational pathways. Visa's top management has been influenced by chaos theory and the theoretical work on self-organizing systems. Dee Hock, founder and former CEO of Visa, which has grown 10,000 percent in the last two decades, coined the word *chaordic* to express the combination of chaos and order that he seeks in an organization. Rival MasterCard, half its size, undertook a sweeping reorganization in 1999, designed to make it more competitive against Visa. Under this scheme, all regional and functional heads will report directly to the chief executive. The change is expected to make it easier for MasterCard to package products in ways that member banks wish. As Drucker observed, "Organization is not an absolute. It is a tool for making people productive in working together." A one-size-fits-all approach to organizational design is not the way to go.

After Alfred Sloan's system became widely adopted over a period of nearly three decades, some corporations saw the need to escape its main drawback, the silo structure in which data and decisions flow up one silo, down another, then back up again, across the top, and again down. The remedy was the matrix, which established dotted-line connections across silos, or between divisions and lines of specialization. In time, it was commonly observed that the matrix is hard to operate effectively. In the 1970s, a number of companies tried and abandoned it, either due to poor implementation or to a poor fit with their strategies. Yet the matrix is far from dead. A 1998 PricewaterhouseCoopers study of nearly 400 CEOs worldwide found that two-thirds of their companies had adopted a more complex matrix-style management structure in recent years. The matrix was more popular in North America than in Europe, and younger CEOs were more likely than older ones to try it.

Such perseverance in the face of obstacles reflects a constant struggle in the corporation to overcome defects of structure. In many ways, companies like to have their cake and eat it, too. Large entities want to capture the advantages of small entrepreneurial outfits—they want the benefits of centralization *and* decentralization. They seek to control against mistakes and risk—and also to liberate their managers from the center's iron hand. The greater these contradictions, the more corporations have to rely on the human factor to reconcile them: to interpret not the design but the intent of an organizational form.

Corporations have always depended heavily on employee creativity to prevail against the organization's irrationalities. In a *Harvard Business Review* article, "Breaking the Mind-Set in Process Organizations" (January/February 1996), Ann Majchrzak and Qianwei Wang looked at the impact of business process reengineering programs in which previously functional/silo organizations were altered to conform to a process-based structure. They found that the new architecture alone did not cause "the people to change their functional mind-sets or forge them instantly into teams intent on achieving common goals." Rather, they found that departments where the new organizational structure worked well "were those whose managers had taken steps to cultivate a collective sense of responsibility among workers that went beyond merely changing the organization structure." To foster this collective sense of responsibility, the authors urged companies to structure jobs with overlapping responsibilities, base rewards on group performance, lay out the work area for maximum visibility of others' work, and design processes that stimulate collaboration.

How Dead Is Hierarchy?

Hierarchy is the "glorious invalid" of organizational theory. Despite the rhetorical assaults of the revolutionaries, despite hundreds of articles in the management literature forecasting its demise, hierarchy is alive and well. As Frederick G. Hilmer and Lex Donaldson observe in the Spring 1998 issue of *Organizational Dynamics,* "The critical issue facing large corporations is not, By how much is our hierarchy bloated? but rather, What degree of hierarchy is optimal? For each organization, there is an optimal height of hierarchy, reflecting its size and feasible spans of control and, importantly, whether it is planning to grow or cut back."

Hilmer and Donaldson deplore the fashion of hierarchy bashing. They write: "Proponents of flatter structures applaud [the resulting] increased spans of control, seeing them as empowering lower level employees and managers. And the applause increases for those companies that form autonomous work groups and remove supervisors—cutting out another level of hierarchy. Although such developments may be valuable, their effect is limited. Substantial hierarchy remains necessary to provide the coordination framework that is required in a large corporation." Drucker is more blunt by far: "One hears a great deal today about 'the end of hierarchy.' This is blatant nonsense."

The appearance of the hierarchy may be the same as ever, but the experience inside it is different in most companies. Hierarchy has been changed, hybridized, in order to increase speed of response, accountability, flexibility, knowledge sharing, and connectivity. That's what Peter Bijur, CEO of Texaco, has done in his persevering effort to pull up his company's performance to compare with rival oil giants. He has changed the formal organization very little, and expectations of behavior a very great deal. Since oil and natural gas are commodity businesses, where strategy differentiation between companies is slight, Bijur has decided that human skills and attributes are the key to performance gains. Along with many contemporary organizational theorists, Bijur believes that leadership style has a profound influence on organizational climate and capability.

Another CEO who knows that leadership style is competitively decisive is Mike Armstrong of AT&T. Two years ago he was recruited to take over one of the biggest and most sluggish enterprises in telecommunications. Heir to the long-distance business of the deregulated Ma Bell, Armstrong runs the company with the cycle times and urgency of a Silicon Valley start-up—because he must. He is convinced that if this elephant can't dance it will lose market share and profitability, and perhaps even perish amid the powerful forces reshaping the telecommunications industry. His predecessors at AT&T believed in feeding the dragon: first building the processes needed to support a strategy, then taking action. They believed in exhaustive strategic studies that took so long to arrive at conclusions that changes in the environment rendered them obsolete. Mike Armstrong's approach is, Let's do it. He says, "The processes will evolve from the strategic decision, people will figure out what is necessary. If there are mistakes, they'll quickly show up and can then be unmade." These attitudes explain why, upon taking charge, in just a few months he realigned the entire company strategy and repositioned it technologically for the future.

A generation ago time was not so scarce. Management theorists and CEOs often compared large corporations to supertankers that could only make slow course corrections. Armstrong is far from alone in promoting a rough-and-ready organization that is designed to change and evolve, based on signals from the marketplace. Many other companies are thinking along the same lines: looking to markets and customers for clues to the best organizational design. An old dilemma for organizational architects is whether to structure activities and resources by market or by function. Function is usually the right approach when economies of scale are critical. However, where there are numerous work-flow interdependencies and processes, organization by market tends to be preferable.

There has been a large increase in the number of companies adopting market-driven organizational forms. In this regard, there was a landmark happening in early 1999. Microsoft scrapped an organization that was technology based and replaced it with a structure focused on customers. Bill Gates and his people were, to be sure, hardly in the vanguard. But that such a powerful and accomplished technology company should take this route was a strong endorsement of the process-driven organization, sometimes referred to as the front-back organization, where the front is the customer-focused piece that gets products or services transferred from the back. Other front-back organizations are Harley-Davidson, Sun Microsystems, AT&T, and IBM's Global Services. In 1999, Hewlett-Packard rolled out a new enterprise strategy much like IBM's. It melded two autonomous divisions to offer global customers a single point of contact for enterprise computing.

Predictably, globalization promotes organizational reconfiguration as scope and complexity increase. Even so, changes are coming quite slowly. In his book *Total Global Strategy* (Prentice Hall, 1995), Professor George S. Yip wrote, "One of the most effective ways to develop and implement a global strategy is to centralize authority so that all units of the same business around the world report to a common *global sector head*. Surprisingly few companies do this. Instead, they are tied for historical reasons to a strong country-based organizational structure, where the main lines of authority run by country rather than by business." A 1997 survey of 400 global CEOs conducted by PricewaterhouseCoopers reported that only 39 percent of companies have reduced the influence of geographical leaders—just those executives who were so characteristic of the preglobal multinational enterprise. However elegant the concept of global sector head may be, companies are reluctant to demolish the baronies and fiefdoms that possess intimate knowledge of regional conditions. There is a well-observed tendency to let loose the hounds of divisional autonomy when times are good, and to rein them in when profits are under pressure. For instance, UBS, Europe's largest bank, initiated in 1999 a cost-saving plan to integrate its worldwide operations and curb the relative autonomy of operations around the world. "This will pose challenges for a management accustomed to a more devolved style," noted *Financial Times*.

The Virtual Organization

Yet another spur to organizational change has been the rise of the virtual organization, which stands on its head the old model of full-scale integration of all the factors of production—research, manufacturing, marketing, and after-service—under one corporate roof. Proponents of the virtual organization ask why a corporation must own all that it is and does. Better, they advocate, to hone a single competency and for the rest depend on alliances, networks, suppliers, consultants, outsourcers—all connected in real time. The virtual organization coordinates economic activity to deliver value to customers, often using resources outside the boundaries of the traditional corporation. It embodies a theory of limits that holds that even the biggest and most accomplished corporations cannot deliver topflight management and world-class scope exclusively through proprietary resources. Unlike the standard organization, say its advocates, the virtual organization thrives in environments where the demand for rapid response is unrelenting. These are some of the proposed merits of the virtual organization:

- Optimum results because each partner/collaborator invests its best competencies in the outcome

- Shared investment and operating costs among participants

- Greater flexibility, more efficient development, faster time to market

- A culture that favors experiment and leverages the best characteristics of each partner/collaborator

- Profit enhancement through better focus, because providers of a narrow range of goods and services, and those that sell to narrow market segments, are frequently more profitable than those that sell a broader range of goods into broader markets.

Outsourcing aside, the virtual dimension in most organizations is not great, in part because of the drawbacks, which include ambiguous frontiers between organizations, vague accountability, the risk posed to the whole by a single weak link, the loss of operating and strategic control, and, above all, the difficulty of acquiring and supporting entirely new management attitudes and skills. Accordingly, corporations are inclined to move with caution. As with boundaryless or horizontal organizations, they seem inclined to view the virtual as identical with flexibility, swift response, and cross-fertilization—but no more than an add-on to the status quo in the form of project teams and new interrelations across disciplines. The virtual is a guiding *metaphor* for organizational change, not yet a structural reality.

The Warwick Study

Our major theme that hierarchy is largely undiminished in its influence, while nonhierarchical features have been integrated or grafted on, is substantially confirmed by recent research. In 1999, Warwick

Business School released a major opinion study on organizational change between the years 1992 and 1996, covering a sample of 450 large European institutions. Internal evidence in the study suggests that results in the United States would be fairly similar. This research was funded by PricewaterhouseCoopers, in cooperation with Britain's Economic and Social Research Council, and led by Professor Andrew Pettigrew. In addition to offering a rare topography of organizational change in a large group of companies, the study broke new ground by examining relationships between organizational change and profit outcomes. The research focused on organizational structure, process, and boundaries. Half the firms made boundary changes; 28 percent made process changes; 20 percent made structural changes.

Structure

There has been some delayering of hierarchy, but far less than a reading of the management literature would suggest. In the study's four-year interval, the average number of organizational levels between the CEO and the lowest-ranked manager with profit responsibilities declined for the whole sample—falling from 3.5 layers to 3.2 layers. This result was influenced by the 30 percent of the sample in which some delayering had occurred. But only a slightly smaller proportion, 20 percent, went in the opposite direction, adding levels of hierarchy in response to increasing scale and complexity and in pursuit of growth opportunities. Half of the companies neither added nor subtracted from their layers of authority.

Another facet of structure is the centralization/decentralization axis. Warwick University researchers recorded greater decentralization in a number of different ways: the rise of project-based structures, more operational autonomy among business units, and increasing divisional freedom in operating areas such as supplier and procurement strategies or production processes. Here again, the management literature frequently suggests that centralization is obsolete. Not so. While the decentralization of operations grew, strategy was retained at the center. Sixty-one percent of the sample in 1996 had a high degree of decentralized operations, versus 32 percent in 1992. Decentralization was much less common for strategic decision making, such as long-term planning and capital investment; only 18 percent in the sample were somewhat more decentralized in these respects than four years earlier.

Although corporations have used project teams for many years, they are more likely than ever to do so—in part because they have become more skilled at maintaining activities outside the regular hierarchy and better at horizontal collaboration across internal boundaries. Project-based organization increased by 175 percent in the 450-company sample. Many projects operated in a virtual or ad hoc mode, achieving goals for which the regular organization was not well equipped.

Processes

The pathways of communication, much influenced by electronic communications technologies, tend to follow corporate structures. In the sample companies of the Warwick study, the use of cross-enterprise IT strategies and technologies like groupware and intranets increased fourfold. Horizontal traffic doubled in 1992–1996, thanks to more lateral networking, the sharing of R&D knowledge across units, joint purchasing, and shared distribution and marketing. But that is not the whole story. Vertical communication increased even more than horizontal traffic—it actually tripled, substantiating our thesis about the endurance of hierarchy. IT capabilities are being deployed to strengthen hierarchical patterns of information and authority.

There is no contradiction in these findings. Rather, they demonstrate that corporations seek to be strong in both dimensions, thereby posing altogether new issues in organizational design. In Alfred Sloan's day, there was a binary choice: Do we or do we not centralize/decentralize this activity? Thanks to IT power, both solutions are possible, but this power has created fresh dilemmas about what information and authority should be placed into which channel, horizontal or vertical, and what information should be placed in both.

The Warwick study found that hierarchy has been modified by the adoption of many new human resource practices. Transfers of people and skills between units and cross-enterprise management training and conditioning effectively make the organization more flexible and responsive than in the past. The surveyed companies have striven to push cross-structural teams and encourage channels of horizontal knowledge transfer.

Boundaries

Companies are reducing their activities to the essential—to core competencies—by entering into outsourcing arrangements and/or strategic alliances. Ten percent of the sample scrapped strategies of unrelated or conglomerate diversification. Another 65 percent reported increases in outsourcing and in long-term external alliances.

Uniquely, the Warwick study found a relationship between corporations with high returns on investment and their organizational structure and practice. High-performance companies are organizational activists, and more likely to be innovating in areas of structure, process, and boundaries. Across the board, they do more outsourcing, more downsizing, more operational and strategic decentralization, and deploy more special projects teams. They are also more inclined to invest in new human relations practices, such as team building and networking, and predictably they are also big spenders on information technology.

High economic returns are associated with a whole system of complementary activities that combine organizational change with innovative human resource applications. The researchers found that "high-performing firms were characterized by denser and more inclusive webs of relationships." Companies that went furthest in terms of changes of structure *and* processes *and* boundaries were associated with superior earnings performance. In contrast, companies that merely had one or two narrow organizational initiatives and pursued piecemeal changes did not get higher economic returns.

Companies that aggressively reworked their organizations represented only about 5 percent of the total survey population, but they registered a 60 percent improvement in performance. They also tended to be international and/or knowledge-based companies. They animated their structures by means of heavy investments in knowledge management, best practice sharing, transfers of people and skills between units, and the frequent use of cross-enterprise managerial training. In the report, Professor Pettigrew notes, "The performance benefits of the new organizational practices depend on the context of other changes in which they are set, and are especially strong when combined within comprehensive organizational change." He adds, "The management implication is that change initiatives should not be piecemeal, but advance across several fronts in careful alignment."

The sequential approach—first the outsourcing, then the horizontal networks, then the alliances and partnerships—fails to benefit from the spillover effects created by numerous measures simultaneously implemented. In short, *organizational changes that increase the effectiveness of some activities in a company will also promote successful adoption of other desired changes.* Why this should be so is open to speculation. But we believe that the occurrence of many initiatives shifts the organization from the background to the foreground of consciousness—beneficially. Managers become aware of connections, of the subtle relations between functions, and of bottlenecks. They become organizationally literate and set aside whatever degree of organizational passivity they once had.

The Warwick Business School data show that the center is maintaining authority to make strategic decisions and formulate a vision of the future. But the center remains vulnerable to criticism. A 1997 PricewaterhouseCoopers survey of chief financial officers found that some 15 percent were "highly dissatisfied" and more than 50 percent "somewhat dissatisfied" with their headquarters environments. Topics of complaint ranged from the excessive cost of oversized centers and inadequate value-adding skills and resources at the center to damaging influences over business units—typically because the center failed to understand the dynamics and risks of a business unit's field of activity. The authors of the report, *Corporate Center Transformation,* clearly agree: "Time and again the ability of the center to focus has been compromised by its natural tendency to drift towards the more traditional role of administrator. Concentration on such 'nanny' function can switch emphasis away from initiatives and responsibilities that truly add value."

The dissatisfaction with sluggish centers expressed by AT&T's Mike Armstrong is widely shared. Many organizations have adopted a "small is beautiful" approach with respect to the corporate center.

In the preceding decade, 85 percent of companies have stripped down the size of their headquarters, according to a 1999 Conference Board study. The main motive given was to increase speed of response and improve organizational clarity and accountability. The 89 companies in the Conference Board study (United States, Europe, and Asia) were divided according to return on assets and credit ratings. Those with the higher returns and ratings generally had smaller centers. These companies had also revised roles and responsibilities at the center and strengthened certain functions, such as business development, procurement, best practices, and knowledge sharing. They also sought to foster "cooperation and synergy" between their business units and to "improve integration" across the board.

The Thrust of the Modern Organization

Integration and synergy have long been the Holy Grail of organizations because very small gains in these respects have powerful economic outcomes. But the mode of realizing this dream has changed materially since Alfred Sloan's day. Some of the difference is summed up in an observation by U.S. pollster Daniel Yankelovich, who a decade ago observed a shift in public opinion data that showed "a shift from the Protestant ethic valuation of work as having intrinsic moral value, to work as a source of potential satisfaction, and therefore less tolerance for work that does not provide personal satisfaction." If people are to find personal satisfaction, they will need an organization that releases trapped energies and fosters creativity. They will not want a command organization that looks like an army's battle order. Nor will they flourish in an external organization that takes no account of their minds and hearts. The entire thrust of the modern organization can now to be summed up: It has built-in discipline. There may always be a degree of control from the top to maintain enterprise-wide cohesion and strategic direction. What is new is the degree of self-reliance and dedication that can be asked, and will be contributed, at every other level.

C. Michael Armstrong
Chairman and Chief Executive Officer, AT&T

Slaying the Dragon

When I came to AT&T in the fall of 1997, the communications industry had reached what Andy Grove of Intel defines as an *inflection point*, a watershed moment when the rules of the past are no longer relevant. Not only are new technology and new market conditions changing the rules of the communications industry, they are creating unprecedented opportunity and double-digit global growth.

Unfortunately, as of fall 1997, AT&T wasn't sharing in the growth. We seemed to be missing the party. Our top-line revenue growth was almost flat while our costs were the highest in the industry. We were defending our lead in the commoditized long-distance phone business instead of aggressively marketing services made possible by new technology.

Clearly AT&T needed to reach an inflection point of its own and redefine the company—from priorities to operating style to product lines. I spent my first 90 days on the AT&T payroll virtually locked up with the senior management team working on a blueprint for the new AT&T. As the industry leader, we had to set our sights on growing at least as fast as our industry. And we wouldn't do that through business as usual. We needed to transform AT&T from a long-distance company into an "any distance/any service" company—a company that could take advantage of the way the Internet and broadband technology are redefining communications. The new AT&T would connect customers to whatever information is useful to them, be it in the form of voice, data, or video. To do so, we needed to reach customers directly with our own broadband connections and move from being a primarily domestic company to being a truly global company.

We had to get AT&T in shape to go the competitive distance, not just against the Bells, which are poised to compete with us in long distance, but against the growing field of familiar and nontraditional companies attracted to the communications market. We had to decommoditize our $23 billion revenue stream from consumer long distance by bundling it in a combined offer with new services like high-speed Internet access, cable TV, and local phone service.

A Vision As Simple As It Is Ambitious

We were, and continue to be, driven by a vision that is as simple as it is ambitious: We want to be the only communications company our customers will ever need. Realizing that vision meant making some big decisions in a very short time. But I learned long ago that the ability to make big decisions quickly comes with the territory of leadership. The only question in my mind was how fast could we get it done. And as I look back on my first year and a half at AT&T, no one could accuse us of dragging our feet. In that time, AT&T:

- Acquired Teleport Communications Group (TCG), America's largest provider of competitive local phone service for business, for $11 billion

- Purchased TeleCommunications Inc. (TCI), one of America's leading cable TV companies, for $48 billion, giving us broadband cable connections to 18 million homes passed by TCI's cable systems

- Announced a joint venture with British Telecom to serve the communications needs of multinational businesses, international carriers, and Internet service providers

- Purchased IBM's Global Network business for $5 billion to expand our global services

- Reached an agreement to purchase the MediaOne Group, another major cable TV company, for $54 billion, which will give us broadband access to 8.4 million homes passed by MediaOne cable systems, in 18 of the top 20 U.S. markets

- Broadened our wireless coverage, now the most extensive of any U.S. provider, by acquiring Vanguard Cellular Systems

- With BT, made a 30 percent investment in Japan Telecom, Japan's third-largest telecom company, to expand our ability to serve multinational corporations and domestic companies in Japan

- Reached agreement with Nippon Telephone and Telegraph (NTT) to collaborate in the fast-growing market for customized networking solutions for large and midsized companies.

We're committed to creating the best, full-service, end-to-end communications company in the world over a five-year period. That's tough stuff. Nothing like it has ever been done before. But that is what happens when you reach an inflection point. You write new rules and redesign your game to stay ahead of changes in the marketplace. We now have the basic new resources we need for the big job ahead—but we also need a new operating style and philosophy.

Five Points of Emphasis

In 1962, when AT&T was still the parent company of the Bell System, AT&T chairman Fred Kappel said: "The Bell System is like a damn big dragon. You kick it in the tail, and two years later it feels it in the head." That was a vivid metaphor, and one I've kept in mind as we push for a new operating style. We're in the process of converting AT&T from a dragon to a jackrabbit—albeit a big jackrabbit, one fast enough to outrun the competition when it spots a new growth opportunity. We're changing the way AT&T does business, and the changes we're making fall into five major categories.

Customer Culture

All elements of our corporate culture should stem from and support a clear customer focus. Every meeting an AT&T executive attends, inside or outside the company, has to be customer oriented. Unless we engage the customer, we will not earn his or her next dollar. In the past, amazingly, customers did not come first at AT&T. There was too much internal focus, too few managers at all levels of the business who were in close personal contact with customers.

We had to cure that, and the first step was to get our executives, at all levels and in all assignments, out of their offices and meeting regularly with customers. I'm a strong believer in leadership by example. If I want to ask my people to do something, they better recognize that I'm out there doing it, too. I've identified four big customer accounts for my personal attention. I visit each of them at least twice yearly, and each of my senior executives has a similar relationship with top customers. Our purpose isn't to sell anything, but to make sure that they are getting full value for the money they are spending with AT&T. We also use the customer as a sounding board that helps us identify issues, problems, and technologies that should be on our radar screens. If we find a generic problem of concern to one customer and come up with a good remedy, that solution is passed on to our entire customer community.

Cost and Competitiveness

All discussions about vision, culture, and strategy are moot if the company isn't cost competitive. The most elegant business plan in the world won't get you anywhere if your costs are too high. From time to time, companies drop out of the front ranks of the Fortune 500, but they are rarely the low-cost producers. AT&T was not and is not the low-cost producer it has to be. Ideally, AT&T should be able to leverage its enormous size and high volume to beat other companies on cost. But its past record is just the opposite. AT&T has been the high-cost producer in its industry. We're going all out to change that.

When I came on board, our SG&A (selling, general, and administrative) expense was 28.6 percent of revenues, compared to an average of 22 percent for our competitors. That was completely unacceptable. We launched a counterattack on costs, and we've made progress. Fortunately, when you aggressively attack costs, you realize other benefits, too. You improve your cycle times, responsiveness, and accountability. It keeps you focused on what actions are producing revenues and what actions are producing costs.

As part of our overall cost reduction effort, we set the goal of a workforce reduction of 18,000 over two years. We made that number in the first year, 1998. We also took $1.6 billion in costs out of the business and brought SG&A down to 24.0 percent by the end of 1998. That's progress. But costs are always a moving target since competitors don't stop their cost reduction efforts and wait for you to catch up. Our current SG&A target for 1999 is 21 percent in our core businesses, and we committed to take another $2 billion in costs out of AT&T by the following year.

In large companies you often hear about high-level task forces, or brain trusts, that have been laboring for many months on this or that important agenda—productivity enhancements, reorganization, or facilities rationalization—with little regard for the pace of change outside, in the marketplace. Instead of participating in brainy task forces, I prefer that AT&T managers tackle competitiveness factors, including cost. A single-minded quest for competitiveness imposes focus and discipline. It produces priorities or remedies for strategic issues. If you have an overhead that is $4 billion higher than that of your competitor, you're not going to be around very long. Rule number one: Get yourself competitive and then, sure enough, the simplifications and the right processes will come into view.

Risk Taking and Decisiveness

In the old AT&T, there was an inclination to "get things right" before taking a new step. A huge amount of executive time and energy went into trying to minimize uncertainty with unlimited analysis, data, and discussion. Yet by the time these executives knew everything they needed to know to make a 100 percent sure solution, it was too late—circumstances had changed. The market had moved away from wherever it was when the analysis began.

Being timely with a decision is more important than crossing the t's and dotting the i's on some report. You have to go with a mixture of information and instinct. You have to accept that some calls will be wrong. No one makes a perfect run on decisions. But in the long term, you'll suffer more damage from consistently delayed decisions than you will from occasional wrong decisions. In the old AT&T, there was a premium on not making mistakes. Managers spent valuable time imagining what could happen and trying to insure themselves against all risks, while opportunities passed them by. The company lost momentum, while rivals took a bigger hand in reshaping the telecommunications business.

Urgency

When an industry is in a rapid state of evolution, no management team has the luxury of figuring out strategic and tactical responses

on a quarterly or even a monthly basis. That job has to be done continuously.

The old AT&T didn't have a monopoly on slo-mo decision making.
There is a tendency in large corporations to look at processes and,
when they are understood, to construct a strategy. My preference is
the other way around. Begin with a strategic direction, then figure
out the processes and everything else you need to get the job done. In
the thick of implementation, managers see what's necessary and the
processes fall into place.

I prize a management team that is decisive, in a situation where
people take risks, where everyone knows that their leaders will
respond promptly (no ideas, good or bad, piling up in the *in* tray). In
an environment like that, mistakes are recognized and corrected
promptly. Too often, big companies are afraid to admit they've made
a mistake. Instead, you hear, "Let's wait two more quarters." And all
you will have done in that time is compound the problem.

I meet with our top management team several Mondays each
month to discuss a single agenda: What must we do to stay competitive? Everyone in AT&T management knows that this is the place to
show up when they need decisions on policy, prices, practices, and
new investment approvals for technological initiatives. In addition,
I've formed an executive council to create a focused environment for
the line executives who are responsible for implementing their piece
of the $7 billion in annual investment.

Achieving urgency, getting managers charged up and committed
around the vision, with a sharp awareness that time is scarce—these
have been some of my chief goals. Some of the present management
team have said that decisions now take a third of the time they used
to. Within a few years, we'll do even better than that.

My confidence on that point reflects my overall confidence in our
senior leadership team. It's always the best team that somehow wins
the Super Bowl. It may not have the best running back, or the best
passer, or the best defensive backfield. But in the end, people recognize that they are a great *team*. Of the 16 senior executives, 8 are in
new assignments, and 4 of these 8 are new to AT&T. I think our team
is a blend of new ideas and priceless experience.

It's my job to bring that team together and focus them on winning. That's what leadership is all about.

Accountability

In the old AT&T, institutional memory was poor. The historical ratio-nale for decisions that we were living with in the present was often weak. Ideas, projects, schedules faded off into the mist. I would ask how the company had gotten into some situation or other, and no clear answer was forthcoming. I was told that the people who had ini-tiated this thing had died, retired, or quit and left no trace.

Obviously we had to build front-end accountability as a key ingre-dient of the AT&T recovery. To encourage this, I've introduced the term *comeback* into our management meetings. When a question is raised or a necessary action is identified, the accountable person is also identified. He or she is given a comeback, which means come back to us with an answer or an action at a specified time. When I became CEO, I gave myself a comeback of 90 days to develop a strate-gic vision for AT&T that I could share with senior leaders and share-owners. Similarly, other executives in the company are given 30-, 60-, and 90-day comebacks, which they are fully expected to meet.

To reinforce accountability, every proposal has identified spon-sors and a clear audit trail of how decisions are made along the way. There is no "going along by humming along," no diluting responsibil-ity in the name of consensus. Within AT&T today, if somebody wants something, getting it requires signatures from these three individu-als: the line executive who is most directly responsible, the division or unit supervisor, and the appropriate executive from our Opera-tions Group. These three know that they own that request or project.

We also aim at a degree of coordination and interdependence between elements of AT&T that has never been tried before. The peo-ple in the consumer long-distance business know that they can't make it unless they integrate with the wireless business, which inte-grates with the international business, which integrates with the Internet business. This is not only desirable—people are accountable for making it happen.

Early Signs of Success, Vast Potential

We've made encouraging progress through 1998 and the first half of 1999. Our revenue growth nearly doubled in 1998 and we're committed to doubling again in 1999. We had a 23.5 percent increase in our share price in 1998. We have a new strategy and a new vision, which take advantage of the fundamental change under way in the communications industry—an industry that should be growing in double digits for another 10 years.

No other company in the world has AT&T's potential to put together local, long distance, international, wireless, and the Internet. How we put it all together will be what sets us apart. The big question among investors, of course, is whether we can execute in the market successfully. Will we be able to go out there and define the service right, price it right, package and market it, carry the traffic, invoice it, and support it? Execution is the mantra, and will be for several years—although we've not finished making investments.

I'm enthused about AT&T's future. In the next few years we look forward to bringing even more excitement to what has to be the world's most exciting industry—and bringing investors the kind of growth in value they deserve. As I told our shareowners in the 1998 annual report, we have the tools and the time is right. The rest is up to us, and we won't disappoint our customers, employees, and shareowners.

Ralph S. Larsen

Chairman and Chief Executive Officer,
Johnson & Johnson

Decentralization Is the
Crucible of Growth

Few corporations have been as unswerving and passionate about decentralization as Johnson & Johnson. Over several generations of managers we have applied this principle with great rigor and never doubted its importance as a source of profitable growth. At Johnson & Johnson, decentralization is more than a form of organization that can be depicted in a chart. It is a deeply held belief that shapes management style and impacts corporate culture. And, in consequence, Johnson & Johnson has racked up one of the best long-term growth records in its industry. In the last decade our sales and earnings have tripled, and market capitalization rose from $14 billion to $113 billion at the high of 1998.

Decentralization is a very important point of difference between us and our competitors, most of whom are either not as radical in their commitment or have opted for a more centralized style. Time— a long period of time—will eventually show which is the wisest path. The centralists emphasize the benefits of strong direction and of focus generated from corporate headquarters. Such advantages are outweighed, in our view, by the center's limited capacity to interpret and react to the flux of market and technological change. Only those in the thick of reality, on the firing line, can know all the options and take the wisest decisions. Accordingly, we give our 180 operating units the autonomy to work out their own destinies.

Without decentralization Johnson & Johnson could not have attained the broadest product base in its industry, nor its market dominance in consumer products, medical devices, and ethical drugs. We are the most comprehensive and broad-based health company on the globe. Approximately three-quarters of our revenues stem from businesses or categories in which we have the number one or number two global market position.

Such extensive market coverage is, in our view, a big advantage at a time when there is a convergence in treatment modalities. We expect that in the years ahead pharmaceuticals, diagnostics, and medical devices will be brought together at earlier stages than they are today, and result in superior prevention, diagnosis, and treatments. We are ideally positioned for this unfolding future.

Our businesses are so distinct and range so widely that the vastness of Johnson & Johnson's market breadth and technological scope is difficult to convey. We operate in every part of the health care business, which has fundamental growth characteristics. Our pharmaceutical business is the sixth-largest in the world: It markets more than 90 prescription products in 150 countries, and 28 of these drugs have annual sales of more than $50 million, 17 of more than $100 million. Professional products used by doctors and hospitals include wound closure devices, cardiology products, disposable contact lenses, surgical instruments, and orthopaedic joints. And then there are the personal care and hygiene products in the consumer segment, which include such powerful brand names as Band-Aid, Mylanta, Tylenol, Neutrogena, and, of course, the Johnson's Baby line of products. These businesses all have very different characteristics and determinants of success. I am convinced that Johnson & Johnson could not attain this extent of market coverage without our managers around the world having extraordinary authority to operate their units as if they owned them.

Trade-Offs

There are trade-offs in organizational choices. No one form or philosophy can be perfect. We recognize that decentralization is inherently disorderly. It demands a high tolerance for ambiguity and complexity. It demands, too, a willingness to bend and compromise. We do not homogenize our businesses. We do not have a corporate pan-global strategy that sets out the direction for tomorrow—although, of course, all the units march to the drumbeat of shareholder value-creation objectives. All the units operate under their own names; all have powerful identities and strong esprit de corps. Decentralization allows us to operate not as one $23 billion company, with all the bureaucracy that implies, but as a federation of 180 small companies, each focused on a specific medical or product franchise and/or geographical area.

Our people on the front lines have wide latitude to pursue their individual strategies and optimize their often enormous opportunities for innovation. We plant a lot of small trees across a very wide base and nurture and grow them simultaneously. We do not attempt to manage a broad-gauged innovation portfolio in all of our market segments from a center perspective. If we had a centralized organization in which people had to get in line for resources and approvals, this company would come to a grinding halt. Many of the opportunities are small, and many are risky. If entrepreneurs in our divisions had to convince headquarters of the wisdom of hundreds of sometimes minuscule investments, the center would be worn down in short order. The number of opportunities pursued would shrink dramatically, and consequently our growth would be negatively affected.

Over the decades most of our businesses have been championed and built by one person, sometimes two. Often these champions faced enormous obstacles—technology challenges, market resistance, and sometimes the struggle to generate the internal support they felt their businesses deserved. A case in point is the contact lens business, in which we are the biggest manufacturer in the world. We basically reinvented that business with the disposable lens. However, in the late 1970s corporate headquarters had an austerity program that was scheduled to kill this business, tiny at the time. Whereupon this product's champion found out that my predecessor, Jim Burke, was flying up to Harvard to give a speech that night. He wangled a ride on the airplane and jawed the chairman on the flight up and the flight down. By the time they landed, the project had been reinstated.

Dynamic Decentralization

Our decentralization is not static. It is dynamic and thus has evolved in recent years. One aspect of this evolution has been caused by diminished protectionism around the world. Twenty and thirty years ago, duty barriers usually forced us to build relatively small local factories to supply local demand. Now that there is freer trade, the scale of many of these plants is no longer viable. Accordingly, we have mutated from a country-centric multinational to a more global and regional structure. In the past our operating companies were mostly managed on a country-by-country basis and encouraged to function independently of one another. Today each of our main product franchises is coordinated globally and regionally in such areas as manufacturing and R&D. In 1998 we initiated a plant reconfiguration program aimed at cutting our global manufacturing facilities from 159 plants to 123. This more regional manufacturing pattern will operate with 4 percent fewer workers and achieve significantly higher productivity levels, lower inventories, and better service to customers.

Faith in decentralization is tempered by common sense. When the structure is inappropriate, we quickly modify it. For example, many of our biggest customers want to interact with a single supply organization, not separately with half a dozen or more of our units. We do what they want. Big customers like Wal-Mart have a single point of contact. Another example: To capture economies of scale in ingredients that several divisions use in large quantities, we have centralized purchasing. In other words, when we see an advantage in company-wide standardization, we do it—as with accounting, information technology, and human resources management.

These are exceptions that prove the rule and do not compromise the basic logic of decentralization, which is to put decision making in the hands of the men and women closest to the ground. That is where the creativity is; that is where managers are going to see and seize opportunities. I believe that our climate of radical decentralization shapes people into independent-minded and self-reliant managers. The environment teaches them to negotiate ambiguity and uncertainty, and to be farsighted in their visions of technological futures.

It is hard to exaggerate the liberation of intellect created by decentralization. Our goal is to generate that fierce intellectual power every day and every week, while retaining the overarching benefits of corporate scale and the assumption of risks that small independent companies might shy away from. The people at headquarters usually have no trouble recognizing the growth potentials of certain broad markets and technologies. But actually seeding and exploiting these opportunities, finding or creating the situations where market needs and technologies come together, requires immersion in the detail and specific circumstances that people at headquarters cannot know except in the most general terms.

There are times, to be sure, when decentralization appears to be a demanding philosophy. Managers in the field can easily feel that headquarters should provide expertise and resources, and give them advice and support, a pat on the back, or a shoulder to cry on. I felt like that as a 30-year-old manager. A defining moment occurred when I was running a plant in Illinois with about 3,000 workers. We had very troubled and volatile labor relations. One day a walkout looked imminent. I called headquarters and anxiously asked our vice president of labor relations what to do—I was sure he would have good advice. I was flabbergasted when he said, "Well, kid, I'm sure you'll do the right thing," and hung up on me.

In that moment I understood that the people at the center in this company are uncompromising in their belief in nonintervention in the domain of the operating unit. I tackled the issues solo, and a walkout was averted.

When I became chief executive I had to relinquish my personal need to be in total control and instead rely on the abilities of the people running the 180 businesses. After all, I have to be willing to give these managers the same kind of rope that I was given. And I had been given tremendous latitude: Nobody looked over my shoulder; nobody wanted to know what last week's numbers were. Freedom from second-guessing by headquarters forced me and my peers in the company to be self-reliant. Real-world successes and failures spurred our growth and development, and honed our managerial skills. Managers who are by nature centralists, who have a need for control, who must have everything cut and dried and directed from the center will not do well at Johnson & Johnson.

The Center Has Its Role

I said earlier that decentralization requires tolerance of ambiguity and contradiction. In contrast to what I've written so far, I shall now look at the one-company perspective and discuss areas in which our lean center adds value. One hundred percent uncompromising decentralization is not a viable option: In exercising their independent judgment, 180 operating companies are bound to affect the corporate commonweal in ways that have to be monitored. For instance, new ventures in new geographical areas need to be orchestrated by headquarters. We wouldn't want half of the operating companies rushing to set up independent subsidiaries—for example, in China—if that resulted in overexposure of the total corporation. Conversely, from a corporate strategy standpoint we cannot have them entirely neglect China, so that some of the operating people might need to be encouraged to consider the potential there. On issues like this there is a push/pull interaction between the center and the decentralized units. Currently we have six joint ventures in China, about the right number for the present. In the case of Russia, we decided at the corporate level not to invest large amounts of capital there because of our perception of risk. I don't recall that any operating company made a proposal to invest significantly in Russia. Had one done so, we would have said no.

Another area where the center plays an important role is the allocation of executive resources throughout the decentralized network. We actively transfer people around the company to get the best fit between particular challenges and individual managers. And another role for the center is, predictably, the larger acquisitions and divestitures made to optimize our product portfolio.

While the center has a hands-off policy on details of decision making, it bears responsibility for addressing the climate and assumptions that surround and influence those decisions of the operating companies. We live in environments of great change and uncertainty and increasing competitive intensity. How, then, do we align the ideas and decision making of the operating units with the overarching realities of our extraordinarily dynamic markets? How do we ensure that the minds of operating managements are in sync with macroeconomic and macrotechnological scenarios? How do we help them divine, capture, and exploit the maximum array of opportunities?

These are difficult questions in a company where there is inherent discomfort with well-intentioned, corporate-wide programs. But they had to be addressed, if the company was to break down organizational, functional, and geographic barriers, and act in unison. The result was a management process dubbed FrameworkS: a tool for identifying and exploring a broad range of important issues with long-term ramifications for the company as a whole, a tool to ensure that we weren't inward-looking.

Here is how it works. A FrameworkS team gets appointed by the executive committee to address a pan-company issue. This team is organized into task forces for doing legwork and research and benchmarking (whatever it takes), and their findings are then thrown open to debate. At the conclusion of debate, management teams create action plans to capitalize on identified opportunities. Since 1993, there have been a dozen FrameworkS initiatives over a wide range of issues and tasks. The results have been several new business initiatives, significant improvement in regional operations (a FrameworkS on Japan came up with 1,000 ideas for strengthening the business there), and scoping of emergent technologies.

FrameworkS is a formal program that reinforces a continuous informal networking and exchange of ideas and perspectives among managers of different units and groupings of units. I'm aware that networking goes on in all large companies. But organizations differ, it seems to me, in the quality, spontaneity, and freedom of these interactions. Our informal networks are fertile because of the underlying decentralization. Managers speak from a base of hard-won practical experience. They command a lot of authority with their colleagues. In some cases, informal networking creates quite unexpected benefits. In Paris, for example, we had nine separate office locations. One day, much to my surprise, the managers there got together and decided to consolidate and rent a single office location with shared services. I never asked them to move into a single office, yet they concluded on their own that it would lower costs and, in consequence, they could reduce prices or contain price increases. Knowledge of this network, and the ability to function within it, is very important.

In conclusion, I would hesitate to recommend decentralization to everyone. Appropriateness depends on circumstances. But in very large companies with a large product range, it seems to me that there is no alternative for releasing the creativity and entrepreneurial fervor that ultimately drive growth.

Two final observations. One, many companies have organization charts that suggest they are decentralized. But the principle of decentralization is often compromised in them by covert or parallel centralism. The ambiguity and complexity are daunting—so they trim a little. Two, rigorous decentralization is not built in a day. It has taken Johnson & Johnson many decades to realize it fully and turn it into a source of sustained competitive advantage.

William J. Henderson
Postmaster General, United States Postal Service

Firing Up the Evangelical Organization

Organizations do not thrive on mind alone. They need heart. Their systems may be great, their strategy cunning, their incentives world-class, but without heart an organization can never reach or go beyond its limits. It is not enough for organizations to conceptualize their goals and put them into people's minds. They must reach managers' hearts, turn them on, and fire them up. Then an amazing thing happens: Managers develop huge energy, mental focus, and drive, far more than if they mentally and coolly did "the right thing." I speak from experience. At the United States Postal Service (USPS), we are zealots about reaching managers' hearts and minds through high-impact rituals of recognition and reward. The results have been fantastic.

"Binding the Nation Together"

The scale and complexity of the USPS organization is unequaled. A workforce of 850,000 delivers mail to 130 million addresses daily—typically, 580 million pieces. Our daily unit volume is equal to a year's volume at FedEx, and about five days' at UPS. Our $62 billion in revenues comes from extremely diverse market segments, ranging from giant commercial mailers to residential customers who put a few letters in the mailbox each month. Unlike our domestic competitors, we have a universal service obligation: We cannot eliminate unprofitable outlets (amounting to more than half of our 39,000 post offices), and we cannot redline service areas because of inadequate revenue, high crime rates, or low population density. We adhere to a 200-year-old mission to "bind the Nation together through the personal, educational, literary, and business correspondence of the people by providing prompt, reliable and efficient services to patrons in all areas and to render postal services to all communities." These are words from the 1970 Postal Reorganization Act, effectively expressing our tradition.

USPS has two identities: It is both a government agency and a highly competitive business entity. As an institution and a brand, USPS is an independent agency of government. It possesses monopolies over letter mail and access to the mailbox but competes in all of its product lines. Our fast-growing advertising mail, for example, competes against TV, radio, and newspapers, and now the Internet. We have been highly aggressive in the international arena. Foreign posts pick up U.S.-originated bulk mail, ship it to home countries by air freight, and distribute it, and we do the same for them. Before the 1997–1998 financial crisis in Southeast Asia, we built a formidable mail-order network in some of those countries. We have recently signed an exclusive alliance with DHL to ship guaranteed two-day service from 11 U.S. cities to 64 foreign countries.

We have repainted ourselves and spruced up our image, sent our employees to customer-oriented training, and worked to get the message across that "the customer is first." The payoff has been dramatic: Customers give us strong ratings both as a service and as a brand. The U.S. letter carrier remains something of a folk hero. Our evolution as a force in the market is reflected in dramatically improved service levels and in the growth of our competitive services, such as Priority Mail. We were an early adopter of economic value added (EVA) as a measure of performance and compensation. Judged by our many awards for performance, from quality processes to advertising, our managerial skills are in the top rank.

Decentralizing for Effectiveness

That's the good news. Notwithstanding our achievements, we face deep uncertainties about the role of paper-based mail in the looming electronic age. Space does not permit a full account of our initiatives to carve out a critical role for USPS in this new environment. There are many possibilities on the drawing boards, in prototype, or in field-testing. We must develop significant new services to compensate for the likely loss of lucrative first-class mail, currently running at about half of total revenues. Meanwhile, there are competitive and political pressures on us to ratchet up levels of service across the entire customer spectrum and also to wisely invest some $4 billion annually in up-to-date facilities and technologies.

Fittingly for a business that daily covers every square mile of the nation, USPS is a model decentralized organization. The postmaster general can speak softly or use a big stick, but actual implementation of mission, strategy, and goals depends on the several leaders of each of 85 regional operating units. We have a detailed reporting system for each operation, but what animates these key managers' hearts and minds is pride, achievement, satisfaction—objective confirmation and reinforcement of a job well done.

Regional leaders annually foregather with the heads of centralized central staff functions at a national executive meeting. About 1,000 of us attend. Over the last four years I have managed this event with two overriding objectives: to celebrate achievements and to sell the direction of the organization. By design, the event is like an evangelical tent meeting—not didactic, not cool. It is fervent, sometimes even a little manic. The purpose of the evangelism is to bring coherence and single focus to an organization that would otherwise be fractured, diffuse, and ill coordinated.

USPS is like a giant organism with 10,000 eyes. How do you get all those eyes to focus on the same point? Without that focus, managers will be looking everywhere: California will have one set of goals, while Louisiana will be chasing something entirely different. Lack of focus has been a legacy problem at USPS. My goal has been to identify a limited number of targets and hit them with all we've got.

We need that degree of focus from the largest civilian workforce in the world. And that is why the National Executive Conference is so critical. It is a chance to get people fired up with zeal and positive images of themselves and the organization. Approximately 400 to 500 hours of planning and preparation ensure that the conference is a moving, action-packed, overwhelming hullabaloo with terrific music, explosive lighting effects, and, most important, an integrated message that focuses everyone on our business objectives. People charge out of there ready to climb Mount Everest.

The Power of Recognition

Many books and articles have been written about the power of employee recognition. In the famous Hawthorne experiments at Western Union in the 1930s, it was found that recognized employees achieved higher productivity. But when senior managers know and use everyone's first name, and there are plenty of office or plant parties, and there are real rewards for employee suggestions, the benefits easily dissipate. I want our managers to have a peak experience so powerful that its effect will last—it will bind, it will direct and release massive personal energy all year long. That's what the conference gives us, and we reinforce these feelings throughout the year in follow-up celebrations and communications.

I learned on the job the power of recognition. Eight years ago I was one of a group of regional managers at a meeting with a former postmaster general, who told us that he wanted a minimum national standard of no more than five minutes for waiting on line at post office windows. The response of most of these regional managers was a chorus of, "It can't be done." On impulse, I decided to be contrarian. I said that I would give it a try in North Carolina. Back at work, I met with a group of postmasters and told them that in three months I planned to launch an advertising campaign claiming the fastest windows of any service organization in the region. We would challenge customers to catch us not making good on our promise. Each and every postmaster could do whatever was necessary to achieve the goal, I didn't care how. There was no special budget, no magic program. I just wanted them to figure out how to speed up window services. In the weeks that followed, the number of phone calls from them saying, "We can't do it," fell from a flood to a trickle. Then we launched the program in every post office in the region. Some local McDonald's franchises took up our challenge, since they had waiting lines, too. We had a great time.

After our initial success, some in my operating group suggested that we go out in the field, identify best practices, and standardize them to achieve the lowest possible line waits. But the postmasters said no. They each said, in effect, "I've done it my way. Don't make me do it by some standard. Let me do it the way I want to." I understood the message: They were *proud* of their achievement; they didn't want it diluted or taken away.

I realized then that if you set high targets, people will strive to reach them. My next scheme seemed even more impossible to many of my colleagues: to guarantee error-free delivery. I had stickers made up and pasted on 650 mailboxes, which said, "We guarantee error-free delivery, or call this 800 number." The unions didn't like it, but I asked them to trust me: We weren't on a witch-hunt for carriers who made mistakes. I simply believed that our delivery was error free, and I wanted data to prove it. So we launched the program. I had sew-on patches for uniforms emblazoned with "ERROR FREE." I took out full-page newspaper ads with the picture of the district letter carrier, saying, "Congratulations! This person has delivered X amount of mail without a single mistake." Publishing that picture began to generate enthusiasm, and the program took off.

Did we achieve absolutely error-free delivery? No. But when mistakes occurred, the local postmaster or the highest-ranking supervisor would personally deliver the misdirected mail, with an apology to the customer. The carrier who had made the error wasn't reprimanded.

At year's end we held a banquet for eligible carriers and their families. They went on stage and received a standing ovation. And at the sight of their spouses and children applauding and cheering in the audience, some of them cried. I felt sure that these men and women would not leave the service—they were our core. And I realized that emotion-charged recognition can be the vital force in any organization for transmitting focus and goals.

Later, as chief operating officer, I met obstacles to applying this approach systemwide. My colleagues felt that inviting spouses to the national executive gatherings could be perceived as a misuse of postal funds, and that view prevailed. We met without spouses, and the meetings were good—but not all they could be. When I became chief executive, spouses were invited to the National Executive Conference, not as tourists but to attend the business meetings like their mates, gain insight into the challenges we face, and understand how they, as spouses, contribute to our success. It became clear that spouses are more than happy to participate. Why? Because a lot of what we address is not about the Postal Service. It is about life: about how you achieve, how you climb mountains, how a person can do extraordinary things. We invite inspiring guest speakers—executives, athletes, people from many walks of life—to tell us how they have won their own battles.

We tightly script these meetings from the opening to the closing bell, with two goals in mind. The first is to deliver an integrated message focused on our goals. For this reason, Marketing doesn't do a sales presentation, and Finance doesn't trot out numbers. Instead, every unit presents its goals in light of total business objectives and the strengthening of the brand. And the second goal is to share emotional peaks. We want recognition to be as memorable as the film industry's Oscars, and generally we succeed. At our last gathering, when managers and spouses were recognized and thanked by the management committee, they came on stage. I remember one manager as he went back down the steps to the audience. His wife joined him, gave him a hug—she was so very happy for him. And I felt that there would be conversation in their home about that manager's life on the job, a dialogue that would give added meaning to everything he did.

The Emotional Bond

It is not my intent to invade private lives. We are not trying to create an organization man or woman who thinks and dreams only of the job. We don't want to surround and envelop the executive. We do mean to forge an emotional bond. That bond is the key to organizational focus, direction, and momentum—and these are the factors that will make USPS governable. We need strong emotional commitment and confidence at the very top of each management center because these feelings have a long way to travel as they are transmitted down through the organization and spatially across our geography. We debate internally whether our area managers should adopt some of the attributes of the national recognition effort. Frankly, the costs of full-scale adoption are prohibitive. Nonetheless, we encourage area managers to apply the same passion to smaller-scale recognition efforts.

Most people who join the Postal Service don't feel as if they are signing up for a crusade. Some 98 percent of people who walk in the door plan on staying 30 years, doing the right thing, and earning their pensions. There is not the same potential for advancement as in a major corporation. For this reason, symbolic recognition is such a potent force in employees' lives, be they letter carriers or top managers. It has also been a powerful antidote to a long history of fatalism at USPS. I recall an early meeting of the National Executive Conference at which I announced the goal of raising on-time overnight delivery to 90 percent from the 40 to 75 percent rate then prevailing. "No way" was the universal response. The executives from New York, whose rate stood at around 40 percent, said, "If we can reach *70 percent*, it will be a miracle!"

I refused to back off from the target. We pushed the regions hard, especially Miami, which had some of the most highly publicized management problems in the system. In less than a year, Miami broke 90 percent. At the next National Executive Conference, we made stars out of the Miami people. We showcased them, laid out the red carpet, acknowledged our debt to them, lit off firecrackers around them. Other regions enviously determined to earn equal acclaim at the next meeting. We had triggered a yearning for achievement and recognition across the entire management team. "Impossibles" fell one by one. New York, for instance, steadily improved and crossed the *97 percent* mark.

A large-scale recognition effort cannot afford to fail. There can be no slacking, no looking back. At USPS, we have to raise the benchmark every year, reach our goals, celebrate—and raise the bar again.

How relevant is our approach to other organizations? Fully relevant, I would say. Setting clear objectives for success, presenting them as symbolic propositions that are consistent with our organization's values and executives' individual values, and rewarding high performance are an unbeatable combination. The emotional investment and focused energy we generate far exceed the investment in time and dollars we must make to support the National Executive Conferences. An organization that duplicates our approach will find its core leaders eager to pour their hearts and minds into the effort to be the best.

Peter I. Bijur

Chairman and Chief Executive Officer, Texaco, Inc.

The Energy of Leadership

Within the last decade, interest in leadership has greatly increased, as evidenced by the huge number of books and articles on the subject today. Yet it did not interest an earlier generation of fabled CEOs such as General Motors' Alfred Sloan, ITT's Harold Geneen, and Reginald Jones of General Electric. So why the interest in leadership now? Clearly something in our present circumstances has dramatized the need for leadership and for the rich associations it can carry.

The largest obstacle to discussing leadership is that the term is so common—we hear it from politicians, businesspeople, the clergy, athletes, and their coaches. The list is endless. What do they mean by it? Usually something rather broad, vague, and by the end of the discussion, elusive. My own goal is not to define the word but to show it in action, to connect it to concrete behavior and familiar situations.

Leadership is what makes the difference between a mediocre and a world-class company. And developing leaders is the best way to ensure a company's long-term success.

People: Our Most Important Resource

CEOs used to say that "people are our most important asset"—and then they would go right out and run their companies with abstract finance tools or by tweaking strategy and organization. With corporations facing new challenges of complexity, turbulence, and competitive intensity, the human contribution has become central to success. *Leadership means enhancing human potential.*

The corporation is an organic community whose competitive ability ultimately resides in the minds of employees at all levels. Leadership influences their states of mind by helping them to better understand the corporation's purposes with respect to colleagues, customers, suppliers, competitors, shareholders—and therefore to make better decisions.

dership begins with understanding the limits of executive
Jo authority structure can *make* people give customers good
No single executive or management team can foresee or program the thousands of decisions—all of them consequential in one
degree or another—that are made every day in a large corporation.
Good leadership imposes unity and cohesion upon decisions up and
down the line. It helps people understand the issues and suggests
modes of conduct.

In large energy companies, the strategies of the major players are
all pretty much alike. Ours is a commodity business. All our competitors have essentially the same assets we do. We have pipelines, we
have oil wells, we have gas wells, we have gathering systems, we have
transportation facilities, we have refineries and service stations, and
we have distribution systems. We are all looking for a competitive
advantage.

Well, our assets will not be fruitful without people. It is people
who seek out the operating efficiencies I just described, people who
understand the diverse needs of the marketplace, and people who
take a promising idea and make it become reality. Without the dedication and creativity of people, what we have is a lot of lifeless assets.
Consequently, I believe that our competitive advantage has got to be
our people.

To harness and direct the energy and creativity of people in every
business function, you must have leaders. And leadership embraces a
lot of things beyond the specific business requirements of the enterprise.

You have to be action oriented and deliver results. You have to
understand that diversity links to business success. You have to moti-
vate people and be aware of what is going on in the world around you.

At the end of the day, our primary competitive differentiator has
to be people and how they are led. The only way my company can
operate refineries and oil wells and rigs better than our rivals is
through people who better understand the sources of value creation.

The End of Command and Control

One or two generations ago, corporate chiefs were like generals. They
stood in front of the troops, waved a sword in the air and hollered,

"That's the hill we're going to take. Charge!" Today's leaders mus
a mixture of coach, preacher, therapist, cheerleader, and role mc
The leader works best through influence, not command.

Leadership must be behavior specific. One of my main goals as a
leader is to get the people in Texaco to speed their reaction time and
reduce product cycle times, lest in delay there is a lost opportunity.
We can, of course, introduce cycle time procedures into some areas of
the business. That's all well and good, but there are thousands of situations in Texaco where cycle time procedures are not practical. It is
leadership that must stir people to shorten time to decisions by clar-
ifying both the substance and the pace of action.

Consider Texaco's acquisitions of other businesses or assets. A
couple of years ago, when Monterrey Resources went on the block,
our people moved with speed and decisiveness to consummate a very
favorable transaction in just a few months, significantly adding to
Texaco's crude oil position. Our people captured opportunity because
they understood the leadership agenda and demonstrated a sense of
urgency not always present in Texaco's past.

Creating a Leadership Environment

I think we can agree upon one characteristic of leadership: It is teachable and can be transmitted throughout large organizations. Peter
Drucker says that leaders develop; they are not born. They are nurtured from their environment. I'm sure there are some people who
have it in their DNA, who are leaders from the get-go. But they are
rare. Many more have the capacity to find the leader in themselves *if*
they are given the right opportunity.

Here is a dimension of leadership that is often overlooked.
CEOs may think that it is up to them to provide leadership for everyone, all the time. In fact, their job is setting up appropriately structured leadership opportunities for others. I've seen people who
looked for all the world like followers, but who, when given an
opportunity to lead, showed that they were willing to accept the
risks of failure and suddenly blossomed into strong leaders. Experience is the only teacher here.

Good leaders spend a large amount of time putting their managers into challenging situations, nurturing and mentoring them,

then giving them the reins. Leadership creates conditions that generate the confidence and authority from which good decisions flow.

On the other hand, there are things a CEO can't hand off. About 60 percent of my time goes to people-related matters, and the rest is spent with things that indirectly involve people. A lot of my focus is matching what we are trying to do as a company with people's personal aspirations. The net-net is that I spend an enormous amount of time thinking about people matters. These are not issues I can hand off to the human relations specialists, much as I respect their talents. If I did so, I'd lose my sense of involvement. Not only would that be less fun for me, but the people in the organization would see that I was holding back.

The Power of Communicating

Leadership also includes the ability to communicate clearly and compellingly. I cannot emphasize this enough. To be an effective leader, you must be able to communicate. This doesn't mean just stringing words together in the way journalists do on TV. It requires the desire to communicate and the skill to engage in dialogue.

When I start looking for leaders, one of the things I look for is the willingness and ambition to communicate. I consider that absolutely key.

I suspect that many CEOs get frustrated at the intractability of human issues. True enough, people are difficult, often slow to change, sometimes unable to understand messages. If a CEO is going to be involved in personnel development activities, he or she must work exceedingly hard to make contact with the people, to build bridges throughout the organization.

My own preference is for open-ended get-togethers with about a dozen employees at a time—to which their managers are not invited. I share with them a lot of my views on things, and I stimulate them to share their views. Sometimes it isn't easy to persuade them to be candid. So I take my jacket off and I sit down and kick off a very informal chat about a wide range of things. I accept that there are things on their minds that I won't hear about. If people are going to ask me questions, it won't be about minutiae. It will be about macro issues that they think I might be interested in.

I also recognize that they are anxious not to embarrass themselves by asking me a question I might regard as dumb. But I try diligently to treat with respect every question that is asked of me. I tell people all the time, "There is no such thing as a stupid question. If it's important to you, I'm happy to answer it." I end these meetings by saying, "I read my e-mail everyday and I always respond."

E-leadership

In these situations, e-mail is a wonderful medium. Just three or four sentences, then the person pushes the "send" button and the dialogue has begun. People feel free to send e-mail where they'd not ever think of writing me a letter.

I was recently at a big CEO conference sponsored by Microsoft. We were asked how many of us made our e-mail address known to the whole wide world, including all employees, as Bill Gates does. To my surprise, less than half of the group raised hands. I think those CEOs who don't broadcast their addresses are missing a great opportunity to create connections outside the executive suite, be it with employees or suppliers.

What does this have to do with leadership? Plenty. Leadership is made up of tiny grains of sand, of many small gestures that cumulatively build powerful meanings. Those CEOs who don't give out their e-mail addresses symbolically convey a message that they live behind some executive barricade. They are also tacitly admitting that they are not good listeners. Listening, sounding out people, taking the pulse of the climate of an organization are a big part of my agenda.

It is my firm belief that more than half the task of leadership lies in teaching, learning, coaching, counseling, inspiring others—all within a framework of intellectual equality and commitment to common goals. When I look to select leaders in our organization, one of the things I focus on is that willingness to give and receive good communication deeply.

Mentoring

The CEO who wishes to lead must also get involved in mentoring. I mentor a number of people throughout the organization. My goal is to create deep bench strength from which we fill future key positions in the company.

I've taken on the careers of about 125 people who have been identified as potential leaders. I strive to know them individually. And I hope to influence how they think about the company, about our future, and about how we should be acting to develop our competitive position.

We use members of this group on special project teams in exceptional situations. If, for example, there is an issue at some place, no matter how distant, that local management cannot resolve, I may very well take three or four of these people out of their current positions and tell them to go handle it. We had a major problem with one of our North Sea facilities several years ago. I took a group of people and told them to find out what was going on, then come back and transfer that learning throughout the rest of the company. And they did just that.

Making Things Happen

Good leaders make things happen. Not everyone can—many don't want to, and that's okay. I have a great respect for managers who are doers, who execute their functional responsibilities really well. But leadership is not simply can-do enthusiasm and know-how. It demands a great deal of thought, judgment, and perception. It does not *necessarily* require knowledge of how to do something, although functional knowledge may be helpful in coaching others. Leaders can step out of their role as doers and find a new dimension to a task because they can communicate complexity and interrelationships where others can't. Leaders shine in situations where multiple tasks have to be handled simultaneously. They don't always have to *do*—but they must be able to orchestrate.

Total Accountability Management

All of these pieces of the leadership puzzle are important. Here's one that's more important than all of them: accountability. Let me approach this concept through our own specific business situation.

Texaco is in a tough commodity business, sensitive to price. We compete by demanding our people's total commitment to performing at the very highest levels of their capability. We can't afford mediocrity.

To achieve maximum performance, we have to give people access to the knowledge, the experience, the training, and the *authority* to do their work. I've told my top management team that we at headquarters must be the resource that is used by the rest of the company. The field operations should come to us when they feel the need. Otherwise, we need to get out of the way and give them a free hand to do their jobs, because they are much better at their jobs than we are. My personal style is, "Show me you can lead and do the job—and it's yours."

I have stressed rigorous accountability in order to underline profit deliverables. If a manager tells me he or she has an investing and operating plan that will add value, then that manager is responsible for the outcome, regardless of any and all external factors, including acts of God, like the weather. I don't want to be told this manager didn't sell as much end product because the weather was bad. That possibility has to be taken into account from the beginning.

Let me give a concrete example of how total accountability management works. We run a number of refineries around the world. These are among the most complex industrial machines in the world because they involve high degrees of heat, pressure, vapors, and explosive gases, and they employ large numbers of people. In other words, there are potential safety problems that can lead to stoppages called "unscheduled downtime" in our business.

When a refinery goes down it creates a very expensive headache, running typically to several millions of dollars a day. Total accountability management means that I expect the people involved to factor unscheduled downtime into their annual operating plans for a simple reason: Something *will* go wrong. There will be downtime.

Total accountability management requires the people responsible to employ forethought to honor the implied contract with me and the shareholders. Such allowances weren't always made, with the result that managers frequently did not make their planned targets.

I want people to say, "Yes, I've taken that into account. I recognize that there are unforeseen acts of God—El Niño, the collapse of crude prices, and so forth. But I have a contingency plan." Total accountability management demands that managers thoroughly canvass likely contingencies and possibilities. *You* are accountable for your job—and for your career at Texaco.

Respect for the Individual

Total accountability also applies to other areas of the business. Texaco is one of the leading proponents of respect for the individual, and not just because of the crisis this company went through in 1996. Treating people with respect and dignity is our number one priority. *Then* we worry about the numbers and the assets. Is that just talk? No. In my view you can't get decent numbers, anyway, unless you treat people with respect and dignity.

So total accountability management has a role to play here, too. For instance, I am not interested in managers telling me that they don't have adequate people to fulfill their demands. Their responsibility is to train people to add value and convince them of its importance.

I want our employees to go home at night, look in the mirror, and ask themselves, "Did I add value? Can I identify one thing I did during the day that added value?" Adding value every day is vitally important in this competitive environment. And good leaders bring value creation out in their team.

CHAPTER 5

E-business

The Internet will lead to many changes in society because it has the potential to be such an efficient way to bring buyers and sellers together.

—BILL GATES, *chairman and CEO, Microsoft, May 1997*

The Internet shakes the foundation of what retail is all about—selling to a mass market. The Internet requires us to cater to each customer . . . and that's something we have to learn. There is no blueprint to follow.

—RAGNER NILSSON, *CIO, Karstadt, Germany, September 1998*

The ubiquity of the Internet—the fact that anyone can link to anyone else—makes it potentially possible for a participant in the value chain to usurp the role of any other participant.

—SHIKHAR GHOSH, *"Making Business Sense of the Internet,"* Harvard Business Review, *March–April 1998*

With the blossoming of the Internet, e-business is entering a new, exciting, and—for many—unsettling realm. As noted by Gates, Nilsson, and Ghosh, the Internet will bring about sweeping change in at least three distinct ways:

- The Internet represents a revolution in the costs of moving information. Low-cost, standardized technology will create huge efficiencies.
- The Internet represents a marketing revolution. The real-time interconnection of people and companies will reduce the cycle

time of market research, market feedback, and product and service innovation.

- The Internet represents a business revolution, where technology not only facilitates but also dictates strategy. The networked nature of the Internet fundamentally alters the way companies can create value.

Electronic business incorporates two distinct yet complementary notions: the marketing, selling, and buying of products and services on the Internet, and the improvement of business performance through Internetworking to connect the value chains between businesses—and between businesses and consumers—in order to improve service, reduce costs, and open new distribution channels. Peter Keen notes two important characteristics of e-business that relate to the preceding definition:

- E-business is not a single technology or tool: It arises from the combination of technologies, applications, strategies, organizations, and processes.
- E-business cannot be accomplished by a single enterprise working alone; it requires multiple parties. In short, e-business is about relationships.

The migration of business-to-business e-business to the Internet actually continues a decades-old evolutionary process, building upon the successful experience of large companies using electronic payments and electronic data interchange (EDI). The movement of business-to-business applications onto the Internet is merely a new way for relatively large companies to achieve greater efficiency, lower transaction costs, and make more direct linkages with customers than are currently available using value-added networks (VANs). Simultaneously, business-to-business e-business lowers the entry bar and makes broader connectivity possible, providing new opportunities for smaller firms. As Don Tapscott, chairman of the Alliance for Converging Technologies, notes: "The new technology networks enable small companies to overcome the main advantages of large companies: economies of scale and access to resources. At the same time, these smaller companies are not burdened with the main disadvantages of large firms: deadening bureaucracy, stifling hierarchy and the inability to change" ("Strategy in the New Economy," *Strategy & Leadership,* November–December 1997).

Indeed, business-to-business e-business is big and is poised to get much bigger. Forrester Research estimates that in 1998 companies buying from other companies on the Internet will account for $17 billion, or roughly 80 percent, of all Internet purchases (excluding financial services). Forrester projects that these sales will increase to $300 billion by 2002 (cited in *Inc. Technology,* September 15, 1998). Whether referring to large or small firms, the Internet advances the ability to create integrated, seamless business-to-business relationships. These electronic relationships cement business alliances and act as entry barriers to competitors seeking to loosen existing relationships to garner business for themselves.

By contrast, Internet-based business-to-consumer e-business represents a revolutionary change. Reaching consumers and creating customer value through increased choice and convenience have never been easier, yet rising above the cacophony and generating company profits have never been harder. The emergence of knowledge as a valued asset and of innovation as a primary driver of value is a key differentiating factor of this new channel. The new business-to-consumer e-business model challenges established roles in the value chain, shifts the locus of where and how value is created, and simultaneously necessitates new models for organization and infrastructure.

To be sure, participation in this new world of e-business is not mandatory; the choice to shape the future or have it shaped for you has always been freely available. But consumer uptake on the Internet is occurring with much greater rapidity than anyone expected, and e-business laggards may face the unenviable and expensive task of trying to pry their own former customers from the electronic web of other providers. As *Fortune* noted in its December 7, 1998, issue on the e-corporation: "Any company that denies its ultimate consumers convenience and value in the interest of protecting an entrenched channel is swimming against the tide of retailing history. Consumers will not be denied."

We hope to offer in this chapter both context and guidance for those who choose to be proactive in shaping this element of their futures.

The Changing Role of Technology

Commerce in developed economies cannot be conducted without the effective deployment of information systems. In a global market that is increasingly shaped by e-business technologies, a strategic response that includes technology is a competitive requirement.

With the rise of the Internet, technology strategy needs to be integrated as an explicit and equal partner with business and operations strategy as firms plot their futures. Information technology platforms and packages that are unable to adapt to the changes brought by e-business, especially changes in the telecommunications arena, will increase costs and challenge the effectiveness of the enterprise. Organizational structures and processes that slow adaptation to a rapidly evolving marketplace will ultimately cripple the performance of the business. Technology strategy needs to sit at the business strategy table, and technology strategy as well as business strategy implementation needs to be flexible and adaptive, providing direction and focus but adapting devices and tactics as new information is gathered.

The openness of the Internet and its technological standards are a competitive strength versus non-Internet-based systems. These characteristics also constitute a major weakness as a differentiator in the marketplace. First, the technology itself is readily available in the marketplace to any and all takers. Second, the business requirements that the technology must satisfy are readily apparent to anyone who visits a competitor's web site. One need only look at the current state of competition among portals or early e-business players—like Amazon.com and Preview Travel—to see copycat strategies being readily deployed. The various Internet portals are all trying to be the storefront of choice and are quickly becoming more and more alike, with their directory, community, shopping and news services, and personalization options. Similarly, the early e-business players are now having to contend with aggressive competition, especially from current physical-world market leaders, often in the form of copycat strategies. Moreover, the Internet is still in its formative years. Technology suppliers are therefore attempting to deploy and drive adoption of their products as quickly as possible. By setting future standards, they hope to ride the Internet growth curve. While manufacturers might gain advantage by establishing standards, their goal is to establish commonality and ubiquity among users as quickly as possible.

The strategic advantage must lie beyond the technology itself. If the technology does not provide strategic advantage in the new world of e-business, what does?

Redefining the Value of the Business

In their seminal article in *Harvard Business Review* (November–December 1995), Jeffrey Rayport and John Sviokla state, "Every business today competes in two worlds: a physical world of resources . . . and a virtual world made of information. The latter has given rise to the world of electronic commerce, a new locus of value creation."

The data and information gathered from e-business transactions and the signals culled from that information bring about this "new locus of value creation." Never before have such detailed data on an individual-consumer or company level been available to sellers of goods. Simultaneously, never before has the technology been available to use that information to create a dialogue and "virtuous cycle" with consumers. The dialogue leads to innovation, which results in new, customized products and services where customer-specific value will be created. This enhances the brand in the eyes of the consumer, which results in repeat interactions, which generates additional dialogue—to begin a new phase of the cycle. *Fortune* (December 12, 1998) describes the emerging situation in this way: "The Web lends itself to immediate customer feedback and rapid adjustment. Learning cycles are much shorter on-line than off-line. Companies that are quick to try, quick to learn and quick to adapt will win. Those that learn fastest, and keep learning, will stay ahead."

To be sure, increased efficiency has been an important and early by-product of e-business, especially in business-to-business relationships. However, innovation based on knowledge, rather than efficiency, especially in business-to-consumer e-business, is now emerging as a primary propellant of value. While efficiency improvements have provided early e-business wins, future battles will be fought over the use of knowledge for creating innovative, customized value anywhere and anytime.

We are already seeing instances in which some of these new Internet-based knowledge businesses have attracted greater value than traditional asset-based businesses. As *Time* magazine reported in its July 20, 1998, issue, "Not since Bill Gates took Microsoft public in 1986 has Wall Street witnessed anything like the wealth-creating power of today's Internet stocks. Consider Amazon.com, an on-line bookseller that has lost more than $30 million since 1995 with nary a penny of profit in sight. No matter. Amazon's $5 billion in market value exceeds the combined capitalization of Barnes & Noble and Borders Group, the two largest U.S. bookstore chains."

What's behind this extraordinary, albeit perhaps temporary, value creation? Amazon.com employs knowledge of purchases to make customized recommendations to individuals returning to their web site, recommendations that are constantly updated to incorporate knowledge gained from subsequent consumer purchases. Hambrecht & Quist, the San Francisco investment bank, reports that, in the quarter ended June 30, 1998, 63 percent of Amazon.com's sales were from repeat buyers. This model threatens to transform business-to-business and business-to-consumer relationships. Relationship-based businesses, with regular and/or frequent customer interactions and transactions, potentially will benefit most from these changes.

To suppose that the revolution will stop at the altar of efficiency shortchanges the underlying power of e-business. The low-cost, standardized architecture will allow many more significant changes to take shape; it will transform industries. Indeed, according to a PricewaterhouseCoopers/World Economic Forum survey, nearly 80 percent of global CEOs surveyed believe that e-business will reshape competition in their industries. The findings show that 20 percent of those surveyed think e-business will completely reshape how they do business, while 59 percent say it will lead to significant change. It will be worthwhile here to look at a few examples of potential e-businesses.

E-business will place retail banks and brokerage houses under an increased threat of disintermediation and reintermediation. Retail banking is a knowledge-based business that has already been widely restructured. Automatic teller machines took many bank customers out of physical branches. Banking by phone and by PC continued that trend. Additionally, third-party processors have pulled away some traditional back-office functions. Smart cards—electronic wallets—threaten to reduce the need for physical cash. What will be left for the retail banks to do? As the *ABA Banking Journal* noted in its September 1998 issue, "Nothing less than the future identity, viability and profitability of many commercial and consumer banking institutions is at stake."

The costs of stock transactions have been dropped by a factor of 100. E*Trade has grown phenomenally as more investors move away from brokerage houses. At the same time, E*Trade faces intense competition from other new entrants competing on price. As a result, E*Trade has started moving into other financial services activities—providing cash management services, multiple account types (individual retirement accounts, Roth IRAs, education IRAs), access to mutual fund investing, research and performance data, and its own Platinum Visa credit card, all of which builds upon its customer knowledge. It now offers customers free e-mail service. Where will the journey end?

The physical infrastructure of universities and schools will diminish in importance. More and more, education materials and libraries are available to subscribers and allow an education to be completed online with supporting summer schools. E-business has expanded degrees by television arrangements by permitting a two way interaction and broader market coverage.

James Sempsey, a professor at Temple University in Philadelphia, noted in the Fall 1998 issue of *Money.com,* "There will be a convergence of universities into consortiums that transfer credits back and forth." Indeed, the magazine reports that Western Governors University (WGU)—"the country's first completely 'virtual' academic institution"—has already combined into a single catalog online programs from colleges in 18 states. Students can get credits from either WGU or another participating institution.

Software development will become increasingly global. Like hard-goods manufacturing before it, software manufacturing is moving overseas, but for a very different reason. A national shortage of software professionals and a restriction on U.S. immigration led high-tech companies to seek resources elsewhere. India and the Philippines, for example, are becoming major sources of software professionals. Software can be written, integrated, and tested entirely in the electronic medium, and no one needs a green card or a business-class reservation to participate effectively in this new pattern.

The Consumer Revolution

Only four years ago, the Internet was largely considered a fad. In 1995, there were 15.3 million online users worldwide, and online commerce totaled roughly $300 million. For the year 2002, IDC estimates 320 million online users worldwide and $420 billion in online commerce (with a business-to-business versus business-to-consumer split of roughly 75:25). As reported by Georgia Institute of Technology, today's average U.S. Internet user is a far cry from the stereotypical male computer nerd. While males still account for the greatest portion of users (roughly two-thirds), females are rapidly catching up; they have grown from 5 percent of Internet users in 1993 to 30 percent (and growing) in 1997. Close to one-third of Internet users are married and roughly 30 percent are home owners. And, reflecting the global reach of the Internet, by 2002 non-U.S. commerce will account for 37 percent of worldwide e-business volumes.

Clearly, within this short period of time, the Internet has established itself as a channel for both business-to-business and mass consumer applications. Business-to-consumer e-business models are making particular impact in several industries: cars; computer software and hardware; music, videos, and CDs; banking and brokerage; and entertainment categories such as gambling, adult entertainment, and children's games and videos. This picture will get even better in coming years. The number of Web users who will purchase goods online will shoot from 18 million in 1997 (26 percent of online users) to 128 million in 2002 (40 percent of users).

What factors drive adoption of the Internet and e-business among consumers? At a macro level, several key factors can be identified for the United States:

- Decreasing costs of going online
- Ease of use
- Increasing familiarity with technology

- Regulatory encouragements, such as sales tax incentives and the curbing of censorship
- Increasing returns on virtual networks
- Variety and convenience of shopping, learning, and entertainment alternatives.

Internet adoption is at different stages of development in other regions of the world. While Europeans have embraced the concept of the Internet and e-business, government regulations and high tariffs on imports such as computers have slowed the pace of progress. Computers are more expensive in Europe than in the United States. Internet access is typically offered through the national telecommunications company. Private Internet service providers (ISPs) are virtually nonexistent or heavily regulated, so that monopolistic pricing is still prevalent. Given these high costs, fewer households in Europe have Internet-ready PCs. Fewer people online make it less attractive for local merchants to invest in e-business capabilities. Fewer merchants online mean there are fewer options available for people to purchase products and services on the Web. Fewer options mean there is less incentive to go online. Thus, while the United States represents 80 percent of Internet users globally, with one in four households owning an Internet-ready PC, Europeans represent roughly 5 percent, with penetration rates by country varying from 0.8 percent to 12.2 percent. The Nordic countries have the greatest Internet penetration, but Switzerland, the United Kingdom, the Netherlands, and Germany are also above the Western European average.

Time magazine, in its July 20, 1998, edition, cites data from World Research identifying the leading reasons individual consumers gave for not buying online (see Table 5.1). Addressing these issues will further propel the uptake of Internet commerce.

E-valuation

How to make money is a crucial, yet largely unproven, element in the evolution of e-business. At the end of calendar year 1997, only America Online (at $2 billion in revenue) and Dell (at an estimated $1 billion in online revenue) had revenues at or exceeding $1 billion. In

Reason	% of Respondents
Fear of hackers	21
Lack of products	16
Can't see the products	15
Must reveal personal information	13
Poorly designed site	8
Companies' reputation	6
Afraid of money or merchandise getting lost	6

Table 5.1 Leading Reasons for Not Buying Online

fact, most of the leading e-business or Internet brands reported revenues far below that figure. Netscape was just over $500 million, Amazon.com and E*Trade were between $100 million and $200 million, and Yahoo! and ONSALE between $50 million and $100 million. All other players were smaller. Yet Amazon.com has carried a market valuation greater than that of its two largest competitors combined, and Yahoo! has created multibillionaires out of two "starving" graduate students. What factors are expected to propel these revenues to the point that profits justify these valuations?

A number of factors drive the perception that revenue will indeed grow dramatically in the not-too-distant future. First of all, the online market will grow enormously in coming years. IDC estimates that online usage will grow from 69 million at the end of 1997 to 320 million in 2002, a fivefold increase in five years and a 36 percent compound annual growth rate. As noted earlier, IDC thinks that 128 million of these individuals will be making purchases over the Internet, up from 18 million in 1997. Continued advances in cellular and television access to the Internet, and the continuing development of a technology-savvy younger generation, will also fuel further growth.

Next, current first-mover e-business players are expected to gather a disproportionate share of this market growth. E-business and other Web-based firms are making aggressive plays for customer acquisition, thus boosting their chances of capturing a large piece of the expanding online pie. They are doing this in a variety of ways, for example:

- Entering into multiyear agreements with portals that provide them with exclusive access to the portal's high traffic flows and large customer base.

- Undertaking aggressive brand building and advertising, in both traditional and Web-based media. E*Trade, a company that generated revenue of just over $215 million in the four quarters to mid-1998, will spend $150 million in the next 12 to 18 months to advertise its new web site.

- Creating revenue-sharing and other referral arrangements.

Third, online customers will continue to exhibit strong repeat buy rates, resulting in a customer base highly productive of revenue. E*Trade notes that its customers trade on average 25 times per year. While this number primarily reflects the behavior of Web commerce's early adopters, this level of activity bodes well for the ability of customer-focused e-business companies to build highly profitable, lifelong customers.

Finally, as the e-business provider gathers customer transaction behavior and preference data, new product and service offerings will heighten customer loyalty and generate additional revenue streams. Innovation will determine the winners in this new "e-conomy." Who better to innovate than those companies with the best customer data? These first-mover e-business companies will offer ongoing, incremental enhancements to keep the experience fresh for customers, continue to cement relationships, and fend off later-stage competitors. Essentially, these companies believe that they will create virtuous cycles.

Overall, the economics of the e-business world do look potentially highly attractive, both on the revenue and cost sides, although underlying assumptions remain to be proven. One of the greatest unknowns is whether customers will maintain the high degree of loyalty and repeat purchase levels exhibited by the early adopters of e-business. There is also the question of how and when marketing expenses of new online entities—which include costs for traditional and online advertising, exclusivity agreements, and the like—can be cut back without adversely affecting revenue growth. A third concern involves whether physical-world competitors will make the transition successfully to the e-business world, enabling them to keep their volume-driven gross margin advantages over newer, online competitors while also reaping the SG&A savings promised by the virtual world. A key consideration here is the ability of physical-world companies to exploit this new channel without undermining their businesses in the near term by antagonizing existing channel partners.

In sum, e-business has the potential to change the world of business radically, especially in business-to-consumer relationships. Technology will become part and parcel of the strategic planning process, rather than an afterthought. Existing companies, especially those involved in business-to-consumer products and services, will come under attack from new and agile players not burdened by the baggage of old systems or processes. Industry and company strategies, technologies, processes, and organization will be transformed. Companies that move aggressively to understand e-business and its implications, and use that knowledge to create business change in their organizations, will be the survivors. With high levels of innovation, customer service, and reliability, they might just prosper.

Esther Dyson
Chairman, EDventure Holdings Inc.

Online Commerce
Changing Everything, or Nothing?

Electronic business is not new. Large companies have been using electronic data interchange (EDI) for more than a decade to connect electronically with established customers. Today, however, the Internet allows companies and customers to interact in an entirely different way. By eliminating the need to prearrange electronic business relationships and by affording to small businesses many of the same capabilities formerly limited to large ones, the Internet has changed the nature of online commerce and the fundamental architecture of business.

But how significant is this change and what will be its ultimate impact? Some argue that online commerce is transforming the global business landscape by rendering obsolete the practices that have supported commerce since the industrial age. Others view it as just another tool—albeit a powerful one—for conducting routine business.

As usual, the truth lies somewhere between the extremes. The basic topics that have defined commerce for over a century   competition, pricing, marketing, expansion into new markets, customer relations—are and will remain at the heart of business, even if much of that business is conducted online. The fundamentals have not changed, but how we apply them has. Furthermore, the essential relationship between buyer and supplier, and between large company and small, will change over time as customers and small firms gain access to better information—and bargaining power. Companies that will prosper in the online world will do so not by abandoning basic principles, but by reconciling what has changed with what remains the same.

Managing the Competition

Online commerce is intensifying competition. As Microsoft chairman Bill Gates memorably termed it, the Internet tends to create a friction-free business environment where better information enables and encourages customers to consider more options. For many businesses—particularly those not well-positioned competitively—this is worrisome news. An environment that empowers customers dramatically fosters competition. I foresee great benefits for customers as result of online commerce; correspondingly, I see challenging times ahead for businesses.

A fundamental tenet of practical economics is that the best markets are made up of healthy competitors. Healthy competition eliminates pricing extremes, drives the development of new products and services, and improves customer service. However, inefficient or low-quality businesses often inflict damage on competitors as well as themselves by cutting prices.

In the online environment, price wars may become endemic, since someone, somewhere, is probably going to be pricing lower than cost, whether to enter a market or—unwillingly—to leave one. Since all one needs to engage in online commerce is access to the Net and a minimum amount of capital, the barriers to entry are lower than they have ever been before. In the world of online commerce, it is impossible to compete on the basis of price alone and succeed.

"Bigger is better" is another traditional concept related to competitiveness. The advantages of size and economies of scale have driven the industrial world for the last 100 years. But the Internet is empowering consumers to be producers, and the sheer number of new businesses that are appearing daily on the Net is turning the "bigger is better" concept on its ear. In an online environment, the competitive dynamic is not big against small; rather, it's good against not-so-good or fast against slow.

As I am writing this chapter, the business press is reporting on a single individual who is going up against the Amazon.com behemoth. Can he compete with them as a full-service provider of books, videos, and CDs? Certainly not. But can he take them on in one small niche of their business, say technical books or best-sellers? Yes, and he is doing so successfully.

Businesses like this are redefining the competitive landscape by underscoring a key point: As long as revenues stay ahead of costs, anyone potentially can run an online business of an arbitrary size and succeed. The advantages of economies of scale are huge, but for non-commodity businesses they pale before other factors, such as adding value through customized information, communicating effectively with customers, and offering personalized customer service. In the new online economy, these factors matter more, while size is often a disadvantage because it reduces flexibility and fosters bureaucracies that frustrate customers. With the Internet, it is possible to have a rewarding life running a small but profitable business that satisfies the people within it. As more people realize this possibility, more such businesses will be formed, and many will start competing successfully against larger, established businesses.

Does this mean that as online commerce proliferates large companies are doomed? Not at all—or anyway, not all of them! There will always be a place for some large companies. In certain commodity-oriented, asset-based businesses—the auto industry for example—size makes sense, as it is a means of benefiting from economies of scale that still matter. But traditional carmakers may find themselves under pressure as consumers become more knowledgeable and squeeze car dealers, who will in turn squeeze the carmakers.

There will always be a need for large companies to provide infrastructure—technical, social, and even legal—in areas of the world that do not have it. Large companies also will be natural outsourcing partners for smaller companies unable or unwilling to invest large amounts of capital in noncore, commodity business processes or assets.

Moreover, companies can be large in scope, though not necessarily large in terms of assets or people. Without owning or even controlling the resources they coordinate, some companies can leverage their size to take advantage of the opportunities the Net offers for integration by forming partnerships and alliances across the whole infrastructure of manufacturing/assembly, fulfillment, delivery, and supply chain management. Such relationships are already moving us away from a particle to a wave economy—in other words, from product-oriented transactions to longer-term relationships involving streams of services.

Large companies, however, will face a unique challenge on the Net. They will need to become more flexible and less bureaucratic. They will need to link up better with their strategic partners and allies to move products and services through the supply chain more smoothly, forecast more accurately, and manage more efficiently. And they will need to understand that a Net presence is more than just another sales channel; it is an opportunity to redefine their business.

Managing Price

As noted, online businesses cannot compete on price alone. This does not mean that pricing tactics cannot be key elements of overall marketing strategies. Like service industries such as airlines and hotels before them, online enterprises are learning to use yield-management techniques. While a terrestrial company manages yield in a single-point way by taking an occasional markdown, for example, the online enterprise is able to use price far more strategically because of its ability to make simultaneous price and strategy adjustments in real time as it communicates and negotiates with customers—and they negotiate back.

In the past, customers could respond to price in one of two ways, by either buying or not buying the product. But by giving customers more control in defining the terms and conditions under which they accept or reject a price, the online company has a greater ability to make price an integral part of the business proposition. As a result, the pricing dynamic between a customer and an online business has evolved from a yes-or-no proposition into something that more closely resembles a genuine negotiation. These changes go well beyond traditional pricing strategies to represent a true shift in traditional business models.

The need to move beyond the compete-on-price-alone paradigm threatened by Web commerce has led to a flowering of new and innovative pricing models. These are redefining traditional approaches to yield management by fostering the single most significant differentiator of the online experience: the two-way interactivity between customer and company. By capitalizing on the factors that consumers desire most—control and interaction—companies are using these models to strategic advantage. Among the most interesting are the variations we are seeing of the online auction.

Auctions are a classic yield-management technique. Traditional auctions are devices used to drive prices up—the highest bidder gets the prize. And there are any number of auctionlike web sites where consumers or businesses bid for products ranging from computers and accessories to travel packages. These sites involve consumers by placing some control of price in their hands and by making the thrill of the bidding experience central to the transaction. And they attract businesses that keep hoping that they'll get a better price at an auction than from a steady supplier.

But an even more interesting model has emerged whereby consumers set the price they are willing to pay, and vendors enter the market looking for unexploited demand at lower prices than list. Priceline.com, a web site that auctions airline tickets and other items, is a good example of company whose approach to price has shifted the traditional business model. Unlike traditional auctions, the concept behind Priceline is to discover people who are willing to pay less. Also unlike traditional auctions, Priceline (and presumably the airlines and other vendors Priceline represents) does not want the prices paid to be visible, since visibility would threaten stated prices. (After all, would any person feel good about paying $1,000 for a ticket to Los Angeles after seeing a Priceline customer purchase it for half that price?) By gauging price against a customer's willingness to tolerate inconvenience, Priceline has discovered an innovative way of collecting an aggregate, unexpressed, and heretofore unknown demand and satisfying it without disrupting a product's stated price.

Such models will, I think, have a number of long-term effects. First, they, are demolishing the notion of fixed costs. In the former Soviet Union, where I have a number of business interests, pencils used to cost, say, 10 kopecks, no matter where they were sold, no matter when. In fact, the price was printed on the pencil. The fixed-cost idea is not carried to such extremes in the United States (discounts and special promotions are staples of the U.S. retail market), but the notion of fixed price nevertheless has been prevalent. Online commerce is changing that.

By contrast, a concept that is spreading is the idea of perishable products: products that, if not sold today, lose value tomorrow. We used to think of only certain products as being perishable. Airline seats are a good example. (If they don't sell before the departure of the flight, they are worth nothing.) However, as products become perceived more as streams of use than as one-time fixed objects, everything becomes perishable. The value of fixed objects gives way to the value of objects used over a period of time. A product will still exist tomorrow, but the stream of its use today is perishable. The result will be a division in the world of online commerce into two camps working side by side: One will be concerned with soft issues such as brand differentiation and customer experience; the other will be extremely mathematical, analyzing the net present values of everything.

Managing Brands

Creative pricing models are one way a company can differentiate itself on the Net. Another is careful brand management. Online commerce is adding some new dimensions to brand management that can't be ignored.

In the world of physical objects, brands imply promises. A new automobile, for example, may promise adventure, excitement, sexuality, safety, or value. In the cyberworld, these promises don't go away. But they do become inextricably bound to a new dimension: the context provided by a web site. In the physical world, a consumer might think about that automobile as a physical object in a variety of contexts: a dealer showroom, a country road, a family outing. But in cyberspace, the web site can provide an additional value for the product through personalized interaction with the buyer.

So far, few companies understand this opportunity and, as a result, many give short shrift to the quality and value-adding potential of their web sites. Many fail to provide any means for interaction between consumer and company. (Stories concerning impenetrable, one-way web sites are legion.) Still others are virtually impossible to navigate, leading to dead ends and user frustration.

There are two critical aspects of managing the context in which an online business presents its product or service to the world, and each has tremendous brand-building potential. The first concerns the basic usability/intelligibility of the web site: Does it in fact add value to the product it is identified with, or is it impenetrable? The second involves the two-way experience that is possible only on the Web.

An analogy will illustrate the first point. A web site is, in many ways, like a city. When you visit any big city you are bombarded by a huge amount of information: street signs, maps, labels on buildings, neon signs, messages in shop windows. All of these contribute to your impression of the character of the city—what it promises, what it offers, what makes it different from other big cities. In a way, you might think of these impressions as defining the city's brand.

Unfortunately, the semiotics of cyberspace are, in many cases, woefully lacking. Entering some web sites is like entering a restaurant where every booth is draped in black; where you don't know if the people there are happy or sad, rich or poor, enjoying their food or gagging on it. By failing to provide a sense of community on the web site or at least a platform for a community, these companies are missing out on a golden opportunity to add value to their brand.

They also miss that opportunity when they fail to provide for interaction on the web site. Brands are a promise, but they are also an experience. A company can have a beautifully designed web site, but if it doesn't offer interactivity, it is failing to leverage the brand. The reason for this is simple. The actual value proposition of a brand is changing as a result of online commerce. Let's take an airline as an example. In the past, positioning the brand as a premium—more planes, better cabin attendants, more comfortable seats, superior worldwide route structure—might have been enough. But because of the interaction made possible by the Web, that is no longer so. I might care deeply about these things, but what I really care about is the number of flights Delta offers to Moscow, the status of my personal mileage account, and access to information, customized for me. Interaction makes it possible for the airline to add value to my flying experience through the information I am given on the site. Companies that view the Web as merely another sales channel are missing out on the strategic value that they can provide. The Web is not just another advertising medium. When online commerce is done right, the Web is a medium for customizing mass-produced products or services, and for delivering value specific to each individual customer, thereby providing more value.

Managing Customers

In the world of online commerce, dealing with customers is not as simple as it used to be. The instant feedback that the Web has enabled is the reason. Feedback has always been possible—through "snail mail" or telephone calls. But in the past, few consumers believed that a letter to the CEO would have any impact, or that a telephone call would get them any further than the switchboard. So they didn't bother to write or call. Now, the expectation of response is higher and the effort required to send the feedback is reduced. Online commerce has empowered consumers, and the tool that enabled that empowerment is e-mail.

There was a time when I knew everyone's telephone number. It was how I interacted with the majority of people with whom I needed to communicate. That's changed. Now, I know their e-mail address. If I don't have it, quite frankly, I rarely take the time to track people down by telephone. Doing so would involve an opportunity cost to me as an economic being; in the same amount of time, I could be sending several e-mails. In the same way, when a consumer or a business deals with other companies, it is going to go to where it can get the quickest return—to someone reachable by e-mail. Take that instinct and multiply it by millions, and one can understand how e-mail has revolutionized customer empowerment and service.

The power of e-mail is not only in consumers' enhanced ability to communicate with a company; it's also in their ability to communicate with each other about the company, to form communities, and to leverage the power of those communities to the benefit or detriment of the companies with which they do business on the Net. News of bad (or good) customer service, or bad (or good) products or services, spreads rapidly on the Web. The Internet is home to virtually thousands of special-interest communities catering to every conceivable interest. Members are generally passionate about at least some of the products they buy or the companies they deal with. They express that passion by posting their experiences—good and bad, affecting the opinions of thousands of other individuals. Companies that ignore the power of this kind of communication capability do so at their own peril.

In short, customers doing business on the Web see themselves as active participants in a two-way experience, not as passive recipients of products and services. Acknowledging these new customer attitudes and capabilities means responding to customers in new ways. Companies that understand this will prosper; those that don't will fail. Far more online businesses commit suicide than are murdered. And the surest way to commit suicide on the Web is to ignore your customers.

Managing the Global Implications

Web-based companies, no matter how large or how small, potentially have global reach. The Web eliminates geography as a relevant issue. Clearly, the future of online commerce is not one in which countries are pitted against countries, but one in which companies are pitted against companies.

Prior to online commerce, forecasts concerning the global economy were based, in part, on a rich-versus-poor paradigm: The low-cost countries would produce the products; the high-consumption countries would buy them. With the spread of online commerce, the place where a company is based is becoming less and less the issue. For instance, the costs of some services—programmers, for example—are rising to world levels in markets where everything else lags behind. In such cases, an electronic market that is globalized coexists with local markets that are not. In other words, the rich-versus-poor-paradigm has not disappeared entirely, but it's definitely becoming less country specific. Companies compete on the basis of what they can do, not where they are from.

Online commerce has brought into relief the incredible diversity and heterogeneity of the global economy, which must be understood and embraced if online businesses are to succeed. This admonition is particularly—though not exclusively—applicable to U.S. companies, which, in my experience, are less sensitive to cultural differences than many companies located outside the United States.

It's easy to see why. United States e-commerce vendors continue, for the moment, to do a brisk business abroad, because little local competition as yet exists, and, unlike Americans, most other peoples of the world understand not only their own cultures but U.S. culture as well. For the time being at least, they are willing to adapt.

But this is gradually changing. The United States is no longer the center of the world, and the day is coming when foreign consumers will prefer to buy books in their own languages rather than English, be informed about their own sports rather than American sports—in short, deal with companies with which they connect through common cultural references. (And like any other customer, foreign consumers don't want to deal with customs!)

There are signs that some U.S. businesses are getting the clue. Yahoo!, for instance, is beginning to show an increased sensitivity to the needs of foreign customers. AltaVista provides an electronic translator that will convert any web page (however poorly) into four different languages and has recently launched a German site.

Can this process be accelerated? It's certainly to our advantage to do so, but that won't happen until certain basic attitudes change. It's distressing, for example, how little interest young people show in international experience. If this attitude doesn't change, it will be difficult to compete in international markets. If you want to penetrate a market, you've got to speak the language. I couldn't do what I do in Russia if I didn't speak Russian. Companies need to place a high priority on international experience now if they expect to compete successfully in the online business environment of tomorrow.

A Wakeup Call for CEOs

CEOs are important people. They are used to defining business trends rather than reacting to them, and they have historically done so. But, in general, CEOs are not defining the direction that online commerce is taking. The Internet is simply too large, too diverse, too democratic, and too unpredictable to be shaped by the hands of a few. CEOs *can* act now to take advantage of the benefits of online commerce. But if that is to happen, certain long-held perceptions must change.

CEOs must come to grips with the nature of the Internet and its commercial potential. The Internet is not just another sales channel. It's not just an advertising medium. It is a tool to change fundamentally how a company does business and how it takes orders from its customers and provides value to them. Most products will have an information component that is delivered over the Internet.

CEOs must stop consigning online commerce decisions to marketing managers and chief information officers. The Internet is not tactical; it's strategic.

CEOs must fundamentally rethink customer service in light of the newly empowered consumer. Never before in history have consumers had more choice and more power. And they are using that power to define the kind of service they expect.

Last, and perhaps most important, CEOs need to get their feet wet and their hands dirty in the world of online commerce. They've got to understand its texture before even thinking about its architecture. How? They must: Learn how to use e-mail, and use it regularly; go online and buy something; look at competitors' web sites and see what they are up to; use a computer to track a Federal Express package; go to a favorite airline's web site and check out their mileage, noting the kind of security issues that are involved; call the factory and ask for a special order as a test of service, or call the company's main number—without identifying themselves as the CEO!

These recommendations may seem obvious, but recent surveys indicate that, for the most part, CEOs are not big e-mail users or Web surfers. That must change. Only committed Internet users can be truly effective online providers. Increasingly, customers will be both.

K. Blake Darcy
Chief Executive Officer, DLJ*direct* Inc.

E-business
New . . . and Not So New

There is general agreement that 1998 was the year that e-business passed its credibility exams, at least in the United States. The volume of e-business revenues online went up dramatically, from $12.4 billion worldwide in 1997 to more than $32 billion. Several companies closely identified with the Internet registered eye-popping market valuations, in some cases outpacing venerable Fortune 500 firms. The press began to concede what the public had already decided: E-business was for real.

This realization was oddly comforting for someone who had been in the online brokerage business since 1988—yes, nineteen *eighty-eight*. We believed our business was for real back then, when we launched on Prodigy, averaging about eight trades and three new customers a day. We thought we were off to a good start, although you didn't read much about a new mode of business that was *exciting, full of promise,* even *revolutionary.*

Exciting? No doubt about it. Today, we have our own web site, visited by approximately 90,000 people each day, and we execute 20,000 trades per day on average. *Full of promise?* We hope so. We took our unit public last spring, and the results have been extremely gratifying. *Revolutionary?* In some respects, certainly—we've all heard about new value propositions and distribution channels and lower barriers to competitive entry. But let's hold on a minute. E-business is a new way of doing business that has changed some of the rules but also had the effect, often overlooked, of validating some of the most hallowed canons of business success.

New Attitudes, New Consumers

Online brokerage has brought out the skeptics and naysayers from the beginning. They raised questions about issues ranging from transaction security to the savvy of "mere" individual investors. The security issues have been largely resolved. As for the day traders' alleged lack of sophistication, I'll let somebody else deliver that message to them. No, with one in seven stock trades in the United States now being conducted online, the trend is enveloping the entire financial services sector as it moves from a flesh-and-blood, bricks-and-mortar industry to one with a large and significant online sector. Mammoth banking institutions that have grown principally by acquisition, such as First Union, are now announcing that they seek future expansion by growing on the Internet. Merrill Lynch, hugely successful with its enormous staff of brokers, has announced that it will enter the online world.

What has wrought this change? Is it simply the computer—its increasing ease of use and affordability? Did "getting America wired" mean Americans were automatically going to manage their finances online? I think a deeper change in human attitudes is at work.

Some months ago, I spoke to an audience of perhaps 300 students at Harvard Business School. They are people of whom it is safe to predict a reasonably affluent future, and so I asked them: How many of you plan, within the next few years, to open a traditional brokerage account? Maybe a dozen hands went up. Then I asked: How many of you plan, within the next few years, to open an online brokerage account? I think every hand in the audience went up, including the first dozen.

Good news for someone in the online brokerage business, but something more important was being registered here. It's not just that this generation grew up with computer technology and feels at ease navigating the Internet. More broadly, I think we see increasing numbers—vast numbers—of people who are more self-directed, more confident about their own abilities, better able to evaluate professional advice and come to informed but ultimately independent decisions. A very few years ago, most of the people in that Harvard audience, for all their business acumen, would have opted for a personal relationship with a broker and let their own investment decisions be guided in substantial part by these professionals. Today, that audience is saying that it will do the heavy lifting, neither ignoring nor depending upon the wisdom of brokers. This cultural change is not confined, by the way, to the young, well-educated, and about-to-be-affluent. Retirees with a little nest egg have gotten wired, discovered online brokerage, and use their free time and resources to make investment decisions. I'm sure there are other groups fitting the same general pattern.

This self-reliant mentality has happily intersected with technology—affordable, more powerful computers and the Internet—to create not so much a new industry as a new means of distribution. The financial services industry is not being transformed into the *online* financial services industry. It is being transformed into an industry with a large online component, a new distribution channel. The same is true for booksellers and clothing merchants and dozens of other retail industries. They will remain the same, only different. DLJ*direct* is a good example. We're guided by principles that are in some respects entirely new and in some respects old.

New Consumers, New Business

In online brokerage, you can't very well have a newly self-reliant and self-confident consumer who is largely responsible for the rapid expansion of your business *and* treat that person like the consumer of old. Everyone knows that the Internet consumer has ease of access to a broad range of buying choices and the ability to terminate a relationship with the flick of a finger. That is enormous power, and people trying to be successful at e-business had better respect it.

Moreover, the power and autonomy of the Internet consumer include the freedom to change opinion with dazzling rapidity. Consumer preferences on Day One might have changed by Day Two, for good but not necessarily obvious reasons. By Day Three, new technology may have broadened the range of choices. By Day Four, new competitors have provided consumers with new opportunities. By Day Five, an entirely new set of consumers has swelled the market and subtly shifted the balance of opinion, while you're still trying to convince yourself that the approach you offered on Day One still makes sense—even though it isn't selling.

In some ways, more than 10 years' experience in this business is no longer all that helpful. Changes in the past 2 years have altered many rules of the game and rendered much that we've learned irrelevant. In some respects, though, our long experience has been invaluable. We grew up with the 286 computer chip and the 1,200-baud modem. We tasted the anguish of the October 1987 market dive, went through the recession of 1991, and have enjoyed the benefits of the bull market since. We have seen changes beyond number in markets, in investors, in competitors—in practically every dimension of the business you can name.

As a result, our own corporate culture is a collection of skill sets and attitudes—not a grasp of how the Internet works, but a grasp of where the Internet is *going,* and what customers who buy over the Net will accept. Perhaps I should say, "will accept today," because one of things we have learned is that customer attitudes change continually. It's not too much to say that our corporate culture is, in three words, *responsiveness to change.* We built this business out of components designed to assess customer needs. Our brokers understand change. Our tech people understand change. Our marketing people understand change. E-businesspeople who don't understand change don't stay e-businesspeople very long.

One more observation on this question of change: It's not enough to listen to customers. You have to *keep* listening to them. When I started out investigating the possibility of such a business roughly a dozen years ago, the people at Prodigy asked me if I would like to attend a focus group. I answered, "What's a focus group?" In my own defense, I can only say that I have become a full-fledged convert. At DLJ*direct*, we do focus groups, we do advisory groups, we keep an eye on bulletin boards and read our e-mail, and we keep doing it—day, week, and year in and out. Nothing less will suffice.

New Business, Old Values

When we took the idea of online brokerage to senior management at Donaldson, Lufkin & Jenrette, we were fortunate to be dealing with people who weren't afraid to try something new and different. They understood immediately that any such venture would have to be a business unit separate from the parent company, because it would need to engage in a variety of activities largely unknown at DLJ— focus groups being one, advertising being another, a heavy emphasis upon operation by teams being a third. At the same time, senior management made clear that the core values of the parent company were to be kept intact at the new entity—values such as complete commitment to integrity, dedication to the highest quality of products and execution, and sensitivity to regulatory issues.

We also discovered, as we went forward, that as new as this world of online business was, it was familiar in certain respects. It wasn't so much a case of "the more things change, the more they stay the same" as it was learning to let the traditional and the new work together side by side.

For instance, the importance of quality doesn't decline when you and the customer enter a virtual experience. Each time a customer enters our site, we want that total experience—reliability, speed, security, but also the overall feel of the experience—to exceed customer expectations. The independence and power of the Internet customer mean that if anything falls short of these expectations, we could be in trouble. While online brokerage is sometimes accused of commoditizing what had been a special experience, we don't see it that way. Our dedication to the highest-quality product and service is complete.

Second, and with interesting connections to quality, price can be a make-or-break decision. Online traders see themselves as executing their own trades. They conclude that they should be paying even less than they pay to a physical discount brokerage. This attitude does nothing to compromise their expectations of quality. There is no Ferrari in this business, a product of such superior quality that people will pay a premium for it. We found out the hard way. Years ago, we refined our Web presence—the ease of access and navigation, the swiftness and sureness of execution, the reliability of our e-mail system—to the point that we unquestionably had the highest-quality site in the trade. We thought it reasonable to charge accordingly. But customers left, and our growth stalled. We were so committed to quality that we assumed customers would pay extra for it—assumed, and didn't ask. When we finally wised up and lowered our prices, we doubled our business in eight weeks. Achieving and maintaining the highest quality at low prices isn't easy; it also isn't negotiable.

Third, as with any retail business, branding is probably decisive. It doesn't matter what you're selling—securities online or suntan lotion over the counter. You must offer consumers what is essentially a *promise,* one that is ownable, repeatable, and relevant. This area is another in which we learned to step more nimbly only after stubbing our toe. We started out focusing so much on quality that we tended to neglect brand. Lesson learned. Once we had gone public, we committed to spending $50 million on marketing the brand during the remainder of 1999.

Quality, price, brand—nothing new there, and for good reason. These have been touchstones of consumer business for many years. We may have to learn how to apply them in new ways, to get them to work with one another differently. But like the fundamental corporate values at DLJ, these basics are known for good reason as *core principles.* We don't know exactly where we're going, and that is one of the challenges that make this business so much fun. But as we navigate the uncharted seas of e-business, however *exciting* and *full of promise* and even *revolutionary* they may be, we must not lose sight of these lodestars.

Robert W. Shaw
Chief Executive Officer, USWeb/CKS

To Portal or Not to Portal?
That Is the Question

To date, the e-business movers and shakers have been venture capital start-ups, feisty guerrillas at the bottom of an industry food chain who saw a chance to gobble up occupants of higher links. The benefits of e-business for Fortune 500 companies were not so clear-cut. Those days of innocence, with a negligible price for inaction, are over.

I know from discussions with management at hundreds of North America's and Europe's largest companies that they are beginning to recognize that the Internet may involve huge repercussions for value creation and relations with customers. Even so, there remains tremendous confusion on what their responses should be, either short or long term. The extent of confusion correlates directly to size of market share, brand power, and investment in distribution. These firms have thrived in the status quo. But the status quo and its determinants of value generation are unraveling. Unless these giants find ways to deploy their economic power in this unfolding environment, they will end up like so many Gullivers, tied down by hundreds of e-business Lilliputians.

For, if nothing else, the Internet as a medium of information and commerce has rendered first-generation corporate web sites obsolete. The next evolutionary phase is more expensive and riskier: Companies are compelled by rising medium standards and consumer expectations to bring to bear a wide range of skills in corporate identity, branding, and electronic marketing. Systems must be sufficiently muscular to manage a large volume of complex transactions and feedback. Old, hobby-type corporate web sites must now be *industrialized*—my term for getting serious about creating a channel to market that is robust, scalable, secure, and interfaced into the company's legacy systems. The site must be quickly refreshed and dynamic, and it must convey the brand of the business accurately, vigorously, and creatively. A space without these properties might as well go offline because it will not engage, far less lock in, the customer—the ultimate goal of every corporate channel.

Two Portal Models

Too many e-business decision points exist to address all or even many of them in a single essay. Let's take up one significant issue and probe into it deeply: the corporate portal. Portals come in two broad types—the *enterprise portal* and the *consumer-centric portal*. Both use basically the same browser technologies and add-ons, such as bots or agents.

Enterprise portals are a major evolutionary advance over static intranets. They offer a fantastic convergence of information from disparate sources. Managers and knowledge workers access real-time and historical information from internal applications, legacy databases, and the Internet. Within my own firm, we have built an enterprise portal called Central, which features databases of active and completed consulting engagements, marketing materials, specific employees' technology expertise, and even pieces of reusable code for software development projects. It is a logical way to get our arms around our intellectual capital.

Customer-directed portals are a different matter and something of a watershed. They offer choices:

- Either taking or building an existing direct channel and then adding some of the features and capabilities of a Yahoo!, a Lycos, or an InfoSeek
- Launching a new portal that would suck in data from disparate sources and offer a wide range of functions from transaction processing to chat rooms, all in an easy-to-use form.

The choice is between the old Amazon.com model and the new one. The old model focuses on a single product—books—and a single channel for that merchandise. The new model offers more consumer goods and hosts an auction site. Presumably other e-business features will be added.

Yet portals don't have to be comprehensive. It may turn out that targeted portals are the way to go. The portal under development at BankAmerica's private banking unit, beamed at high-net-worth individuals, will generate customer-specific reports on cash projections or current net worth and also connect to mortgage loan and credit card facilities and accounts. In theory, this or any other customer-centric portal could adopt a "gateway to the world" model and deliver all manner of real-time data (stock quotes, weather forecasts, currencies) and tailor information to individual customers—thus taking mass customization to a new level.

While the compilation of data from disparate sources is hardly new—data mining and data warehousing are now familiar disciplines—the browser-based portal is many times easier and often cheaper to construct and operate. There is a booming industry, of which my company is a part, dedicated to supplying software packages, consulting, and outsourcing services for those companies that don't, or can't, develop such sites on their own. The portal's amazing power to handle large amounts of information and offer continuous interactivity is not, however, ideal for most businesses. Some will do better as a button on somebody else's portal, so as to piggyback on better audience demographics, traffic flows, and marketing pizzazz.

Behind the Portal Decision: Questions, Questions, Questions

What overall conditions support the portal of a company in the widget business? Frankly, I'm not sure that anybody knows the answer to this critical question. Consumers probably don't want a smorgasbord of portals—perhaps two or three, surely no more than half a dozen. Telephone companies and local power utilities have a very large piece of the total universe of customers in their customer base. But are they the logical developers of portals that generate strong customer following? Will banks and financial service companies have greater opportunities, because personal financial management is more important than paying the utility bill? Perhaps so, but by enlarging their scope, portal operators will also greatly increase the number of businesses they are in and the number of their competitors. A bank that creates a portal with stock and currency feeds is competing with Reuters and Bloomberg. Then, too, any newcomer to the portal game will go up against established portals that boast name recognition, good traffic flows, and good "stick" effects (how long customers stay at the site). Further, many of the established portals are currently increasing consumer delight by creating customized interfaces with tailored databases and agent capabilities.

As I write in mid-1999, deal making abounds in the portal space. There have been several big mergers and consolidations. Meanwhile, free and low-cost Internet service providers (ISPs) have been mutating into portals, offering e-commerce services and advertising. I suspect many of the existing portals won't be around in a couple of years, especially if advertising proves to be but one—and not the most effective—way to make money. Even so, many new venture capital–backed start-up portals have been launched, while more established portals are busy vying for new services.

The likely outcome is that the portal market could fragment. The Gartner Group has forecast that the current attractiveness of general-interest portals will fade in favor of niche interest portals that aggregate content for specific communities of interest, such as the medical profession or day traders in stocks. "By 2000, niche portals will replace portals as the most desirable piece of cyber real estate," predicts a Gartner Group report.

If this prediction is right, then there are opportunities for new entrants with the financial resources to create and retain a commanding role in communities of interest. These new portal builders are likely to be companies with very deep pockets and powerful brands—for example, global financial services behemoths or auto giants. Imagine for a moment that you are the CEO of one of the latter. You have taken the first step of recognizing that your web site, which offers a static array of current models in the showrooms ("brochureware," in Net slang) needs to be scrapped. Your technical people dazzle you with a demo of dynamic virtual imaging and show you how customers can build their own models, choose colors and interiors, and even simulate behind-the-wheel experiences. Maybe there are chat rooms with experts on picking the best tire for variable local conditions. Imagine further that you've somehow got the dealers to accept some degree of disintermediation, so that they no longer earn their bread and butter selling cars but offer support services, instead, such as delivery, after-sales service, and so forth. Now the question for you is this: Do you want to just be an assembler of cars? Maybe you should build a portal that runs electronic used car auctions, sells auto insurance, helps with travel planning, offers credit cards and banking capabilities. Indeed, as you have suddenly plunged into financial services, why not go further—into home mortgages or discount brokerage?

Such freedom of choice is a new and scary dimension for the old-line corporate strategist. General Motors, Ford, Daimler/Chrysler, and Toyota all have the possibility (at least in theory) of being nontraditional competitors in some or all of these businesses where they are not, at present, players. Unlike Amazon.com, which started with next to no financial resources, the CEOs of these companies have billions at their fingertips. Could they be thinking, "Hmm . . . I might do that, too—if I can get it right"? A big "if," yet a reasonable reaction to incursion into their domain by such Internet car outlets as Carpoint or Autoweb.

It may also be that some factor or other—the periodicity of automobile purchase by the average consumer, public perceptions of automobile manufacturers, or something else—does not promote the community of interest at the core of a portal's appeal. Indeed, highly successful direct channels should probably stand pat but others should consider shifting their models. Levi Strauss, for example, created a direct e-tail channel through which the company sold millions more jeans than through retail outlets. Sales were built to order: Instead of buying a standard size, the customer went into the electronic waiting room and was fitted for a pair with his or her unique measurements. Although traffic to the site was reaching satisfactory levels, Levi's began to realize that the cost of direct channel sales was too high. Alternately, they recognized that large mass retailers like Macy's may be the logical ones to create portals for all wearables. So, in October 1999, they decided to halt direct channel sales and increase their work with their largest retailer instead of doing it themselves.

I say "may be" because neither I nor anyone else can see how all elements of electronic markets will evolve. I don't know everything that a portal for wearables should contain, although I believe that one is inevitable because it rationalizes distribution at the same time that it adds value to the consumer. If the traditional department store is disintermediated at its physical location, it can take steps to reintermediate itself by means of a portal and thereby benefit from the expected large shifts in consumer purchasing behavior. That's why this whole issue is so immensely important. Moreover, the decision has to be made fast, because windows of opportunity are shrinking. Do you, Mr. or Ms. CEO, want to be a portal or a button on someone else's portal—or will a highly efficient, stand-alone web site be sufficient? The same question needs to be addressed by media conglomerates and by big manufacturers of an array of consumer goods. Should Time Warner have a portal for its entire product range, or will it do better with discrete, targeted web sites for magazines, cable, and all the rest?

No Answers, but Lots of Free Advice

Nobody should doubt how tough it is to find your way through uncharted territory. The best I can offer here is a half dozen tips that may be useful.

- While portal technology is well established, actual execution faces some uncertainties about feasibility within a reasonable time frame. There has to be a good Internet infrastructure aligned with existing company data, combining high-performance output with reliability and scalability. While current Internet users are willing to accept some unreliability of execution (in stock trading, for instance), this tolerance is vanishing. A big automobile maker with a poorly executing site invites devastating public perceptions of the site's products.

- Corporate Internet sites have only begun to be advertised in other media. These sites demand compelling and often costly marketing programs to drive traffic and buyers to their site.

- Capital outlays and ongoing upgrades and redesigns are expensive. The annual cost of a major licensing deal on a high-traffic portal runs into well over eight figures. Amazon.com has several such deals. Only a handful of the most popular portals with real drawing power will be spared years of subsidies from the corporate exchequer. However, rate-of-return calculations are irrelevant, at least initially, when the stake is ultimate survival.

- As in *The Sorcerer's Apprentice,* this dance cannot be stopped once begun. Companies that go down the portal path must commit to staying on the edge of future technological developments. They must continually seek new ways to create convenience and personalization for the consumer—perhaps tailored e-mail advisories of special products and prices, which American Airlines does currently; perhaps the use of agents, or bots, or inferencing engines. For high-end dishwasher consumers, Bosch has a site that can be accessed to troubleshoot a repair. The consumer describes the problem to the inferencing software and then is guided step by step through the fix, which sometimes takes but a few minutes. Such capabilities will be necessary for portals to earn recognition. They will have to demonstrate continually the best in customer service and self-service. Such requirements will mean, too, that the supply chain and company knowledge management will be directed to serve the customer interface more effectively.

- A portal puts a bank, an auto giant, or a major book publisher some part of the way into the entertainment business. Internet customers want functionality—and magnetism. Sites earn acceptance through style as well as content. Skills in audience development are crucial. But the portal relationship with this audience will be like nothing the company has known. For example, some portals will link up customers in electronic communities of interest, a connection that has not existed in the past. The content of the interactions in these communities will be outside the control of the space provider, and this could make corporate bureaucracies nervous. In a customer chat room, the site provider will find that customer suggestions for design and product improvements will be freely offered. Will this be perceived as a fantastic resource or as a trivial pursuit?

- Audience development raises complex issues of partnership with other sites. These are essential for a wide-ranging Net presence. Should these arrangements be long term or short term and opportunistic? And with whom? With other big brand names that want to march and fight together on the Internet? Or with smaller players, agile and bristling with street smarts?

In structuring these deals, what is the value of a brand with huge real-world recognition but no identity on the Internet? Clearly, some brands will move to the Internet because of an affinity between medium and product, while others will not.

This list of issues is far from exhaustive. But it indicates, I believe, the range of decisions that go into any high-end interactive and transaction processing site (portal or not), and the numerous strategic effects that flow from an Internet-based business-to-consumer interaction. The one element I've not conveyed vividly enough is the urgency. In the past two to three years there has been terrific flux in this environment, a lot of experimentation and uncertainty. Fence-sitting was a reasonable option.

No longer. Huge incremental gains will be reaped by established corporations that are the first to junk their old home pages and move aggressively to the next level of Internet presence. My guess is that these responses must be fashioned and implemented within the 18 months after this book is published in January 2000. After mid-2001, roughly, the environment will have hardened. Those companies that haven't made a place for themselves may never get in.

James J. Schiro

Chief Executive Officer, PricewaterhouseCoopers

Consumer Empowerment
The Internet and the Art of Management

As a business advisor to multinational companies and as CEO of a global professional services firm, I am fortunate to have had an insider's view of the development of e-commerce from its inception. I've watched with great interest as clients made their first, and by today's standard, rudimentary attempts to connect electronically to vendors and suppliers. I've seen those attempts grow in sophistication as electronic data interchange (EDI) technology rapidly matured. Today, we are all witnessing a massive expansion and redefinition of e-commerce, thanks to the Internet, which places it somewhere toward the center of the twenty-first-century economy.

Before the Internet, e-commerce was exclusively a business-to-business phenomenon, a behind-the-scenes affair visible only to a company and its business partners. Perhaps the most profound commercial impact of the Internet—and the most fascinating to me—is its introduction into the transaction of a third powerful factor, the consumer. Consumers participate in new electronic markets, but they also shape those markets. The Net is a catalyst. By accelerating consumer empowerment, it obliges management to reconsider many features of its business model.

Managing Upside Down

Envision the business environment from the 1950s to the mid-1990s as a pyramid. Market power flows from the tip of the pyramid toward its base. Occupying the peak are corporate management and brands. The media offer efficient distribution channels for information about these brands, while a fairly coherent channel structure facilitates physical distribution. At the base of the pyramid sits a relatively homogeneous mass of consumers who are the brands' target audience. (See Figure 5.1.) And consumers are typically viewed as commodities—undifferen-

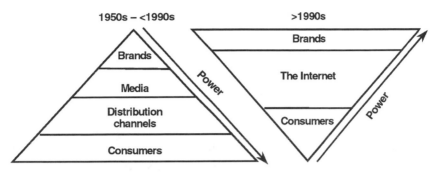

Figure 5.1 Market power then and now.

tiated, fungible, passive participants, the last link in the value chain. Yes, market segmentation is a developed discipline by the mid-1990s, but the segments remain general categories. Few consumers are known by name and by individual preferences, needs, and wishes.

The Internet has altered this once effective model; in fact, the Internet has turned it upside down. In this newly inverted pyramid, power still flows from the apex—but consumers, not brands, occupy the apex, and each Internet consumer is his or her own individual target audience and market segment. Online, the consumer no longer finds a homogeneous marketing environment, but instead a tremendous degree of differentiation. The base of the pyramid, where businesses and brands now reside, has become the commodity position in the eyes of customers.

The key to managing successfully in this upside-down world is understanding that the Internet alone did not cause this fundamental power shift; rather, the Net found a fertile environment in which it accelerated changes already under way. The Net draws power from the most fundamental of consumer behavior axioms: People will make for themselves the decisions they feel capable of making. Those people who feel that they can make the majority of decisions for themselves are today's Internet users, and managers do well to pay close attention to this new breed of active, exciting, individualistic online consumers.

Why Now?

What accounts for this surge in consumer decision-making power that prompts millions to trade their own stocks, buy cars sight unseen, book their own travel? I believe that the Internet arrived at a time when the fundamental demographics of the marketplace demanded it. In a well-educated society that includes burgeoning numbers of knowledge workers and working women, customers perceive themselves as supremely competent decision makers. The way they work has changed the way they consume. Add to this what I call the "consumer learning curve." Because customers have been exposed to a greater amount of media information and a larger number of product choices than our parents ever were, they have learned to be better buyers. In short, consumers are going online because the Net offers them the largest possible arena for transactional decisions.

What evidence do I have for these assertions? I recently spoke at a conference where John Naisbitt, the famous futurist, was also a speaker. I have always thought that futurists have the easiest job in the world; no one ever goes back to confront them with the gaps between their earlier visions and present reality. I did go back, however, and reread John's 1980 book, *Megatrends*. Not only had the changes he forecast come to pass, but they were all driven by the rise of confident, decision-making consumers. Twenty years ago, John foresaw that America was restructuring itself because consumers wanted to make the decisions they felt capable of making. *Megatrends* predicted not only the following powerful trends, but also that they would flourish with the rise of something that would be much like . . . the Internet:

- *Decentralization:* No longer centralized, power is flowing back to the local community and the individual. Citizens who once needed fireside chats to tell them what to think and feel now want to decide which issues mean the most to them and make choices for themselves. Issues-oriented Internet chat forums are already deepening that personal involvement.

- *Deinstitutionalization:* The classic institutions that we trusted to be our intermediaries (for example, hospitals, airlines, the media) are being reconceptualized, and their legitimacy as the final arbiters of our choices is being questioned. Consumers are able to find alternatives that take care of their needs in ways that call on their personal judgment and decision-making power. The wealth of information and news on the Net and the ease of access to shared-interest communities places traditional institutions under pressure to be more transparent and interactive.

- *The move from "organization man" to entrepreneur:* The days of the corporate patriot are waning. Increasingly, individuals want to be their own bosses and make decisions for themselves, even within the structure of large corporations. The Internet has invigorated the entrepreneurial spirit in unprecedented ways. Intranets and extranets are giving employees, suppliers, and business partners new access to information and an enhanced ability to participate in decisions.

- *Biology as the dominant science:* Replacing physics and chemistry as the primary basis of our metaphors, biology is ultimately the science of information transfer. On a molecular level, DNA is simply a method of storing and transferring information; in ecology, subsystems within communities interact by transferring information. Biology's focus on inner space provides us with apt metaphors for an information-based age. The Internet is best understood as a vast, living, information-creating, -storing, and -sharing organism.

- *Multiple options:* We have moved from a nation that values conformity to one that encourages diversity, increasingly tolerates ambiguity and alternative lifestyles, and champions new kinds of careers and relationships. This shift is an expression of the increasing decision-making freedom in our lives. The range of options available online fosters this search for personal meaning.

- *High tech/high touch:* Every new element of high technology requires a compensatory humanizing element. On the Internet, one of the most popular sites is called Yahoo!, not "Web Content Aggregator"; Sony calls the amazing chip in its new PlayStation the Emotion Engine, and millions of people are creating personalized home pages. The Internet consumer is actively shaping this new environment. Computers found their way into homes in part because people could use them to play games; online, these same people can re-create their own worlds.

Marketing on the Internet

How has the Internet affected the media level of the market pyramid? The media philosopher, Marshall McLuhan, suggested that each new medium subsumes its immediate predecessor. Thus, books become the content of plays, plays of radio, radio of television. In that sense, the Internet is the culmination of all preceding media, for it absorbs and offers back print, video, telephony, recorded music, mail, and chat.

The fragmentation of today's media audiences is well documented. Media consumers thrive in the ever expanding environment of cable, satellite, and targeted magazine choices. How does one reach an audience in constant motion? Unlike their media-customer predecessors, Internet consumers do not passively allow their evenings to be programmed. They no longer expose themselves to advertising simply because it flows along as part of a total programming mix. Consumers are now active participants in deciding which messages to embrace and which to reject. Therefore, the real challenge for brand building in all media, and especially on the Internet, is learning how to market unique messages.

Marketing can be defined in part as the study of transactions. Marketers need to ask what they must *give* of value in order to *get* something of value in return. Online marketing goes beyond deciding whether to advertise with banners or pop-ups. Internet marketers must determine what value to provide to Internet users in return for their attention and, perhaps, their retention of a company message.

The great impresario Sol Hurok once said, "When the people don't want to come, nothing in the world will make them." If online businesses don't find ways to justify repeat visits to their web sites, no one will visit them more than once. Mastering the factors that bring visitors to a web site, turn them into buyers, and then into loyal patrons who spread the good word is clearly the path to success online. The challenge is to learn to manage customers' decisions. Marketers today are passionate about the potential of the Internet as a tool to build relationships with individual customers. Understanding and influencing consumer decision-making processes help to determine whether these individuals will want a relationship with that business, and what the nature of that relationship will be.

Understanding Consumer Decision Processes

What will be the ultimate impact on business and the management of Internet-accelerated consumer empowerment? The online retail environment provides a clue. Even before the Internet, the newly confident customer was driving the restructuring of retailing. Consumers make two basic types of decisions, and they choose channels congruent with the decisions they seek to make. *High-involvement* decisions are those in which the buyer is deeply and personally involved (buying a car, a dress, a PC, a vacation, a stock, a book, or a CD). On the other hand, for *low-involvement* decisions, the consumer needs little information, and price, not brand, is the ultimate criterion.

The recent past has shown that traditional retailers who try to be all things to all people lose market share to other formats that explicitly match the consumer's level of involvement in the purchasing decision. Note the rise of high-involvement designer boutiques, gourmet take-out shops, and bookstores with coffee bars, and the simultaneous success of low-involvement discounters, superstores, and designer outlets. Similarly, on the Web, high-involvement decision sites like Amazon, Expedia, and Schwab coexist with purely price-driven auctions and search bots.

While most visible in retail e-commerce, the consequences of consumer empowerment are also having a profound impact across the entire business spectrum. With access to the Internet, consumers are not just empowered purchasers of goods and services, they are also empowered investors in the companies that provide these goods and services. Moreover, consumer or end-customer empowerment has flowed upward to redefine relationships among businesses and their vendors and suppliers. With end-customer satisfaction raised to the highest priority by the Internet, companies are compelled to use this technology to enhance their customer relationships. Many forge Internet-enabled alliances and strategic partnerships with vendors and suppliers, which ultimately result in better customer service.

Through consumer empowerment, the Internet is melting the links of value chains; it is breaking down the barriers that separated companies from their customers, their channels, their suppliers, and their employees. Rather than a value chain, the Internet has set in motion a constantly changing *value stream*, which is unceasingly carving out new channels and creating new tributaries. The art of management in the Internet world may depend on executives' ability to shape the direction of the flow of value along the length of that stream. But, more and more, the key to perfecting that art will also lie in recognizing that the consumer controls the flow.

CHAPTER 6

Disruptive Technology and the Large Corporation

John Maynard Keynes once quipped that the trick to progress lies more in escaping old ideas than embracing new ones. Although directed toward his fellow economists, Keynes's insight is just as valid for modern business leaders who must live with the effects of disruptive technology.

Technology as a driving force in business is nothing new. However, the impact of technology on business has now reached a qualitatively different level. The management of technology has joined with the management of capital to define the context of competition for twenty-first-century firms and markets. Yet simply adding more technology to business processes does not adequately address future strategy. Business history is replete with examples of well-managed, technically savvy market leaders who failed nonetheless, because they could not respond—until too late—to a changed landscape of opportunity and risk opened by new technology.

Technologies, Not Technology

Clayton Christensen of Harvard Business School wrote in his book, *The Innovator's Dilemma* (Harvard Business School Press, 1997), that there is a vital distinction between what he calls *sustaining* technologies and those that are *disruptive*. Many new technologies foster improved performance of established products according to the preferences of mainstream customers. Regardless of whether innovation in these established products is incremental or dramatic, the value proposition surrounding sustaining technologies is more or less clear.

The value of disruptive technologies is initially less clear. These technologies usually have features that only a few (and generally new) customers value. Products based on disruptive technologies are typically cheaper, simpler, smaller, and more convenient to use, even though they often underperform the mainstream market. They underperform, that is, until an inflection point is reached where they break out of their niche markets and chew upward into established markets with significant cost advantages. It is no surprise, therefore, that the disruptive impact of such technologies lies more in how they upset existing business models than in how they enable new business models.

Yet we believe that there is an important class of technology changes that go beyond Christensen's depiction of sustaining versus disruptive. These technologies cannot be reduced to an improvement in cost or performance over the present state of the art, but constitute an entirely new system. They are the radically new technology waves that occur infrequently, with enormous lasting impact.

The transistor is a case in point. Its Nobel Prize–winning inventor, William Shockley, realized early in the process something that his contemporaries did not. Shockley and his collaborators knew that the transistor was far more than a replacement for vacuum tubes and crossbar switches. The transistor made possible entirely new realms of electronic innovation. Before the transistor it was a fantasy to conceive of portable radios, let alone something as mind-boggling as a personal computer. After the transistor, not only did these consumer products become feasible, the supporting capital and talent to create a new industry was born.

Radical technologies provide the basis for entirely new industries even as they destroy (the correct term) the mainstream economic justification of other industries. They have such vast impact because they enable inventors and users to identify and serve human needs in ways or contexts that have not yet been articulated.

Until recently, the interplay between sustaining, disruptive, and radical technologies occurred largely at the level of research and engineering departments within firms and organizations. However, those days are largely past, due not only to increased board-level appreciation of the power of technology, but also because of a new and radical technology—the Internet—that has captured world attention.

The open network model of the Internet provides an entirely new infrastructure for developing and leveraging technologies and techniques that upset legacy businesses. Think back to the development of the transistor at Bell Laboratories. Granted that a lone inventor or a small clutch of inventors outside of Bell Labs could have grasped the solid-state physics that underpinned the transistor, it is highly unlikely that they would have had the capital and intellectual wherewithal to establish a facility and processes for mass-producing transistors. The main obstacle would have been the high cost of communicating and coordinating the activities not only of inventors, but also of partners, investors, and customers.

The Internet grants individuals and small teams the communications and coordination power that was previously possible only for the largest corporations. This newfound capability allows small, nimble firms to link across geographic, disciplinary, and industrial boundaries. The end result is that the tools for mapping knowledge to products and services to markets are within reach of a far wider population.

In such a world, technology-led advances seem to pop out from all directions. For this reason, today's corporations can expect an avalanche of technology-led disruption as global competition shifts away from an infrastructure-intensive business environment toward an intelligence-intensive business environment. In this world, the primary sustainable advantage is an organization's capacity for rapid and relentless innovation.

This chapter analyzes the impact of disruptive technologies on business from the point of view that corporations have means at their disposal for making disruption a virtue. Creating structures around which new enterprises can be born and, more important, managing the sunset of legacy businesses *profitably* lies at the heart of future strategy. To get to that point requires new concepts of how technology (especially information processing and transport technologies) affects the economics of risk, organization, and markets. We focus initially on the primary disruptive attribute of the most pervasive technology of modern business: the microchip. We then map that phenomenon into the framework of the Internet and explore some of the strategies that organizations employ to leverage innovation, and we conclude with comments on management skills needed to thrive on disruption.

Creating Disruption

While preparing a speech in 1965, Intel Corporation cofounder Gordon Moore observed that when he graphed data about the growth in silicon chip performance, each new chip generation contained roughly twice as much information storage and/or processing power as its predecessor. Additionally, new chips were coming to market every 18 months to two years. Moore reasoned that if this trend continued, computing power would rise exponentially over relatively brief periods of time.

Moore's Law has proven remarkably resilient. In the 27 years since the introduction of the first microprocessor, the number of transistors on a silicon chip has increased more than 3,200 times, from 2,300 transistors on the Intel 4004 in 1971 to 7.5 million transistors on the latest Pentium II processor. This multiplication has translated into ever more powerful and inexpensive information processing. Yet the impact of Moore's Law on business has been consistently misunderstood. While rapid improvement in silicon technology has been important for developing the global computer market, it is a second-order phenomenon. More important for business is how silicon technology has changed the economics of calculating, managing, and leveraging risk.

Information processing has made the developed economies rich because it has enabled organizations to package and circulate risk (corporate, technical, financial, market, competitive, and so forth) ever more precisely, ever more frequently in real time, as ever more differentiated, and in ever larger amounts. Computing has revolutionized how capital is created, bought, and sold because information-processing power has given decision makers exponential gain in their ability to put a price on the risk/reward trade-off that typifies any business endeavor.

Silicon technology is also decisive for coordinating the business processes that turn such calculation into action. Whenever people are organized for work, they must somehow communicate, allocate resources, make decisions, enact those decisions, and test them in the market. Whenever people use markets to obtain goods and services, they must somehow search, compare, communicate, and buy.

Information processing decisively lowers the cost of doing both while increasing their speed and quality. As a result, information technologies enable people to coordinate more effectively, to coordinate on a far larger scale, and to form new, coordination-intensive business and consumer structures. Thus, leaps in information-processing power through silicon technology have allowed more scale and scope to put a price on risk, and this motivates the coordination of capital, labor, materials, and information to seize attractive opportunities—all at a technology cost that halves every 18 months. This development not only creates new industries and markets, it redefines the competitive context for *all other industries.*

During the 1970s and early 1980s, the steel industry in North America and Europe appeared to be in the grip of a rapid, permanent decline vis-à-vis overseas rivals. The U.S. steel industry, in fact, reduced total output by one-third in the period from 1975 to 1985 as many companies went bankrupt or underwent reorganization.

Yet in the midst of this chaotic period, a group of relatively small steel companies was able to expand output at nearly 20 percent lower cost by using computer-controlled electric arc furnaces (EAFs) and continuous casting technology to make steel products from scrap. The "minimills," as they were called, employed a unique way of doing business that fundamentally disrupted an industry model that had remained largely unchanged since the nineteenth century.

Minimills did not achieve their productivity gains by investing greater amounts of capital. Indeed, in 1995 it cost about $400 million to build a minimill versus $6 billion to build an integrated steel mill.

Minimills did not add more labor. In fact, the number of workers required for a minimill is significantly lower than for an integrated operation. Minimill operators leveraged their information-processing capability to conceive, cost, and organize around entirely new ways of conducting the steel business. Instead of viewing impurities in scrap steel as a barrier to market entry, minimills went for low-end markets such as the one for steel reinforcing bars (rebars), products that integrated mill owners almost gratefully ceded to the new organizations.

The minimill operators saw the rebar market differently and used it to generate cash flows to finance their upward march. After capturing the rebar market, minimills went after other markets such as rods and angle irons, again low-end market segments that the integrated operators were relieved to exit.

As became all too clear to the legacy steelmakers, minimill operators were quickly learning how to improve the quality of their products to the point where more substantial steel markets, such as the one for structural beams, became accessible to them. In response, traditional steelmakers moved further up the value chain, investing huge amounts of capital to focus on the high-quality rolled sheet steel favored by automotive, appliance, and can manufacturers.

The respite of integrated steel from the minimill onslaught proved to be short-lived. In the late 1980s, continuous thin-slab casting technology was developed in Germany. This disruptive innovation did not *quite* match the defect-free quality required by the main customers of the integrated mills, but it did allow minimill operators to address new markets such as the one for construction decking. More important, the German innovation gave minimills a toehold at the bottom of integrated steel's most important market.

The disruptive impact of the minimill model for the steel business went beyond new efficiencies in production. Minimill operators again turned to information processing to accelerate the number of inventory turns in steel distribution—that is, minimills used silicon technology to provide them with the flexibility to synchronize their production runs more closely with the needs of customers.

At certain minimills, such as North Star Inc.'s Kingman, Arizona, plant, the ambition is to run a steel mill with little or no inventory in the scrap yard, between the caster and the rolling mill, or in the shipping yard. The plant currently keeps about one week's supply of scrap in its inventory. This low number is possible mainly because of the plant's ability to backhaul scrap on roughly 80 to 90 percent of its deliveries by scheduling trucks so that they are either leaving the plant with finished steel or arriving with new scrap.

Backhauling scrap requires that the sales and scrap departments communicate and coordinate their activities to an extremely high degree. By scheduling operations to such a fine granularity, it takes North Star's plant about three hours after scrap is unloaded from trucks to melt and cast it into billets, then roll and ship it as final steel products to the makers of cans, automobiles, or appliances.

This refinement not only reduces the capital cost and interest payments on excess inventory, it also provides a minimill operator with more opportunities in a shorter time to learn about producing and distributing steel. Such learning is then translated into new products and, more important, into new ways of modeling and pricing the risks and opportunities of the steel business.

The numbers tell what can happen when the creative use of disruptive technology changes the opportunity and risk profile of a market. In 1981, EAF carbon steel companies accounted for only 15 percent of U.S. steel production. By 1991, they accounted for 22.7 percent. In 1998, minimills using EAF and related technology accounted for nearly half of U.S. steel capacity, according to the Steel Manufacturer's Association (SMA).

Without Moore's Law, it is doubtful that the productivity gains enjoyed by the minimills would have been possible. The risks of entering the steel business at the time of the first minimills would have been likely to defeat even the best management teams unless they had the power to calculate the price of market entry while coordinating business processes in an entirely new way.

While minimills represent but one example of the profound effect of silicon technology outside of the computer business, they illustrate the overall disruptive impact of Moore's Law: The cost of information processing is no longer a significant market entry barrier for *any* industry. While the disruptive effect of Moore's Law will continue to accelerate because of further improvements in silicon technology, we anticipate even greater disruption of the risk/reward profile in legacy industries caused by a new product of silicon technology—the Internet.

Communicating Disruption

Ask any classically trained telecommunications engineer an opinion of the Internet and he or she may well tell you that, from a design perspective, the Internet model is a disaster. It has none of the hard systems engineering and quality-of-service attributes that make the public switched telecommunications network (PSTN) one of the most successful infrastructures ever built. Ask that same engineer about the future of communications, and he or she will unhesitatingly reply that it is packet-switching that uses Internet protocols.

Why the contradiction? The exploding demand for Internet connectivity in the telecommunications business may come to mind. However, just like the effect of silicon technology on the computer industry, it is a second-order phenomenon. Instead, the strategic impact of the Internet on business (and, hence, the opportunity that drives the network industry) is how the Internet changes the economics of information sharing over the wide area. This transforms market structures.

Lending Tree Inc. is a privately held firm of 20 employees that operates out of Charlotte, North Carolina, and uses Internet-based technology to address the consumer loan and mortgage market. Lending Tree is not about manipulating money. Rather, Lending Tree uses Internet technology to disrupt the legacy loan brokerage business by matching a variety of third-party loan vendors to a network (as opposed to geographic) consumer base.

Consumers visiting the Lending Tree web site complete a loan qualification form, which varies with the type of loan they are seeking, but which includes the same baseline information as the familiar printed forms of the past. When the customer has submitted his or her qualification form, Lending Tree obtains an industry standard three-digit credit bureau score from Fair, Issac & Com (FICO). Lending Tree then runs the application through its proprietary filtering technology, which matches lender, loan product, and borrower.

On the customer side, once a loan qualification form is submitted through the web site, Lending Tree assigns that customer a password. Using the password, the customer can access a secure web page from

Lending Tree, where he or she can examine the condition of the offers and accept or decline each proposal. Lending Tree will provide a customer with up to four offers. Thus, Lending Tree gives consumers the opportunity to interrogate a wider base of possible lenders than would have been possible or cost effective via traditional communications channels.

On the vendor side, Lending Tree originates loan applications, so that lenders receive a pool of prequalified applicants for their loan products. Lenders know that any borrower referred to them by Lending Tree has been prequalified. Identically, borrowers prequalified by Lending Tree know that any lender from the list of institutions returned to them will lend money.

The main point to remember about Lending Tree is that a 20-person organization has acquired the capacity to mass-customize a primary consumer service over the wide area. But the disruptive impact of the Internet goes beyond how it changes the cost of organizing and sharing information about products or services over the wide area. The Internet also enables organizations and individuals to share and leverage information about prices. A multitude of Internet-based auction sites such as eBay, Priceline.com, Travelocity, and Autobytel.com are redefining how customers search, compare, and bid on prices for goods and services. As a result, the idea of one standard price or a static price catalog for goods and services will seem as archaic to twenty-first-century business as medieval restrictions on interest-bearing loans seem to twentieth-century business.

Personalized pricing, forward auctions (where a firm posts a sell offer at a likely price point for buyers), and reverse or "Dutch" auctions (a buyer posts a price he or she is willing to pay, and firms respond) would be impossible without inexpensive yet powerful information processing and transport capability. Consequently, fundamental conceptions of the cost of inventory, the cost of distribution, and the new risks and rewards of managing both effectively must change as well.

Silicon and Internet technology disrupt the current structure of markets not by changing what they *are* (price-based information structures for exchanging goods and services) but by changing the standard for *efficient* markets. According to Dan Geer, vice president and senior strategist at CertCo, there was once no question that the fundamental reason for a stock exchange was to provide "an advantage of time and place" to those who would trade on it and, in so doing, establish the efficiency and liquidity baselines against which other markets would be judged.

The Internet makes the concept of time and place more or less meaningless for trading goods and services. As a result, new metrics such as oversight, fair play, or quality of service are becoming the baselines for benchmarking markets. Speed and liquidity are nearly taken for granted.

Inexpensive information processing, courtesy of Moore's Law, combined with inexpensive information transport via the Internet moves *all* markets closer to the dynamics of today's stock exchanges. The result is shorter product and service cycles, more ephemeral competitive barriers, and a decisively lowered cost for firms and consumers to participate in larger, faster, deeper, and more disruptive market spaces. Most important, we cannot regard this new configuration as transitional. It is a taste, now, of how economic life will be organized in the next millennium.

Capitalizing Disruption

Pundits have declared that size is the enemy for corporations attempting to catch the next wave of innovation before it crashes over them. Yet large companies are not necessarily passive spectators watching disruptive technologies take shape elsewhere. Many of the technologies that transform markets are born in large corporate labs. The problem with size is that markets that initially coalesce around a new technology are usually small or contested by a host of incompatible technologies where no clear winner has emerged. For large corporations, it is perfectly rational in the short term to concentrate resources on proven technologies and business models that generate cash flow. In so doing, however, they lay themselves open to the disruptive effects of new technology.

The conundrum for large corporations is how to be a player in markets that, from a certain perspective, are too immature to warrant their interest. Strategies to allow large organizations to stay close to the sources of innovation take many forms: acquiring smaller technology companies, building their own venture portfolios, participating in external venture capital funds, and spinning off independent subsidiaries charged with cultivating specific technologies.

Acquisition is a time-honored method for bringing new blood, expertise, and/or intellectual property into a firm. The problem, however, is that many acquisitions founder due to cultural as opposed to commercial, financial, or technological reasons. The cultural factors go beyond the common perception of victor (acquiring firm) and vanquished (acquired firm). More important is the competitive context within which technical assets have to be integrated.

The $4.3-billion acquisition of Netscape by America Online (AOL) has spawned many rumors in the trade press over the fate of Netscape's cutting-edge Web technologies. Although AOL characterizes the deal as a major technical victory, it plans to keep Microsoft's Internet Explorer as its default browser. The CEO of AOL, Steve Case, has been quoted to the effect that keeping AOL's placement on the Windows desktop is worth more to the Virginia-based media company than adopting Netscape's browser.

Another aspect of the acquisition involves AOL's changed relationship with Excite, the Internet portal company. AOL owns a little more than 9 percent of Excite—ownership that includes a seat on the board. Excite also provides cobranded search services for both Netscape and AOL. As part of its original deal with Netscape, Excite agreed to license its search technology to Netscape in May 2000. Whether this means that AOL, as Netscape's new owner, will have access to this technology on the same terms has yet to be determined. In other words, it is nearly impossible to acquire another firm's technology without also acquiring the firm's market relationships for good or ill.

Another strategy for new technology produced in-house by a large enterprise is to create an independent subsidiary that acts as a keeper of the flame for the innovation, without bringing it into direct conflict with existing lines of business. This idea was behind the creation in January 1996 of JavaSoft by Sun Microsystems, as a means of developing, marketing, and supporting products based on Java technology. JavaSoft had the authority to develop its business model and market channels largely independently of the legacy structures of Sun Microsystems. As a result, JavaSoft has been able to push into the market at its own pace and grow the platform, while Sun has been able to concentrate on its high-margin server hardware business.

Moreover, the business model for Java technology has been allowed to incubate and be modified by JavaSoft far more quickly than likely would have been the case, had the task of marketing Java remained within Sun's central corporate structure. Whereas Java technology was originally conceived as a way of attacking the Wintel grip on desktop operating systems, it is becoming apparent that Java's current commercial value lies more in the embedded-systems area of cellular phones, intelligent peripherals, and the evolving network-appliance space.

There are still other strategies to attack the problem of finding, evaluating, embracing, and adapting disruptive technologies developed outside of a parent company. Large corporations are the latest venture capitalists, creating huge pools of investment capital to be made available to start-up partners pursuing attractive new technologies. The telecommunications industry has seen a spate of start-up funds in some of the biggest names in the business—MCI WorldCom, Siemens, Nokia, and Lucent to name a few. In August 1998, Siemens AG announced plans for a $300-million fund to tap the ingenuity of small high-tech companies. The Siemens Mustang Fund, as it is called, targets networking and telecommunications start-ups.

According to industry observers, leading-edge technology is Siemens's first priority. Making money is a close second. Such concentration on intellectual, as opposed to financial, assets is echoed by Nokia vice president John Malloy, who has been quoted as saying that the Finnish telecommunications company's $100-million venture fund would allow it "early insight into new technologies that have normally been the province of start-ups."

Large organizations also outsource their funding activities to dedicated venture capitalists. Accel Partners, a leading venture firm in Silicon Valley, announced in April 1998 the participation of several large corporations in its Internet Technology Fund II. This fund is a $35-million component of a larger $310-million fund base, and will serve as a vehicle for major technology companies to invest in and work with new Accel-funded start-ups. Investors include Microsoft, Compaq, Lucent Technologies, Nortel, and the chairman of both CSK Corporation and Sega Enterprises, Isao Okawa. The Accel fund represents the first time that Microsoft, Lucent, and Nortel have invested in a U.S. venture fund.

Comprehending Disruption

While the heightened pace of acquisitions, spin-offs, and corporate venture funding vehicles indicates a willingness among large organizations to abandon the "not invented here" syndrome that plagued corporations during the 1970s and 1980s, these sustaining strategies are not the complete answer to success in the age of disruption. All three strategies take for granted that the organization is grafting another revenue stream onto its existing business. This assumption is perfectly valid for sustaining technology. However, the brutal truth of a disruptive technology is that it destroys the market advantage that enabled the mainstream businesses in the first place. Entry barriers long thought inviolate—such as ownership of switching infrastructure or scarce radio spectrum—suddenly drop in cost by several orders of magnitude in a very short time. As a result, the market walls built by sustaining technologies begin to lock a company in rather than keep the barbarians out.

When that happens, management is faced with its most important decision: whether to fight the inevitable or use it to advantage. This decision is based not on how companies grow new enterprises but on how they engineer the *demise* of a legacy. A neglected area of corporate strategy is how to create incentive structures, benchmarks, and processes for managing the sunset of businesses while managing the rise of new businesses. This legacy issue cuts to the heart of strategy in the age of disruptive technology. New ways of conceiving the life cycle of *companies*, not just *products*, are the touchstone for thriving on disruption. The march of Moore's Law and the Internet ensure that fragmented information processing and communications infrastructures will be replaced by a ubiquitous, relatively inexpensive, definitely powerful *converged* infrastructure for organizing firms and markets.

Consequently, the life cycle of business opportunity and risk will be redefined. It is incumbent upon business leaders to view firms in a more flexible, organic light. As any biologist will testify, death is as important as birth for a thriving ecosystem. To achieve a thriving corporate ecosystem in our era of disruptive technologies, some tall trees must fall in order to promote new growth.

Michael C. Ruettgers

President and Chief Executive Officer, EMC Corporation

Disrupt or Be Disrupted
Overturning Conventional Thinking in the Information Storage Industry

In the fall of 1990, EMC Corporation introduced what proved to be its first in a series of disruptive technologies. That year, we launched a breakthrough method for accessing, transferring, and storing large quantities of mainframe computer data. Our system worked faster, more reliably, and at lower operating costs than anything else on the market. And just four years later, we had overturned IBM's predominance in the mainframe storage market. Our share of market soared from zero to leadership and then to commanding leadership, hitting 50 percent in 1997 and more than 60 percent in 1999.

More important, we had transformed computer storage from a passive container without strategic value to the first and only solution for making information immediately and continuously available across a corporation. From the Global 2000 to the ".com" companies, customers now view EMC Enterprise Storage as an intelligent information infrastructure, a must-have foundation for operating information-intensive businesses.

And so it's no overstatement to say that we understand the power of stealth technologies that can quietly invade an industry, quickly advance in capability, and precipitously steal large numbers of customers from established companies. Some portray these technologies as a spontaneously forming, destructive force over which even the most able companies have little control. We don't share this view. Our philosophy is: Disrupt or be disrupted.

In fact, we have identified four preconditions for creating a disruptive technology, three of which are within a company's control:

- Stay intimately in tune with your marketplace and take the widest possible view of that marketplace—not just your existing customers but potential and even unlikely customers.

- Have a special lens through which to view and interpret customers' current and future needs.

- Offer a new solution that meets these needs precisely while, ideally, redefining your own industry.

- Scour the landscape for changes in market dynamics or customer attitudes, which suggest that your new solution can quickly gain a large, receptive audience.

All of these factors first came into play for EMC in the early 1990s. The pendulum was swinging back from distributed computing to centralized computing. More and more customers were consolidating information into the strategic hub of their technology operations. Businesses were awakening to the essence of their ability to compete: their ability to seize upon and harness all of the critical information in their enterprise. This volume of information was mushrooming. And they needed access to it for many more hours each day.

Concurrently, EMC had come to the insight—rare in those pre-Internet days—that the most important thing about computing was not the power of the processor but the speed and reliability of access to the data. This insight planted the seed for disruptive technology from EMC.

The criterion of fast, reliable access to data shaped and continues to shape our product development and marketing. It has helped us create product features that our customers couldn't fully articulate at the time but have come to love. If anything, this criterion is even more relevant today as new torrents of data pour onto the Internet.

Let's take a closer look at the factors that can create a disruptive technology as well as ways to avoid being overtaken by a disruptive innovation.

In Tune with a Shifting Marketplace

Staying in tune with your marketplace seems so straightforward, yet there is quicksand along the path. Many customers know only their immediate requirements and tend to ask for refinements—faster, cheaper, better—in what they already have. They are often unable or unwilling to articulate their most important, longer-term needs. And most do not know what you can do for them until you tell and show them.

For their part, technology suppliers can easily become too wedded to existing customers and become a prisoner of their customers' assumptions about the technology and the market. There is, however, a way around all this quicksand.

EMC uses five approaches to identify promising technologies and transform them into products:

- Our market requirements group looks out 18 months and focuses on the special requirements of customers in key industry segments such as financial services, telecommunications, and airlines.

- Our emerging technologies organization focuses on technologies that will become important to EMC 19 to 60 months out.

- Our world-class engineering organization interacts intensively and regularly with customers and concentrates on applying emerging technologies to solve customers' emerging requirements. As Thomas Stewart, the author of *Intellectual Capital* (Doubleday, 1997), notes: "When human capital, in the form of top-notch engineers and state-of-the-art technology, doesn't intersect with customer capital, the result is called an Edsel." At EMC, we make sure that these intersections occur daily.

- We build into every one of our intelligent storage systems onboard self-diagnostic technology that communicates by dedicated, high-speed telephone lines the minute-by-minute environmental status of our machines to a customer center, which is staffed 24 hours a day, seven days a week. Unique in the industry, this built-in services approach detects errors before they become serious enough to threaten data availability. Just as important, it enables our engineers to experience the daily problems of our customers and translate that learning into future versions of software that will prevent those problems from recurring.

- In addition, our company engages a wide array of strategic partners who apply their complementary skills to help us make the future happen sooner for our customers.

At the same time, we have two processes for bringing the right technology to market at the right time. First, we convene numerous forums to test our product and solution ideas with customers. And, second, we operate advanced customer testing sites where we put our products in customers' test environments for rigorous product validation.

Listening to Customers

We listen to customers. Each year I meet with about 500 customers. During these visits I'm able to plug directly in to their frustrations, their most pressing problems, their long-term objectives, as well as their insights into new ways to apply our technology. I also listen to senior executives in data-intensive businesses who are not yet EMC customers. These discussions often force me to question and revalidate my assumptions about where the world of information technology is going and where it should go.

As we instruct our sales force, persuading customers to confide in us is the essential first step in relationship building. There is no substitute for getting customers to tell us what their problems are, what they need done, and what their objectives are for the long haul. And the only way to create this trust is to repeatedly act on what customers tell us and then deliver what we say we will deliver, on schedule.

Of course, simply spending time with customers is just the ante. You have to have a real system in place for finding out what they want and then directing this information, unfiltered, to those who can act on it. Over the years, we have formalized our interactions with customers and our approach to identifying, collecting, interpreting, and prioritizing market requirements.

Yes, every company with a pulse asks itself, what is value to our customers? The trouble lies in knowing whether our perspective on what matters to customers is in fact their perspective, and whether our products really satisfy their needs—needs that are in constant flux. In light of all these customer-related information needs, we have created a *customer trust loop.*

The Customer Trust Loop

One key to creating our customer trust loop is our Customer Advisory Councils. These are neither sales meetings nor conventional user groups. Instead, the sessions are about methodically extracting product requirements from customers, validating product concepts and long-term business directions, and, above all, creating a climate for collaborative innovation.

Twice yearly in North America and Europe, and annually in other parts of the world, we bring together 50 to 60 customers to join our product management and engineering executives for 20 hours of intense discussion spread over 2½ days. Our customers do not bring their golf clubs. They bring completed homework assignments. We choose these highly motivated customers with great care. We select only those who are their companies' acknowledged visionaries and decision makers. They agree to a minimum 18-month commitment and sign nondisclosure agreements.

Our discussions follow a certain sequence. First, we present what we believe to be the most troublesome short- and longer-term problems facing our industry and their businesses. Next, we confirm that our perspectives dovetail with their experience—that the problems we have isolated are in fact the problems they find most challenging. After validating that we're in sync, we present a detailed look at EMC's work-in-process solutions to these problems.

At this point, the validation process heats up. We probe to learn whether our proposed solutions will solve the problems and whether our solutions will have a big and positive business impact. Through hours of back-and-forth discussion, we discover new requirements and fine-tune our offering. We also discuss how to best implement the solutions and seek customer recommendations concerning which (if any) strategic partners we might invite to work with us.

And then we feed all of this newly acquired knowledge back into EMC and integrate it into a coherent product design.

The Power of Lead Users

None of this is to suggest that we blindly follow our customers. As Harvard Business School professor Clayton Christensen notes, "There are times when it is right *not* to listen to customers." I would amend that statement: There are times when it's right not to listen to your *average* customers.

Not all customers are equal. EMC has a large handful of customers whom we consider to be *lead users*. These businesses tend to
be early adopters of technology, and they always have technology
experiments under way. They view technology as an enabler of business growth and continuous reinvention. Therefore, they will try
unconventional approaches to increase the number of hours each day
during which their core strategic data are available to employees and
customers worldwide. These customers tend to push EMC toward
customized, out-of-the-box solutions—solutions that we later modify
for wider customer use.

For example, lead users have been behind a few of our most successful software products. One such customer was looking for a product that would allow its business to continue without interruption,
even if a natural disaster or other unforeseen event were to shut
down its main data center. In response, we developed a software product that lets customers create an absolutely up-to-the-minute copy of
their main database at another physically distant site. The database is
available for recovery instantly, and the business can run without any
interruption. Just a few years after its development, this product
(known as Symmetrix Remote Data Facility, or SRDF) has already
sold thousands of licenses, and no competitor has a comparable product. Entirely new categories of customers, among them Internet-
based e-commerce sites, now rely on SRDF to keep their businesses
running around the clock.

I should mention that the success of this software product
prompted us to rapidly expand our software portfolio in order to
make our storage systems still more flexible, adaptable, and multi-
functional. This in turn has served to widen the already large technology and market share gap between EMC and our competitors.

New Lenses for Competitive Advantage

The key to our ability to fully satisfy and at times delight our customers is our "theory of business," to borrow Peter Drucker's phrase.
Every company accumulates customer data, but few seem to put
these data to great use. I believe they may lack a lens through which
to view and interpret their customers' world. EMC's lens keeps us
focused on the sine qua non for customers: fast, reliable access to all

of their corporate information, no matter where in the enterprise it resides.

Where did this lens come from? The answer is our abiding focus on storage—and only storage. In an industry littered with companies that try to be everything to everyone, EMC stands out for its singularity of purpose. Every dollar we spend, we spend on storage. Every one of our engineers and marketing people thinks all day long about how enterprise storage can help our customers.

This focus creates insight. EMC was able to see that the computer industry had lost sight of its reason for being. It had been so consumed with the "T" in information technology that it had pretty much forgotten about the "I"—information. Yet it's the "I" that customers care about.

The entire history of business can be summed up as the search for better ways to find, create, store, retrieve, protect, access, and manage information. But through much of the computer age, this search has not been especially productive because corporate information has long been isolated on different computing platforms, creating an archipelago of information. We decided that what was needed was the creation of a total information environment—an environment where information is an active, living force that an entire company can tap into.

Achieving that, we saw, would involve more than faster processors and speedier networks. It would also require a new concept of storage. This led us to create enterprise storage, a shared, consolidated repository of centrally protected and managed information accessible to all authorized users, no matter what computer system they're using. By transforming storage from a passive receptacle to a dynamic manager of enterprise-wide information, EMC reshaped the information technology industry as substantially as the PC changed the computing world—and we changed it more quickly.

Throughout the 1990s, as customers have shifted the locus of their computing activity from one platform to another—from mainframes, to Unix systems, to Windows NT systems, and now to the Internet—we have tested the continuing relevance of our theory of business. And in each case we have found that the original customer need we answered—fast, reliable access to data—is not only still relevant, but increasingly more relevant.

As *Fortune* magazine noted in a February 1999 article, "A company called EMC has tapped into one of the central truths of the computer age: every time you hit 'send,' buy a stock online, or click on an ad, you generate data that has to be put somewhere for safekeeping. Finding that space—creating that space—is crucial to the infotech revolution."

Storage as a Disruptive Technology

With the knowledge that our business theory remains sound, we have been able to continually expand the reach and relevance of our core storage technology. Our newest disruptive technology is the EMC Enterprise Storage Network. It extends the information sharing, management, and protection cocoon of our storage systems well beyond the data center to virtually all of the mission-critical information in a customer's extended enterprise, including the Internet.

What makes the enterprise storage network a disruptive technology? Three things: First, it's the one place—the only place—that can bring together all forms of information from all kinds of computer systems. Second, it creates a new model of information management. The use of information can remain distributed, but the management of information—the management of its structure, availability, and security—can now be centralized. And third, it brings together the best characteristics of data and voice networks with our software to create an intelligent, specialized network for sharing all of the information distributed throughout today's global organizations.

How do we ensure the staying power of this technology? By investing an additional $1.2 billion in R&D over the next three years, 80 percent of it directed to extending our software portfolio. This does not include the hundreds of millions of dollars we have already invested to guarantee that our storage systems work with every major computing platform and every major operating system. In addition, EMC has spearheaded the creation of open standards—and done so in a matter of months, not years—so that our systems will work with products from many other vendors.

We remain tremendously optimistic about the opportunity ahead for our storage technology. Even though the new millennium is here, we are still in the Stone Age when it comes to the volume of online data that will ultimately be in play, driving the global economy to new levels. All of that online information raises the demand for intelligent information storage and transforms EMC storage into a must-have, enabling foundation for this e-world of ours.

Staying Ahead of the Disruptive Wave

Navigators continually improve their instruments. Cartographers continually revise their maps. And scientists actively seek to refute their own theories. Business leaders must do the same. They must test and retest their theories of business and eliminate those that no longer explain the realities of the marketplace as effectively as newer theories.

That is EMC's philosophy. We were fortunate to develop a lens for understanding our customers' needs that continues to be accurate and relevant. But we agree with the historian Daniel Boorstin, who has written that "the great menace to progress is not ignorance but the illusion of knowledge."

The illusion of knowledge is often a by-product of success—and EMC has had tremendous success in recent years. We are accelerating toward the goal of $10 billion in sales in the year 2001, up from $4 billion in 1998. That said, we are acutely aware that more companies fail because of their success than for any other reason. We have taken several measures to counteract complacency.

We have seen all too many high-tech firms look in exactly the wrong place for signs of impending challenges—namely, among their traditional competitors. So we watch closely not only our traditional competitors but also obscure, emerging competitors.

As a corollary to this, we methodically immerse ourselves in our customers' experience while also immersing ourselves in the experience of those who are not yet our customers—but someday will be. We further broaden our perspective by partnering with a who's who of the information technology world. And we keep reaching out to new markets and new end users to force ourselves to revalidate our theory of business and to push our core technology beyond its apparent limits.

Most important, we recognize that the one resource our competitors cannot duplicate—perhaps the only one—is the team of people we assemble. We are obsessed with recruiting the very best. In fact, we apply a proprietary leadership competency model that identifies the special traits employees at different levels of the business must have if they are to excel at EMC, and if EMC's workforce is to remain one of the world's most focused, aggressive, and productive.

Finally, we reinvent our entire business about every two years. And at each reinvention we communicate to Wall Street our plan to achieve an ever more ambitious growth goal, tied to an aggressive deadline.

Roger G. Ackerman
Chairman and Chief Executive Officer, Corning Incorporated

Walking the Precipice
Achieving the Right Technology Balance

In 1969, Amory Houghton, Sr., a former chairman of our company and ambassador to France during the Eisenhower administration, retired from his position at Corning. At the conclusion of a celebration held at the Corning Glass Center to honor his career, the ambassador addressed those attending with the following remarks: "I want to leave you all with one thought: I lived every day of my business life as if I were walking on the edge of a precipice. Don't you ever forget it!"

I never have forgotten and I never will, since no analogy can better capture the essential dilemmas that confront all technology companies—particularly large, established companies like Corning. The technology business is rife with hungry entrepreneurs whose sole purpose in life is to grab market share away from established companies by blindsiding them with new and potentially disruptive technologies that can reshape the landscape of an industry virtually overnight.

Dealing with such technologies is truly a balancing act. How much do you invest in developing revolutionary technologies? How much in advancing the ones you already have? How many resources do you dedicate to monitoring technological developments? How do you fend off competitors who claim to have the next trailblazing solution? Like other CEOs of technology companies, I am sure, I spend some portion of every day pondering these questions. When I do so, I feel as if I am walking on the edge of Ambassador Houghton's precipice. The right answers will keep our company on solid ground; the wrong ones could move us toward the edge.

Defining Disruptive Technologies

In his seminal book entitled *The Innovator's Dilemma* and other writings, Harvard Business School professor Clayton M. Christensen uses the term *disruptive technologies* to refer to those technological advances that begin life as "cheap," "down-and-dirty," and usually performance-challenged alternatives to existing technologies. As examples, he refers to small-capacity hard disk drives, which, when they made their first appearance, could not even approximate the data-storage capabilities of existing mainframe technology, and to steel minimills, which, by challenging manufacturing processes in place for over a century, disrupted an entire industry. Such technologies run counter to the traditional R&D mind-set, where the goal is to push the functionality and performance of established technology. They also rely on exploiting customers and markets not yet even dreamed of by established companies.

Christensen's concept is surely an important one, but, I think, a bit too confining to encompass fully the broader issues of technological disruption. Disruptive technologies need not be only those that come out of left field and take an industry by complete surprise. From my perspective, they can also be those that represent tremendous advances in existing technologies. That's why I prefer to think of disruptive technologies as being of two kinds: low end and high end. Low-end disruptive technologies enter the market at a lower cost and deliver, initially, lower performance than existing technologies. High-end disruptive technologies do just the opposite. All companies need to be concerned about both kinds, and both, although in different ways, can be characterized as *breakthrough*.

Since its founding in 1851, Corning has had its share of success by introducing into various markets technologies that can be considered breakthrough or disruptive (as I define the terms). Some, like optical fiber, come close to being disruptive in the Christensen sense. Others, like our advances in ceramic, laboratory testing, and silicon chip technologies, have been more broadly disruptive. As I see it, the challenge for any technology company CEO is to find the right balance between disruptive technologies narrowly and broadly defined, to satisfy existing customers and markets while seeking out new ones, to discover the truly unthought-of while not ignoring those things that tremendously advance the tried and true. In short, walking the precipice between the safe haven of established solutions and the uncharted territory of the truly undiscovered.

Achieving Balance

At Corning, we are acutely aware of the necessity of both monitoring the technological advances of competitors and discovering opportunities to create our own advances and disruptive breakthroughs. We have a number of processes in place—both informal and formal—to help us do that.

Informally, we rely on our external orientation to keep us informed of what's going on in our industries. We may be comfortably nestled in a little valley in upstate New York, but we are not an insular company. We have labs around the world—for example, in Russia, Western Europe, and Japan. An important part of their mission is to report on current developments. This network of highly trained scientists serves as a worldwide radar system, alerting us to new discoveries and emerging needs. In addition, our company-wide intranet not only enables dissemination of important information across the enterprise, but also allows us to communicate with each other instantaneously. And then, we have a strong patent department at Corning. Like good field generals, our patent attorneys are constantly on the lookout for new scientific advances or opportunities of which we need to be aware.

Formally we have, in recent years, codified the dimensions of what we like to refer to as our operating environment. These dimensions, each of which is closely aligned with our core values, include a strong focus on satisfying customer needs; achieving extraordinary results; looking forward to anticipate where markets, technologies, and customer needs are heading; providing an environment that fosters entrepreneurial behavior and appropriate risk taking; insisting on the rigor from which result well-defined processes and standards to provide effective control; creating a climate that supports informality and openness; sharing information to gain the active commitment and involvement of everyone; and leveraging the diverse backgrounds, experiences, and perspectives of our workforce.

These general dimensions of our operating environment come alive through a number of specific applications at Corning. For example, every 6 to 18 months—depending on our judgment of the pace of change—we ask each of our major businesses to present what we call their deep-dive strategies. Developing these strategies forces us to ask a number of critical questions: Where are we weak, strong, or hazy? Can we really play for the long term in the area of telecommunications technology? In what sectors do we have the ability and sustaining power to win? How far up the value chain are those sectors? Where is the profit zone and who else is out there? What start-ups do we need to be concerned about? What can go wrong, and what do we—no kidding—need to win?

We also have our businesses participate in three Growth Days per year. During these days, our scientists and product development professionals get together to rigorously analyze and challenge our top 15 projects in terms of R&D investment. In their assessment of milestones, these Growth Days closely resemble venture capital meetings. Their purpose is to judge our ability to win and to determine what it will take to win, where we are falling behind, and whether we have made good on our commitments.

Another important exercise that we demand of every business is the development of technology road maps that look out at least 5 years, and in some cases as many as 10. The purpose of these road maps is to speculate on future needs. For example, Corning supplies semiconductor manufacturers with the material used to produce the advanced optics that lie at the heart of the microlithography stepper systems that create today's complex integrated computer circuitry (an expertise that derives from our more than 70 years of experience with silicon dioxide). But while our High-Purity Fused Silica (HPFS) meets current standards for the deep-ultraviolet krypton fluoride laser steppers of the emerging generation in the semiconductor manufacturing equipment industry, we need to know what stepper cameras are going to look like in the year 2010. We need similar forecasts for each of our businesses. Technology road maps help us achieve that.

Last, we submit the most promising new product ideas or initiatives that result from any of the preceding exercises to a five-stage innovation process that reduces the time it takes for us to bring new products to market, helps ensure that these products are commercially feasible, and isolates the winners from the losers as early as possible. Each new product idea must pass a rigorous set of tests before moving on to the next stage of the process, tests that help us identify and measure the potential risks against the potential rewards. The process ends when a commercially viable product emerges, having withstood rigorous analysis and testing. I don't want to imply, however, that this process can be followed as one would follow a recipe in a cookbook. Without parallel processing against our core values and the dimensions of our operating environment, the process has limited value.

In addition to helping us strike the right balance with respect to disruptive technologies, all of these exercises and processes help us to achieve another, equally important goal: ensuring that we are *in* businesses in which we can change the technology to win—and *out* of those in which we cannot. In 1989, we dropped the words "Glass Works" from our name to reflect the fact that we are primarily a technology, not a glass company. In 1998, we sold 98 percent of Corning Consumer Products for the same reason. We have also exited the blood testing market, in which at one time we were bigger than today's industry leader. In short, these processes have helped us refocus on our roots, but with far more discipline than in the past. They have provided us with the rigor that helps us maintain the all-important balance between creativity and discipline.

Going from Process to Product

All the processes in the world mean little unless they result in commercially viable, technologically advanced products. Have our efforts to achieve the right balance at Corning paid off? I believe they have. Right now, we are engaged in the most exciting research we have ever undertaken in our company's history—research that is not only dramatically enhancing our existing products, but also resulting in breakthrough products. We are working to push the technology envelope in five areas that we consider our growth platforms: telecommunications (fiber and photonics); information display products; advanced optics for microlithography; environmental products; and advanced life sciences.

For the foreseeable future, high bandwidth will continue to be the Holy Grail in the telecommunications industry. In an ongoing effort to capture that prize, we developed Large Effective Area Fiber (LEAF), a technologically advanced fiber that greatly increases the speed and information-carrying capacity of highly developed telecommunications networks. We also believe that, broadly speaking, the next disruptive advance in telecom technology will be driven by optical networking, and we are investing heavily in this area.

In 1947, we invented the processes for mass-producing the all-glass television bulb, making TV affordable for millions. Today we produce the ultrathin glass used in liquid crystal displays. Looking to the future, we are focusing our efforts on new information display technologies to supply the laptop and desktop computer, digital camera, personal digital assistant, and automotive and projection display markets with increasingly faster, higher-resolution, larger, and less expensive LCDs.

Advanced optics for microlithography offer numerous opportunities for new technologies. Materials now in development will enable future argon fluoride laser systems to print lines on computer circuits that are $\frac{1}{800}$ the diameter of a human hair. Meanwhile, research into photomask technologies has yielded products now in beta test with implications for the next 15 years of lithography.

Our work in cellular ceramic technology is leading to a new generation of products that will enable vehicle manufacturers to meet the increasingly stringent standards projected for the United States and Western Europe. We are also applying this technology in other areas, including new solutions for the control of pollutants from power plants and other stationary sources. An extremely promising new technology involves the use of ceramic monoliths as a means of delivering increased yields and process enhancements to the petrochemical industry.

Finally, the revolution under way in the areas of genomics, combinatorial chemistry, and high-throughput screening offers us additional opportunities for technology leadership. Scientists around the world are seeking genetic solutions to the problem of human disease—solutions involving literally trillions of genetic combinations and permutations. Corning is using its evolving expertise in polymers and surface chemistry, coupled with our understanding of molecular biology, to produce the next generation of tools to enable this research.

While separate and distinct from each other, all of these areas are held together by a common thread: our expertise in advanced materials. At Corning, that expertise allows us to leverage technological advances in one area to the benefit of another. Again, balance is the key. We feel we have achieved the right level of complexity, and we are not going to change that—at least for now. Will our results be disruptive in either the narrow or broad sense of the term? We think so, but we'll let our customers and the marketplace be the judge.

Role of the CEO

Achieving the right technology balance at Corning is everybody's job, from our division heads, scientists, and product development people to our sales and marketing professionals and support staff. Yet it seems to me that the CEO has a special role to play, particularly with respect to the company's collective attitude toward disruptive technologies.

First of all, the CEO should know at all times where his or her company and its competitors are heading. If there is a technology out there that threatens to blindside the company, the CEO should know about it and, more important, know what steps to take to neutralize that threat or, in the best-case scenario, turn it into an opportunity.

Second, the CEO should cultivate an attitude that I like to characterize as "confident nervousness." Confidence is great, but not when it translates into complacency. To ensure that all of our leaders feel that nervous edge, I personally bought and handed out 25 copies of Andrew Grove's book, *Only the Paranoid Survive* (Bantam, 1999)— and was only partially tongue-in-cheek when I did so.

Third, CEOs should surround themselves with people capable of thinking better and smarter than themselves. At Corning, we do not encourage the cult of the CEO. An arrogant, egomaniacal leader may be effective at a small start-up, but not at a large and successful organization like Corning. I spend a lot of time cultivating 40-year-olds who I think are smart enough and skilled enough to run their own companies. I want to ensure that their knowledge and skills are fully engaged for Corning's benefit. I particularly seek out those who are likely to contradict me. I surely don't know everything, and the more ideas—even diametrically opposed to my own—to which I am exposed, the better technology company Corning will be.

Fourth, technology company CEOs must take an active role in formulating, quantifying, and promulgating values that encourage the development of sustainable, evolvable, and/or breakthrough technologies. This process must unfold at the top. If the leadership isn't truly interested in the company's values, everyone in the organization senses it. Phonies, especially at the top, are easy to spot. I spent two years working on Corning's values with my predecessor, Jamie Houghton, and two years on defining the operating environment implied by those values. Gaining consensus on what they are and what they mean was a key part of the process. Our values encourage openness and free thinking, backed up by rigor. We live those values every day, and I believe they are in large measure responsible for our success.

The last point may seem obvious: Technology company CEOs need to be passionate believers in and users of technology. "Walking the talk" is a phrase we often use around Corning. You can't preach the technology gospel without living it. That would be dishonest, hypocritical, and ultimately dangerous. The outward signs of our commitment to technology as a day-to-day way of life are evident throughout our organization—in our display cases, on our desktops, through our state-of-the-art corporate intranet. Everyone at Corning knows that I am a heavy Internet user. I track hundreds of companies every day on the Net. I have 17 newspapers channeled to my browser every morning. The Internet is my first stop when I need information. I use e-mail regularly and encourage everyone to do the same. I'm not mentioning all of this just to make myself or my colleagues look good, but rather because it has a practical and important application: Enthusiasm for and comfort with technology translate into the excitement and inquisitiveness that create breakthrough and even disruptive technology products.

Maintaining a Balanced Approach

In this chapter, I've tried to explain my views on disruptive technologies and shed light on the informal and formal processes that protect us against the unpredictable and guide our efforts to develop technologically advanced products. In today's environment of accelerated change, technologies that are disruptive in Christensen's sense are more likely to appear than at any other time. For example, I recently became aware of a new digital wireless technology that uses 10 to 40 million pulses of radio energy per second to transmit phone, data, or video information over an ultrawide bandwidth. Undoubtedly, other radical technologies are at this moment being developed in small labs around the world or being nurtured in the minds of as yet unknown budding geniuses.

Should the pursuit of such technologies be the primary goal of a company like Corning? It's tempting to say yes—but we've found that long-term success lies in a more balanced approach that accommodates today's *and* tomorrow's customers' needs. Those needs vary widely along the technology spectrum and range from significant product enhancements to radical breakthroughs on both the low and high ends. In pursuing this approach, we sometimes succeed and sometimes fail. Both experiences are useful in that they each keep us on the right side of the ambassador's precipice.

Lawrence A. Bossidy
Chairman and Chief Executive Officer, AlliedSignal Inc.

Driver or Enabler?
The Internet's Role in Twenty-First-Century Business

About a year ago, I was having dinner at a restaurant in the Czech Republic that was heavily frequented by locals. As is the case with many such restaurants throughout Europe, I was seated at a long table that I shared with other diners. While waiting for my food, I struck up a conversation with the woman sitting next to me, who must have been in her mid-fifties. I was interested in getting her take on the sweeping changes that have occurred in her part of the world since the fall of communism. "I don't like it," she said. When I asked her why not, she replied, "When you wake up every morning and you're told what to do every day, and then one day, somebody tells you you're free, it's a shocking thing. My kids love it, but for older people, it's difficult."

This woman's reaction crystallizes for me the disruptive effects of change—even positive change—and the difficulty that some have in adapting to altered circumstances. It also serves as a good analogy for what is happening in business as we enter a new century. Sweeping changes are forever altering the global business landscape, shattering old models faster than we can create new ones to take their place. Like my dinner companion, some companies will be overwhelmed by change. Failing to adapt, they will be left behind. Others will embrace change as a positive force and seize upon it as an opportunity to redefine the way they do business.

Some would argue that radical technologies are at the heart of disruptive changes impacting global business. The Internet is the most visible, accessible, and profound example. And as a low-cost tool that has the power to transform industries, it certainly fits within the classic definition of a disruptive technology. But I would like to take that argument a bit further. In my view, the truly disruptive impact of the Internet is not so much on industries but on the models by which companies conduct business and on the social and economic assumptions that underlie those models. The Internet is a driver of change, but more important, it is an enabler. It is, in short, the tool that makes possible a new business model for the twenty-first century.

Envisioning a New Model

As an enabler, the Internet is having a transformative effect on business. It is changing the way we deal with customers and suppliers, the way we access capital, the way we deal with employees, and even the way we bring our products to market. All of these changes can make a company more competitive and more profitable. And all of them provide key inputs into what I view as the biggest change of all: a new business model for the next century.

The business model most large companies have been following has its roots in the industrial age and emphasizes fixed assets, working capital, and economies of scale. Under this model, companies work hard to reduce cycle time and do their best to compress working capital by portfolio changes or various efficiencies. They also provide some education for employees, perform some downsizing when necessary, and sustain a focus on R&D. And then, almost as an afterthought, they begin to think about ways to be more sensitive to customers. This model has worked well and, I believe, was responsible for propelling the United States into the top competitive position worldwide. It certainly served AlliedSignal well. Using such a model, our return on investment has gone from 10 to 20 percent; our return on equity, from 15 to 28 percent; and our revenue per employee, from $112,000 to $215,000—a growth of 79 percent, or 10 percent compounded annually.

Toward the end of the 1990s, computer technology increased dramatically, capital markets began to globalize, and computers and telecommunications finally became productive. But what really made these developments revolutionary was the rise of the Internet as a dominant force. Let's look at just one example—deregulation. Initially, when the airline, financial services, and telecommunications industries were deregulated, most people considered it business as usual. With the appearance of the Internet, however, these industries are being transformed in ways we wouldn't have thought possible at the time. Using the Internet, customers can not only buy airline tickets, they can bid for them at auction. Internet banking and investment services are now commonplace. And telecommunications companies that were formerly just providers of local and long-distance telephone service are now becoming multimedia giants involved in cable, cellular, and Internet services.

The Net has also caused significant changes in the workforce. Thirty years of computers and telecommunications have produced a very literate workforce. However, the second generation of computer literacy is already much better than the first, and the third will be much better than the second. Most of the young men and women entering the workforce today are completely comfortable with technology. It is part of the fabric of their daily lives. They have PCs in their homes; they use the Internet to access information and buy products. For these individuals, e-mail has virtually supplanted regular mail (or as it has come to be called, "snail" mail). They are excited about technology and welcome its growing significance in the workplace.

And finally, there is the customer. Worldwide overcapacity and oversupply have already significantly empowered the customer. But with the seemingly limitless choices and ease of access offered by the Internet, the customer has truly become king. Customers can now demand speed, quality, service, and information. And if they can't get these from one source, they'll click their mouse and get them somewhere else.

What has all of this done to the old business model? Quite simply, it has turned it upside down. Because of the Internet, the most important assets any company today can possess are not bricks and mortar, but nimbleness and flexibility. Therefore, under the new model, companies need to deemphasize, rather than build upon, fixed assets; use as little working capital as possible; and strike the right balance between "owned" employees and a virtual workforce. They should no longer seek to protect intellectual property; they should merchandise it. They will need to develop new kinds of relationships with customers, such as cooperative partnerships that add value to both sides. And they will need to farm out pieces of their supply chains and make those that remain far more substantial, so that suppliers, too, are partners.

Implementing Change

Implementing a new business model requires openness to change. At AlliedSignal, we haven't always been at the forefront of change when we should have been, and we have paid a price for that. We have, however, implemented several major change programs. We began some years ago with Total Quality Management (TQM). We have also implemented an operational excellence program—a first look at how to make our factories better and more efficient. And today we have placed a company-wide focus on six sigma principles, with the goal of achieving zero defects in everything we do. When you look at the degree of difficulty in implementing change, flexibility is the key to success. I believe that these change initiatives have prepared us to take the next steps.

First and most important is to foster a culture that has the ability to change rapidly. Of course, you can't force people to change, but you can make them receptive to it. At most organizations—even AlliedSignal—change is somewhat countercultural. Some of our most experienced manufacturing people were brought up with the idea that if AlliedSignal doesn't make a product, it can't be any good. We've got to change that, but not by stripping experience out of our organization. I don't want to surround myself exclusively with 29-year-old MBAs, even if they are more receptive to change. I need experienced people—they bring with them the lore and history of the organization that places change in the right context. They may be more resistant to change, and I might have to work harder to get them to change. But when they do, they are my most valuable asset. What I need, in short, is a distribution of age among my employees that provides for both experience and openness to change.

How do I go about doing this? First, I hire people who are willing to go through these transformations. Second, I consider the strategic impact of these hiring decisions. And third, I make sure that I get my people to execute strategic change throughout the organization.

The third element is key, and, I believe, the primary responsibility of the CEO. As CEO, I have to clearly define what it is we're trying to do—what our goals are. I have to follow up all the time. I have to make sure that my leadership team is out in the field constantly promoting change. The first thing I do when I visit an AlliedSignal location is ask change-related questions, such as how are you doing with six sigma? Or what steps are you taking to implement the new business model? I can never tire of the message; I have to be relentless in order to make sure that change happens. In an organization as large as ours, there will always be people who are just beginning to get the message. I sometimes get tired of hearing myself talk about change, but I've got to pursue it until everyone is on board.

Articulating the message, however, is not enough. People also must have the right tools to accomplish the mission, and that's where education comes into play. Employee education is an absolute necessity for any company, and at AlliedSignal we have an aggressive internal education program that we consider a competitive advantage. Each of our employees receives a minimum of 40 hours of job-related training per year, and all of our managers have evolved into aggressive trainers. Moreover, our training programs must keep pace with the rapid changes occurring in our business. Therefore, each year, we discard approximately 10 percent of our program and replace it with new content to reflect new realities.

As with everything else in our business, effective education also depends on how fast we can permeate our organization with new ideas and new thought processes. We make every effort to provide our people with the tools they need to change because the better equipped they are, the faster things will happen. And technology is again a key enabler. We recently linked up more than 700 of our people located in various cities across the United States with our Learning Center in Morristown, New Jersey. The information placed on this network is immediately accessible, easily downloadable, and ready to be put to work for the benefit of AlliedSignal.

Will everyone adapt to this accelerated pace of change? Or should they? Some would say that by fostering rapid change I am threatening the stability of my organization and depriving our employees of a sense of ownership in the company. I, too, was taught to worry about such things, but I've come to reject that argument because the other side of the coin is so radical. In other words, if you don't change, you're dead. Those that can't change should leave the organization and go where they will be happy (though I doubt that there is any place left where change can be avoided). However, I believe that if I tell people why change is important, and what will be the result, the overwhelming majority will embrace it and be energized by what we are trying to do.

Role of the Internet

Many people talk about an Internet or e-commerce strategy. I believe they are wrong to do so. The Internet is a powerful tool that enables a business to implement different strategies, but it is not a strategy in and of itself. There is no such thing as an Internet or e-commerce strategy. There is, however, an Internet or e-commerce enabled strategy. In such a formulation, the Internet doesn't create opportunities but makes them far more exciting than they were before. It also changes the dynamics of how companies do business.

At AlliedSignal, the Internet will help us to radically reengineer ourselves in a number of areas. For example, we currently mail benefits statements to more than 70,000 people every quarter. Not only is that expensive, but it is extremely inefficient. That information will soon be available to our employees on the Internet. We also plan on placing all of our product catalogs on the Net in order to reduce costs and make it easier for our customers to do business with us. Those kinds of efficiencies are important, but the real impact of the Internet on our business will be how it enables us to redefine our relationships with customers and suppliers, and, in so doing, helps us implement a new business model that reduces working capital and fixed assets, and results in greater value.

The interconnectivity enabled by the Internet will bind us ever closer to our customers and suppliers, transforming relationships into value-added partnerships. For example, we might propose projects that involve joint design and joint engineering. We might suggest that we manufacture some products currently produced by our customers and suppliers, and vice versa. We want to be able to go beyond the basics—speed, quality, and price—to form relationships based on combined thinking that results in better, less costly, and more profitable products. We also will be able to seek out new customers and suppliers that, before the Internet, would not have been economically feasible. For example, we currently purchase about 6 percent of our materials offshore. E-commerce might enable us to boost that to 35 percent.

All of this is still very much in the planning stage, but the Internet enables us to see the possibilities and work toward making them realities. Moreover, it helps us see how AlliedSignal and its customers and suppliers will jointly benefit from a new business model. With fewer fixed assets and lower inventory, and with a more efficient supply chain and labor force, each of our businesses will have more working capital to employ elsewhere or to grow our businesses faster. In short, if we find new ways to increase connectivity and, therefore, to work more collaboratively with our customers and suppliers, all of our businesses will benefit.

The Payoff

The Internet-enabled business plan is still in its infancy at Allied-Signal, and, quite frankly, we don't know yet, beyond cost savings, what all of the consequences will be. It's hard to place a dollar value on enhanced customer relationships, but I feel instinctively that such relationships will result in increased sales. In the area of cost savings, there is more certainty. Implementing this model well could be a billion-dollar opportunity for AlliedSignal, even if we reduce working capital by just 5 to 7 percent.

Beyond dollars and cents, there are less quantifiable but equally significant benefits. While AlliedSignal and its partners stand to achieve massive gains through this new approach, the impact on people will be equally great. This new model rejuvenates people, and people rejuvenate businesses. It galvanizes people to action and increases their commitment. And, finally, it creates a new excitement that attracts the best and brightest—which, in turn, fosters excellence throughout the organization.

Social and Economic Implications

I began this section by noting that the Internet will disrupt not only existing business models, but also the social and economic assumptions that underlie them. In order for the new business model to succeed, companies must be culturally able to embrace speed, flexibility, and change. And this is where I think the United States, at least for the time being, is at a great advantage. In Europe and the Far East, for example, many companies are still wedded to the very things that work counter to the new business model: economies of scale, fixed assets, and high working capital. But this is changing, because it must.

Some would speculate that deeply held cultural and ethnic beliefs will result in a greater division between the haves and the have-nots in the twenty-first century. I do not believe this. I think that more and more companies are viewing themselves as global enterprises, rather than as American, Japanese, Chinese, or German businesses. As global markets continue to expand, all businesses will have to compete in the same way. But the competitive battle will be among companies that see themselves as multinationals not defined by geographic boundaries. There will be winners and losers, but victory will not be determined by cultural and/or ethnic orientation. The winners will be those that embrace change and react to it in the ways I've discussed. The losers will be those that do not.

Recommendations for CEOs

Like it or not, the changes I have discussed are coming, and many are already here. Fortunately, the wave of change has brought with it a powerful tool—the Internet—that companies can use to define a new business model for the twenty-first century. At this point in time, I can't provide a precise blueprint for such a plan and, in fact, each company will need to develop its own. I can, however, provide some general recommendations for CEOs who, like myself, want not only to survive in the years ahead but to succeed:

- Take your relationships with customers and suppliers to a new level. Form partnerships that add value to both sides. Develop creative ways to foster collaboration.
- Constantly evaluate your supply chain.
- Outsource what is not a core competency.
- Don't build more plants; build more partner relationships.

- Automate as many mechanical tasks as you can; leave your people more time to be creative.

- Constantly improve your products and the speed with which you can get them to market.

- Reduce your working capital; use the money to grow your business, support R&D, and develop new products.

- Educate your people; give them the tools they need to succeed.

- Throw away your multiyear strategic plans; as soon as you complete them, they're out of date.

Last and most important, don't, like my Czech dinner companion, be fearful of change. Rather, be open to change and nimble enough to take advantage of it. If you don't, your competitors surely will.

Thierry Breton
Chairman and Chief Executive Officer, THOMSON multimedia

Marketing Reshaped by Technology

In 1997, at THOMSON multimedia, we adopted a recovery and development strategy based on a comprehensive revamping of all of our processes and the way we manage the business, which is now thoroughly focused on the market. Breakthrough technologies are one of the key vectors used to leverage this strategy.

Global enterprises like THOMSON multimedia, the world's fourth-largest consumer electronics manufacturer, operate in the three principal market regions: the Americas, Asia, and Europe. Most consumer electronics products around the world have many features in common, but there are differences due to specific consumer preferences in each region. Americans, for example, like televisions with bright pictures and Europeans prefer flat screens, while Asians put a premium on sound quality.

Customers everywhere are looking for products that give them what they really want. Therefore, products have to be almost custom-made at the last minute, and customers want them immediately upon ordering. This demand for customized products delivered in the shortest possible time is a recent phenomenon, and part of a trend clearly parallel to the Internet explosion, which offers consumers immediate access to information or goods.

Bringing Customers into the Factory

Every major player in the consumer electronics market has set up manufacturing operations in each of the world's three main regions. Since production facilities tend to offer roughly equivalent quality and costs, they stand out from the competition mainly thanks to the quality of their customer service. Facilities must be flexible, adaptable, proactive, quick to respond, reliable, faithful to commitments, capable of providing prompt delivery tracking information, and more.

These results can be achieved only through the intensive use of information technology.

We decided to integrate our information systems closely with those of our customers in order to save time and provide them better service. As a result, it can truly be said that our customers have come into our factories: We make and store their products in our facilities, adapt them to fit specific needs, and deliver them wherever customers require in the shortest possible time. Part of our finished product inventories therefore already belongs to customers, and we have naturally made it possible for them to have instant access to information about the status of their goods.

This innovation was part of a wide-ranging program initiated to reengineer our working methods and information systems. We dedicated a billion and a half French francs to the program, called SAFE (Sales Administration, Focus and Efficiency), and spent 350 million francs more on information technology.

The changes required were—and continue to be—substantial. New information systems have been installed. Business processes have to be thoroughly modified and people's behaviors have to adapt to the new realities. We entrust this task to outside consultants, each working in one special area. Our business is making multimedia products, and we leave it to the experts to adapt our organization, information systems, and operating methods.

Smart Products and Individual-Focused Marketing

Because our market environment includes two dimensions—one geographical on a continental scale, the other focused on the individual customer—technology presents new challenges and opportunities. Extensive, individualized knowledge of consumers is a source of profit and helps to anticipate demand.

New information systems are indeed bringing us closer to customers and changing the retailing landscape. In the United States, retailing structures have already changed considerably and are now highly concentrated. THOMSON multimedia currently does twice as much business with Wal-Mart as it does in all of France; 60 percent of our total U.S. sales are generated by only eight retail customers. The quality of customer relationships is always more critical in situations like that. In Europe, the market is more fragmented and the language barrier raises an additional hurdle, but the development of large retail chains on a continental level is going forward.

The concentration of retailing structures is clearly benefiting consumers. Manufacturers, however, have lost contact with consumers. Our goal is to reestablish that contact. The question is, How? Again, information technology is transforming the conventional business model. Products alone no longer ensure a company's success, but as service vehicles they can restore contact between the manufacturer and the consumer. One example of this is the interactive television set equipped with software and modems to access new services. We have signed an agreement with Microsoft to develop a television set that offers basic services, including Internet access but also such integrated applications as family budget management and games. The set will permit feedback concerning user patterns of shopping, voting, gaming, and much else—for example, participation in TV programs.

THOMSON multimedia is using this approach to get back in touch with customers by redesigning our products and offering additional layers of services. Such developments explain why we are welcoming new shareholders, such as Microsoft, Direct TV, and NEC. This alliance strategy is at the other end of the spectrum from the previous industry-driven approach that prompted THOMSON to team up with partners in the same industry sector. Today's approach leverages complementary expertise to create new sources of revenue. Upstream, you have key components such as plasma devices or DVD-ROMs jointly developed with NEC. THOMSON multimedia continues to develop its core expertise in manufacturing and retailing finished consumer electronics products. Downstream, we work with Microsoft and Direct TV to develop value-added services.

These are not merely cosmetic changes in the kinds of alliances formed, but genuinely radical transformations of a marketing model reshaped by information and telecommunications technology. If content providers or broadcasters come calling on us now, it's because technology has challenged the conventional business model. Technologies can be used to refine our offering to fit specific demands, gather detailed data about consumers, and thus create new businesses. For example, THOMSON multimedia now manages television commercials embedded in TV electronic guides. Tomorrow, improved storage data technology and considerably faster data transmission speeds will further enhance the potential for diversifying the interactive services we offer.

I decided to redeploy research and development forces in our business units so that we can seize emerging technologies and stimulate related innovation. As a result, our central R&D staff has shrunk from 2,000 to 400, while the main operating units have gained resources. We have also created our own venture capital fund to invest in innovative start-ups. These start-ups are expanding our capacity to innovate and give us access to new technologies.

Feedback of retail information has also helped us seize the initiative. We work within our retailers' sales outlets—for example, Radio Shack stores in the United States, where special areas are provided for consumers to share their views. To my mind, however, innovation is subordinate to two key management criteria: cost reduction and time to market. In the consumer electronics market, there is no room for error; the slightest price difference literally ejects us from the market.

Breakthrough Technology and Chaos Management

Repeated technology breakthroughs that alter our business models call for strengthened management by short-term objectives. The market changes quickly, and quick response is a strategic imperative. At THOMSON multimedia, we operate with a six-month timeline, with six-month budgets and six-month closure periods that require short- and medium-range management objectives. Some 80 percent of our objectives are short range, while 20 percent are more qualitative and medium range (that is, they cover more than six months). Our short- and medium-range perspective looks carefully at the cost performance of the business units, while our longer-range perspective, spanning one to three years, looks for major gains in profitability and performance ratios. The same timelines apply to the development of products, which require very quick marketing to meet changing demand, while allowing for longer-range trends related to changing consumer preferences.

To tie everything together, I have introduced a network-based management system. The group is organized into six operational and six corporate strategic business units. One of these is a special corporate department that goes by the name of *entrepreneurship*. Its mission is to manage a network of group executives and senior executives with specifically assigned objectives. The network is headed by an executive committee member, on a full-time basis, who leads a close-knit team of knowledge workers dedicated to implementing the adopted strategy. In the operational business units, management is more linear and based on people, numbers, and incentives.

Our experience shows that neither we nor anybody else should be afraid of managing new and complex business models and revolutionary technologies. Great discipline is nonetheless required to achieve agreed business objectives, as well as transparent working methods and financial results. We must also recognize each person's right to make mistakes—that recognition is essential to fostering initiative. Everyone is entitled to make mistakes, but never the same one twice. If someone makes the same mistake twice, it will happen again and again. At that point, I would rather it happen when that person is working for a competitor.

Innovation

New Ideas, Dangerous Ideas

Innovation is one of those flags that command salutes. Does any corporate manager dare to be publicly against it? Yet this homage rarely translates into real value for shareholders. When genuinely embraced by senior management and woven into the texture of a corporate culture, innovation can produce dramatic results. Our research has revealed that more than 75 percent of revenues in such firms can come from products and services that did not exist five years earlier. Those at the other end of the innovation spectrum find that less than 10 percent of revenues comes from new products.

The failure to generate significant revenue through innovation is not simply a result of stopping with verbal tribute. It may stem from genuine difficulties: determining how much innovation is needed, and where; identifying precisely the structural and cultural changes required to foster innovation; not merely nurturing innovative ideas, but translating them into concrete programs with commercial value. In this chapter, we examine some proven methods of making innovation a profitable reality.

What Is Innovation?

Innovation means both "altering something established" and "introducing something new." Therefore, it involves a broad spectrum of change, from small improvements to far-reaching revolutions. We refer to the poles of this spectrum as, respectively, *adaptive innovation* and *transformational innovation,* and both types are important across virtually all enterprise functions, not only in R&D and new products. A company that depends on just one extremity of the spectrum will not achieve the best possible financial performance and, in the long run, will be at risk from more agile competitors.

"An idea that isn't dangerous," said Oscar Wilde, "doesn't deserve to be called an idea at all." Because sweeping innovations are perceived as in some sense dangerous, most companies concentrate on adaptive innovation—improving the way customers are acquired and served, upgrading all aspects of operations, and hence delivering additional value. Many authors of these adaptive changes see them as radical, but they could be in for some nasty surprises as more ambitious competitors change the way markets operate. When America Online (AOL) started out, competitors stressed their own technical advantages, while AOL emphasized its user-friendly environment—at a time when most people were still befuddled by programming their VCRs. Ultimately, AOL convinced vast numbers of people that they could easily gain proficiency in the use of an online service and the Internet.

Regrettably, the structures and processes of many large companies obstruct innovation. The management process protects the status quo rather than creating a new future; the annual budget cycle occupies executive time with little gain to shareholders. Both budgeting and conventional strategic plans are endangered species.

The base case of many strategic decisions—that the present is sustainable—is simply wrong. Managers with an eye to a career do not normally put decline into a five-year plan even where that is the inevitable outcome of their actions. As a result, real innovation is frequently underfunded, financially and emotionally; the merely rational crowds out the imaginative vision. Safeway's new Shop & Go system allows shoppers to scan their own purchases, swipe their own cards, and leave. The rational analysis held that people wouldn't pay in full, they would deliberately avoid scanning some items. But in practice thus far, Shop & Go customers have been overwhelmingly honest. "The technology was available fifteen years ago," says a Safeway spokesperson. "The [management] mindset wasn't."

The reasonably rare innovative companies in our research focus their long-term thinking on change rather than stability, as in the following examples:

- *Innovators use their historical understanding of the market as a springboard.* Expertise and experience are sources of innovation, provided that they do not limit creative imagination. The belief that anything is understood, resolved, or fixed forever is dangerous; it prevents other stimuli or interpretations from being recognized and stifles curiosity. At various points not so long ago, the received wisdom held that there was no market for personal computers, that people prefer bank tellers to ATMs, and that the Internet had little potential to support sales transactions.

- *Innovators are curious about how the world around them could evolve and they see many possibilities.* Two-time Nobel laureate Linus Pauling liked to say, "The best way to have a good idea is to have lots of ideas." True corporate innovators are restlessly curious; they extensively explore new possibilities and examine many different scenarios in search of breakaway possibilities. Scenario planning is often underexploited because the voice of today's reason is allowed to intrude too early in the conception of what might be. The fault lies not in the ability to imagine very different possibilities, but, more commonly, in the process of narrowing down possibilities to a set manageable for planning purposes.

- *Innovators focus on creating a future that will bring new value to customers.* The innovative company looks beyond existing customers as buyers of the competencies they are developing and seeks new value chains in which it can participate. It uses existing capabilities and intellectual capital as springboards toward new applications in new customer segments. The firm with a new killer app doesn't charge an up-front premium; it gives away its development products and cashes in on the upgrades.

- *Innovators carefully map where innovation is required and recognize how much can be sustained.* The really successful innovators manage a spectrum of adaptive and transformational changes that are within the ability of their organizations to sustain. At Jim Henson's Academy Award–winning Creature Shop, the Henson Performance System works on incremental improvements on traditional folk arts—but also on the latest in digital imaging. At the Creature Shop, nobody waits for the next big idea; they're all too busy implementing every idea.

- *Innovators find ways of destroying the past.* Successful companies almost invariably have strong cultures. They have embedded the rules of past success into the way they do things. Unlearning these patterns of behavior is extremely difficult. Most change programs devote too little time to "rooting out the things we need to stop." People hear "new" as "additional"— the rules that served well in the past don't get changed. And the past crowds out the future. Innovative companies have institutionalized means to propel themselves away from the present and into a new future. As Charles G. Koch, the CEO of Koch Industries Inc. (privately held, $35 billion in annual sales), likes to insist, "The process of generating value for our customers and ourselves is inevitably a process of creative destruction." Koch employees at one plant applied so much entrepreneurial vision to improving performance that the maintenance force could be cut by 50 people—to whom management promptly gave the opportunity to create new jobs. This group formed an internal construction service function that competed against all comers and ultimately provided superior, and cheaper, service than outside contractors.

- *Innovators create funds that enable would-be entrepreneurs to pursue their ideas within the company.* More and more companies are providing an internal venture fund to back selective concepts that do not fit the current paradigm, but that could ultimately be relevant. One global diversified business has established a blue-sky fund of $75 million for such purposes. Any employee can call a hot line for access to the fund; oral approval from Corporate Finance can start the flow of money. In the first year of operation, the flow of ideas actually implemented rose from 5 per 1,000 to 100 per 1,000 employees. Increasingly, companies are turning to this form of venturing to sustain breakthrough innovation. Freed from conventional financial constraints, projects can operate as virtual subsidiaries with their own rules and very different reward structures.

Styles of Innovation

Our research has revealed two successful styles of innovation. Both styles lead to superior financial returns, but what we call the open style produces outstanding financial results. In our research, fully three-quarters of all respondents among innovative companies employed the open style, including the top 5 percent of financial performers.

In the *managed* style, a clear process drives innovation. There is a systematic search for new ways of doing things and new things to do. Processes of innovation are clearly defined and priorities are thought through. Resources are rationally allocated. There are clear approval procedures and targets. Motivation is extrinsic, based on a monetary compensation for contribution to change. Rational search for the future, rather than passionate or intuitive search, is uppermost in this style.

In the *open* style, progress is less ordered but not without discipline. The process is driven less by formal corporate encouragement than by personal enthusiasm. Motivation is intrinsic. The desire to challenge everything is deeply ingrained and actively supported by the corporate culture. Change is seen as natural and desirable; innovation, an enjoyable way of life. There is sufficient order and process to pull the company back from the brink, but only just. The passionate or intuitive rather than the rational is preeminent.

PeopleSoft's CEO, Dave Duffield, exemplifies the business leader who favors an open innovation management style. His personal style is relaxed. His clarity concerning which values he personally advocates provides a rallying point for employees. Words like *passion* frequently crop up in his conversation, and the implication is clear: Intrinsic motivation will make the difference when it comes to finding new ideas and new ways of competing.

The open style builds on the managed style. It retains the rational analysis of the open style, but at its heart is the notion that idea contribution is a core value of the business. Successful innovation requires maintaining the tension between the analytic and the intuitive. Every CEO needs to choose between managed innovation and open innovation. This choice will determine the development of three key capabilities that underlie successful innovation.

Leadership/Followership Contracts

There is much more written about leadership than there is about followership. In today's complex and rapidly changing world, we need to be much more explicit on how leaders and followers interact in order to ignite innovation. In all organizations, a code—typically implicit— underpins the interactions of managers and their subordinates. The nature of these interactions is partly at the discretion of the individuals involved, but it is hard to depart from the social norms of the organization as a whole. There are four key points in this implicit code, which can be thought of as a leadership/followership contract:

- *The degree of collaboration or involvement in decisions.* The more complex and more rapidly changing the environment, the more leaders and followers must pool their knowledge to reach decisions. However, the involvement of greater numbers of people means that more antidotes to indecision are required. Strong processes to converge on a decision are necessary. A carefully conceived mission statement can help. According to Ber Pieper, president of the construction firm Brown & Root, "When I was told we needed a mission statement, I thought it was just a lot of MBA jargon—but it's been a powerful tool to get our people working and moving in the same direction." The critical word here is *moving:* The mission statement fosters action.

- *The acceptable degree of creativity.* How much deviation from the norm is tolerated? Obviously, companies interested in transformational adaptation must find a way to encourage imaginative thinking without deviating from their overall strategic vision. At British Aerospace, managers in the leadership development program learn to think creatively while still staying within a framework of guiding principles that helps them implement the corporate vision.

- *How learning happens.* How open is the learning process? Are mistakes buried or used to enhance corporate performance? How well does the company understand the old proverb, "We get very little wisdom from success"? Dr. Bill Hollins, a university professor of design management in the United Kingdom, set out to design a safety interlocking device to prevent people from getting injured in industrial plant accidents. His starting point: the previous model on the market, which was a failure. The failed device taught lessons that led to a new one—which performs perfectly and has generated impressive sales.

- *The monetary and social rewards of success.* How will high performance be recognized and rewarded? Are incentive systems flexible and widely understood? Do they reward avoiding or cutting short a loss, as well as traditional achievement? Are there recognitions beyond the monetary? Pitney Bowes has an Inventor of the Year Award, which gives a financial reward, but also high-level publicity, to the inventor or team that has added the most value to the firm's intellectual capital and to shareholder value.

Above all, the code governing interactions must be honest, so that the social norms as stated are the ones enacted in practice. The honesty of the culture is more important than the nature of the social contract itself. An aggressive, performance-driven culture based on "up or out" can produce innovation as effectively as a more gentle, supportive, and encouraging environment. They will operate differently, but each will be internally consistent. On the other hand, a stated social contract that emphasizes performance in an aggressive manner but fails to address how poor performance will be handled undermines itself. In many businesses, dishonesty in the social contract undermines the relationship between leaders and followers, and sabotages innovation.

Idea Management

An idea is a potential solution to a problem or opportunity. Ideas are conceived in a *possibility space,* where improvement is hypothesized—to make a manufacturing process more reliable, make a product perform better, or bring new markets within reach. So-called half-baked ideas are much maligned, but they are an important part of the asset pool. It is essential to maintain a flow of ideas that are apparently not practicable and work on them until they are. High-performing innovators have a vastly greater flow of ideas than low performers. Idea management is the process whereby a company develops its stock of ideas and manages their exploitation. It is an active process rather than an administrative one, and it is formalized in relatively few companies.

We have identified three versions of the idea management process, requiring different skills and support:

- *Background* idea management deals with small improvements that are essential to the progressive business. The possibility space is narrow and defined: For example, how do we reduce scrap by 14 percent? The vast majority of ideas will be adaptive in nature. Many can and will be implemented locally without formal approval. At Pillsbury, the suggestion-box tradition has been updated to an outsourced telephone hot line for new ideas.

- In *opportunistic* idea management, the possibility space is less well defined. It may involve creation of a product that will counter a competitive launch or improve performance by a stated amount. Dow Chemical saved $25 million and generated an additional $125 million in revenue by mining existing patents to respond to opportunities in the marketplace. Chevron used cross-functional teams to find innovative ways of reducing power and fuel expenses—and saved $150 million in the process.

- In *strategic* idea management, output cannot be clearly defined. What will the next generation of computers look like? How will health care evolve as we learn more about the human genome? This possibility space is less susceptible to routine process. There is no single model for managing this process. Shell uses workshops that allow people to generate scenarios projected well into the future. IBM employs futurists. Automobile manufacturers create concept cars.

Managing Climate

Research indicates that specific aspects of climate are conducive to innovation and that these factors are created by the behaviors of leaders. Innovative business leaders recognize that one of their prime responsibilities is to create a climate that will stimulate innovation and growth. Our experience suggests that the most predictive measure of whether an organization will be innovative is the level of trust between people in the organization.

Innovation requires playing with ideas that may not seem immediately practical and run the risk of going nowhere. People only take risks in an environment where they know that they will retain the respect of their colleagues even if this particular venture doesn't work out. Trust enables people to hold different views because of different overall perspectives and to explore these differences constructively. Trust is built when personal values and interests are aligned with the mission of the business. The CEO of one highly innovative business, a timber and paper company, revealed that, in recruiting, the company promotes itself as an environmentally friendly business. Equally important, the company delivers on that promise. This external focus provides a firm foundation for trust within the business.

We have identified a number of behaviors that enhance the climate for innovation:

- *Allowing time for ideas incubation.* Managers who run their lives with back-to-back meetings, dealing with essentially repetitive but comforting tasks, will be unlikely to come up with new ideas. Managers often use this "too busy" tactic as a defense against change. Leaders need to be much more ruthless in weeding out unnecessary sources of busyness that constrain performance and inhibit change. 3M wrote the book on this subject, budgeting 15 percent of management time to pursuing personal projects and elaborating new ideas.

- *Seeking value and relevance before seeking problems.* Most managers are programmed to spot problems routinely. The temptation is great to respond to an innovative suggestion by spotting problems rather than considering potentials.

- *Creating idea conflict, not personality conflict.* A striking characteristic of the most innovative companies is their ability to manage diverse points of view. People engage in serious debate over the issues, recognize different views openly, and seek to understand why these differences occur and to resolve them. In less innovative companies, this debate is stifled. Consensus prevails over exploration. People are too timid to risk ridicule by raising an alternative point of view or challenging decisions. Swedish researcher Göran Ekvall distinguished between *debate* (tension between ideas) and *conflict* (tension between people). In 30 years of study, he has identified clear associations among high debate, low conflict, and innovation success.

- *Encouraging diversity and tolerating ambiguity.* Diversified groups generate more creative output, provided that they are more given to debate than to conflict. They create more novel views of the future and widen the problem/solution space in which the company operates. They can prevent catastrophe by pointing out when accepted wisdom is no longer supported by observable fact. There is little stability in an innovative environment—it is constantly migrating from one view of the world to another, and rules and procedures change as new learning accumulates. Many people find these ambiguities difficult to tolerate. Managers who overlook or avoid ambiguity do little to stimulate debate or the quest for new solutions.

- *Stretching people—with integrity.* Struggling to meet an arbitrary deadline is not motivational. A manager who repeatedly asks this of his or her group depletes a hidden but very real emotional bank account. People treated in this way will limit their commitments wherever they can, and they will avoid debate even when there are critical issues to discuss. The job gets done, but not the job that yields innovation. At PeopleSoft, the charge from management is rather: We trust you, but you'll be tested, and you'll get the support you need.

- *Being clear about deliverables, flexible about means.* People need freedom to accomplish their tasks in their own way. There are checkpoints in any process, but the more freedom people have to navigate between checkpoints, the more productive they will be. Nokia CEO Jorma Ollilia says, "The heroes are the ones who do, not those who talk—not those who comply with all of the rules, but the ones who get things done."

Innovation Leadership: The CEO

In our experience and research, the CEOs who most successfully lead innovative companies have certain personal traits in common. In the first place, they *orient themselves to change*. Their restlessness of spirit communicates a constant desire to improve, to modify, to reorient. The more this is harnessed into a real understanding of how the company can produce a better future for customers, the more focused and purposeful the desire to change will become. We all know senior managers who are guardians of tradition, who adapt and adopt at the last possible moment. There will be few places for such people in tomorrow's world. Dr. Heinrich von Pierer, CEO of Siemens, puts it persuasively: "Today's increasing competitive pressures are not forgiving to the superships of the corporate world. They must transform themselves into a flotilla of high-speed motorboats with all the maneuverability needed to react to the twists and turns of the market . . ."

CEOs who manage innovative companies are *committed to transformational learning*. Two sorts of learning accompany the two categories of innovation we identified at the outset. Adaptive learning builds on current understanding and requires a company or individual to match new information to our current world. This is the basis of continual steady improvement. Transformational learning requires not only learning the new but also unlearning past patterns. This is much more difficult, both for leaders and for followers. Programs intended to foster transformational change frequently founder because too little time is devoted to unlearning. Embedded learning then crowds out the intended patterns and stifles innovation.

CEOs who know their way around innovation *extend the scope of behaviors in which they operate effectively*. Each will have his or her personal style, perhaps adaptive, perhaps transformational. What is important is to recognize where and what one is, and to work to extend the range of styles in which one can operate effectively and draw the best from colleagues who may be quite different in style and temperament.

CEOs for whom innovation is second nature *play with intuitions.* Some are driven by intuition, others suppress intuition in favor of structural and operational clarity. But intuition is the product of an active subconscious, building and rebuilding new patterns from the unique experiences and character of each person. The intuitive mind makes unexpected connections—and some of these may be enormously innovative yet practical.

Innovative CEOs *expand the scope of the possible.* They may be engineers, marketers, or accountants by initial training, but in their role as innovation leaders they go beyond any and all narrow mindsets. They look at the entire company—at its people, its capacities, its markets, its future. They see beyond the horizon.

Pasquale Pistorio

President, Chief Financial Officer, and Chief Executive Officer, STMicroelectronics NV

Environmental Compliance Helps the Bottom Line

Most companies do not list respect for the environment as a source of competitive advantage. Yet I hope to demonstrate that when a company is proactive on environmental issues, it can obtain significant bottom-line benefits.

STMicroelectronics now ranks as the world's ninth-largest semiconductor manufacturer, and one of the very few major players that have been profitable during the recent downturn. We owe our success to many factors, among them a growing volume in custom chips for a wide variety of markets and our focus on applications in PC monitors, disk drives, digital TV set-top boxes, smart cards, digital video disks, and cell phones. The company was formed in 1987 through the merger of two entities owned by conglomerates in Italy and France, in which governments had significant investments. Given the poor track record of state-owned electronics companies in the prior decade, predictions about our survival were not very optimistic.

Skeptics were confounded by our turnaround as we left behind our status as a very small player to become a major force in the industry. In 1998, we recorded sales of $4.25 billion and a net profit of $411 million. During the past three years, our return on equity was 13.9 percent, while that of comparable competitors was only 2.8 percent.

A distinguishing feature of STMicroelectronics' management style was the early and intense adoption of quality goals. Nowadays TQM (Total Quality Management) is treated by some management writers as if it were a fad that had run its course. Not in our company, where the pursuit of TQM was and remains an obsession. In September 1997, the prestigious European Foundation for Quality Management (EFQM) gave us its European Quality Award for Business Excellence. This well-known award, recognizing quality in the broadest sense, is an imprimatur of managerial ability. To win the award, a company must demonstrate extraordinary accomplishments in the fields of innovation, customer satisfaction and service, employee involvement and motivation, market share, and other key variables. I mention this here to establish our credentials as a company that thinks and executes well. One part of that thinking and execution is our somewhat unconventional views on the environment. They deserve the reader's attention.

To many businesspeople, the word *environment* is like a red rag to a bull. Business groups frequently complain that demands by governments and international bodies for environmental compliance limit corporate freedom of action and impose costs on corporations that are as unnecessary as they are unfair. In some countries there is a powerful identification of shareholder interest with minimal environmental compliance. Many companies spend quite significant amounts of money on lobbying for lax or ineffectual environmental legislation. I hope to demonstrate that there are alternatives to these attitudes and actions—that the polarized debate of the corporation versus the environmentalist obscures the facts.

The Benefits Outweigh the Costs

The battle cry of the quality movement was Quality is free!, by which was meant that quality is there for the taking, and that the additional costs of striving for maximum quality are lower than the costs of nonquality. Similarly, for corporations the environment is free; that is, the benefits of compliance far outweigh the costs. What's more, the environment is shared by all of us, including employees. Public opinion polls repeatedly tell us of citizens' yearning for a clean environment. A company that acts with sensitivity to the environment is also fulfilling the aspirations of its employees, suppliers, customers, and shareholders.

Let's look at the issue from the perspective of employees. There has lately been a widespread shift of perception among business executives and business thinkers about the role and place of the individual in the production process. No longer is it possible for businesses to dehumanize individuals and treat them in ways that are alienating or that frustrate their deep aspirations. People empowerment is essential for corporate success as we move further into the Information Age and key decisions are no longer made in a remote corporate center but on the actual firing line where relatively low-ranking people work. Employees want to and must be actors in the creation of goods and services; they are not merely "factors of production."

Coincidentally, there is a strong demand among all people that industrial progress inflict the least possible damage on earth, sea, and air. Companies that do more than others to fulfill these aspirations—both personal and environmental—develop a workforce that is more loyal and better motivated. Conversely, companies that are environmentally destructive taint their employee relations. The recruiting efforts of STMicroelectronics and the zeal for day-to-day work across our organization are helped by the fact that we have an outstanding environmental record. Worker dedication and pride are the foundation for high performance. It is simply impossible for a company to reach high TQM standards without strong technical engagement and emotional commitment on the part of the workforce. Our corporate respect for the environment is a powerful animating, motivating force.

STMicroelectronics is at the confluence of two large social movements: first, people's growing sensitivity to the environment and, second, new and empowered employee relationships based on recognition of individual needs for self-respect and personal fulfillment at work. Lest I be accused of excessive idealism, let me demonstrate how these notions work in practice at STMicroelectronics.

We approach environmental issues with the goal of exceeding our peers' performance and of staying ahead of the industry's learning curve. One area of focus has been the use of forest products; another has been water and chemicals recycling. Since 1994, we have cut our paper usage by 40 percent. Our 40 printed product catalogs have been all but retired, and their contents inputted on CD-ROM. We were the first company in our industry to do this, for a savings of slightly under a million dollars. At many of our main facilities we now recycle half of the water used. Five years ago we were unable to recycle any water at all. We also recycle sulphuric acid and other key chemicals used in chip manufacture.

An Environmental Decalogue

In 1995, we created a corporate vision of our environmental strategies. We called it our environmental decalogue. It sets the following very ambitious goals:

Conservation

- Energy conservation: Achieve 5 percent annual reduction of total energy consumed, with a target of 25 percent reduction by 1999.
- Water conservation: Reduce water drawdown from conduits, streams, and aquifers by 10 percent annually.
- Tree conservation: Reduce use of paper and paper products by 10 percent annually.

Recycling

- Launch pilot programs using alternative energy.
- Reach 90 percent water recycling by 1999.
- Use 90 percent recycled paper.
- Recycle chemicals. The goal for sulphuric acid: 80 percent recycling by year-end 1999.

Pollution Control

- Air emissions: Phase out high-emission equipment (Class 1 ODS), and reduce greenhouse gases and gases that generate acid rain.
- Water emissions: Meet the standards of the most restrictive communities for wastewater discharge.
- Landfill: Achieve 100 percent treatment of waste.
- Noise: Adhere to a "noise to neighbors" policy, on the perimeter of all property, of less than 60 dB.

Contamination Control

- Meet or exceed strictest safety standards for handling and disposal of contaminants and hazardous substances.

Waste Management

- Manufacturing: Recycle 80 percent of manufacturing by-product waste (metal, plastic, quartz, glass).

- Packaging: Move to 80 percent recyclable, reused, or biodegradable packing materials such as cartons, tubes, reels, bags, trays, padding.

New Technologies Research

- Push our efforts to design products for decreased energy consumption or higher input/output ratios.

Proactivity

- Support local environmental initiatives such as Clean Up the World and Adopt a Highway. Ride-share at every site. Encourage workers to participate in environmental committees.
- STMicroelectronics will sponsor an annual environmental day at every facility. Employee training in environmental awareness will also be offered to customers and suppliers.

We buy capital equipment to lower resource usage or diminish discharges, typically sooner than a company with no commitment to environmental quality might have done. For example, we refitted our factory in Agrate, outside Milan, with new cooling units that have better environmental compliance characteristics. We found that the newer equipment incorporated many other desirable new design and performance characteristics. Consequently, there was a very short payback on these resource-conserving investments.

Our policy is global, affecting all of our 17 production sites, 9 R&D centers, and 31 design and application centers. From California to Sicily to China, we take the most demanding local standard that exists for treatment of a resource or a discharge and apply it company wide. Since 1997, all of our plants meet or exceed the requirements of the European Eco-Management and Audit Scheme (EMAS) regulation and the internationally recognized ISO 14001 environmental standard. (EMAS is a voluntary scheme for companies to benchmark environmental performance.) What's more, we have demanded that our suppliers also adhere to this standard.

A global company views the world as its field of action and its responsibility. Therefore, we do not take advantage of local regulatory laxity, where it exists. It is our goal to anticipate, not simply follow, local rules and standards on environmental compliance. For this reason, we comply with any ecological legislation at least one year in advance of deadline. In so doing, we express our belief that it is mandatory for the TQM-driven company to be at the forefront of ecological commitment (1) for ethical and social reasons, and (2) for financial return and the ability to attract responsible, high-performance people.

We've Already Achieved Much of It

Our decalogue is not a wish list. The large majority of these targets has been met or exceeded, or will be met by the foreseen date. STMicroelectronics is currently working on a new decalogue, in which still more exigent milestones will be identified. The new decalogue will focus in particular on greenhouse gases and on energy consumption, two closely linked aspects of the global warming problem.

When STMicroelectronics first started down this road, we found no companies to which we could turn for advice and best practices. Lately, however, I am happy to see that a small but growing number of companies have adopted a fairly radical approach to the environment. Many of these are in consumer products, where cultivating an environmentally concerned image can boost sales. I have read of a billion-dollar U.S. carpet company, Interface Incorporated, that has shaved $67 million of costs in 3½ years by means of drastic waste-cutting and energy-saving programs. It has also promoted a program whereby customers lease but do not own carpets. Upon return of the carpets to the manufacturer, they are reconditioned and leased again, or recycled. There are other encouraging signs, such as the increased visibility of think tanks and business-oriented foundations that promote ecological values.

Their posture, however, is often more idealistic than pragmatic. And that, I feel, is an obstacle to the sweeping adoption of pro-environment values across the entire spectrum of business. There must be a link between a corporation's search for high performance and its need for profit. More managers should consider an observation made several years ago by Harvard Business School professor Michael Porter. He said, in essence, that both excellence and mediocrity are contagious. Companies that pursue excellence in all key functions find that excellence diffuses throughout the organization. Identically, tolerance of second-class standards, performance, and values is contagious.

A company that aspires to be great at research, yet treats the environment casually and exploitatively, will find that research excellence is unobtainable. The environment is free only for corporations that take their full share of responsibility in the quest to fulfill the citizen's and the employee's aspiration for the finest possible environment.

Göran Lindahl
President and Co-Chief Executive Officer, ABB

Cool Head, Firm Hand, Warm Heart
The ABB Approach to Innovation

At ABB, we start by envisioning how the marketplace will function 10 years from now: What services will be in demand then? Then we ask ourselves, *Why not do it today?* There are so many new materials, so many promising conceptual solutions not yet converted into products and services. We are entering an era when ABB once again has the opportunity to break through to important innovations. That is where I place my bet and that is why I push to make it happen.

Innovation at ABB has to do with technology but is not limited to technology. We use three words to explain this larger view: innovation, creativity, and passion. Innovation originates the novel solution that will make a real difference for our customers. Creativity, in our working definition, has to do with making that solution real: It sets in motion and governs the dynamic forces that lead, step by step, to the hardware, service, or whatever is needed to make a customer more competitive. And passion drives the project; it sustains the enthusiasm of all participants through the difficulties that are sure to crop up on the way toward success. I often say that we need a cool head, a firm hand, and a warm heart. This describes the individual who embodies innovation, creativity, and passion.

In order to encourage innovation, we need to ensure the space and time for individuals to use both brain and emotion. Space is intellectual space, not just physical space. It is an environment that cultivates strong and useful ideas. It needs to be relaxed, but not in the least lax. Pressure is, in fact, a critical condition for innovation—pressure from a competitive situation or from a superior. Pressure can be managed by carefully adjusting performance measurements applied across the enterprise.

Engineering Breakthroughs

One of the means by which ABB creates pressure in the field of technological innovation is a new ventures fund. We set aside money for what we call High Rs—High Risks, High Rewards. These are projects with a success probability of not more than 50 percent, driven by someone with a fire inside, whom we have learned to trust. Our message to that person is simple and candid: Take the money, take your time, but if it doesn't work out, think really hard before you come back with another idea.

Our new Powerformer is a good example. It is a single unit capable of generating and transforming electricity. For some 10 years, our engineers had been thinking about this possibility and they had eliminated it—impossible, they said. But one of our engineers found a promising way in. We gave him seed money, set milestones in cooperation with him. And in less than two years, he and his team developed the Powerformer. This was a very considerable achievement: The technology it replaces had remained much the same for a century. Powerformer establishes an entirely new class of machine and lowers costs for the customer by some 30 percent.

Mats Leijon of ABB corporate research was its inventor. The recognition he received has gone far beyond his expectation. ABB rewarded him financially to convey our high level of appreciation, but perhaps even more significant to him was recognition within his profession, including a medal from the Association for Engineering Sciences.

Both financial and social recognition are important to stimulate a community of innovators. I have always felt that people are more driven by social recognition, which goes to the core of our humanness. The opportunity to achieve, the intellectual satisfaction, and the self-esteem that accompany publicly acknowledged achievement, are the strongest motivators. These values, and the resulting value creation within a company, remain long after the financial reward is forgotten.

What about the large percentage of ideas that don't deliver? Failure is sometimes the richest learning experience for an organization or individual. Thomas Edison once conducted 50,000 experiments to develop a new storage battery. Asked if it was frustrating to experience so many failures, he said, "What failures? I now know 50,000 things that won't work." You have to accept that there will be failure. And you have to communicate that, like Edison, one can learn from failure. Yet you must discourage the same individual from repeating the same failure!

I have the idea that there is a strong relationship between "no more than 50 percent chance of success" and highly significant breakthroughs, but I can't prove my point statistically. What matters in innovation is not statistics but brainpower.

The Truly Global Enterprise Is Just Emerging

In the early 1980s, businesses like ABB started to globalize. We were already doing business in many different countries, but a truly global business is not just a multinational. Until recently, our multinational organization resembled a great wheel, with all the spokes connected to a corporate hub. The organization toward which we are working now is quite different: It is a boundaryless network.

The path toward that has been very gradual. Fifteen years ago, we developed sales and marketing forces in distant markets while continuing to manufacture and develop new services in Europe. Some seven years later, we began to transfer technology and know-how, and in some cases R&D resources, to important local markets in order to benefit from the intellectual resources out there. Today, we are going still further by creating a new kind of global network that will, I believe, distinguish the successful firms in the next century. Our objective is to derive full potential from a culturally and geographically diverse organization. This third step is very complex, and I think few leaders are well prepared for it.

Issues of cultural diversity cannot be ignored. Since the 1960s, the predominant global management style and values have been based on American management books, so to speak—on Western values. But in Indonesia, Malaysia, Saudi Arabia, or Tanzania there are a different population, different customers, different employees, a different culture, and, of course, different values. It stands to reason that we need to recognize and manage by a universal value system that people around the world can respect.

I recently invited 12 people with 12 different mother tongues, 12 different backgrounds, and several different religions to review our ABB policy manual. I said, in effect, "Consider this book. You're not allowed to change the goals, but please suggest how we should change the way *toward* those goals." The participants literally lived together day and night for a week and emerged with a new book that represents at least a long step toward a universal value system applicable in a truly global corporation. What they returned to us is not a glossy brochure but practical advice on how we should behave in the outside world and internally among ourselves.

A value endorsed and rephrased by the group is this: It is better to be fast and roughly right than 100 percent right but slow. This makes sense, and I was gratified to see that it was given importance by an extremely diverse group of ABB managers. Today's market circumstances require us to be on real time all the time. In real-time management, you can't say that you'll meet about an issue three weeks from now—you must act at once. When a customer calls, you can't call back later—you must respond immediately. When shareholders want to know what a newly announced contract means for shareholder value, you have to respond that day. This new sense of urgency represents an exponential change for management. We need to find ways to cope within an organization that demands responses in real time all the time. This is what the world demands from top companies. By incorporating this value into our vision for ABB, we give our managers around the world the cue they need to decide and act in real time.

What of the Future?

The two areas that I believe will most influence corporate success in the future are information technology (IT) and human resources (HR). Ten years ago, no one would have said that—one might have thought, first of all, of R&D, global penetration, or still other factors. But I believe that IT and HR will make the difference between success and survival. IT is a generational issue. For my children, IT has always existed, whereas I and many managers of my generation are BCs (Before Computers), who were, at best, taught how to use punch cards. Obviously, we must draw on the innovation, creativity, and passion of the ACs (After Computers). The key role of IT is to help us become real-time managers and to convert data into information, information into knowledge.

In essence, HR concerns attracting and retaining the best people, and ensuring that they recognize your company as by far the best for their careers. A long-term mind-set and loyalty are not very common today, but they remain tremendously important. I believe that there are only two ways to bring this about in a corporation like ours. The first is *genuine challenge:* giving people short- and midterm targets and long-term goals that are challenging but soundly conceived. The other is *genuine participation:* ensuring that each person has opportunities to contribute massively and can see just how his or her contribution furthers our shared success. Only through these two means will people feel empowered.

When we created ABB, the top 400 managers were 43 or 44 years of age. A few months ago, their average age was about 50. In 10 years' time, we'll be retirees. Who will lead the company? We need to change extremely quickly, to get more 35-year-olds into our company, if we want to prosper.

I hold regular meetings with the 400 most senior managers. Participation is something of a competition. I nearly started a revolution two years ago when I reassigned 25 seats to new participants not above 33 years of age—and I have repeated this practice three times since then. It is an act of tremendous symbolism, making clear to everyone the value we place on younger managers. Of course, the trick is to value the younger without disqualifying the older and more experienced. We realize the value of experience; it's the combination of experienced managers and relative newcomers that leads to success.

Fingerspitzengefühl

At ABB, we want to be more knowledge driven, more service driven, more high-tech driven. We want to be known as a technology *and* engineering company. In earlier years, we sold products. Now we sell functions and whole solutions. For example, we sell components for a steel mill, and as part of the new package we guarantee improvements in production efficiency. This introduces new complexity and demands new creativity. The product has no meaning on its own any longer—we sell full functionality. Today I even avoid using the word *product;* we have to look at a function and at how that function helps our customer to be more competitive. This is our new mind-set: selling complete solutions.

Eventually, you come to a point in your career when you realize that you can do only so much directly, but you can accomplish a great deal simply through influence. I've come to call this *management by touch*—not physical touch, but mind touch. I believe that this is essential for corporate leadership in the future. This is how we can achieve the right mix of cool head, firm hand, warm heart. The German language has a good term for it: *Fingerspitzengefühl.* You feel it in your fingertips.

Nobuyuki Idei
President and Chief Executive Officer, Sony Corporation

Teams on Fire:
Sony's Innovation Culture

On May 11, 1999, Sony launched a new industry, or so we firmly think. The occasion was a product launch in central Tokyo, to which video and print journalists had been invited from Japanese and international media. All eyes and cameras were focused on a shiny white tabletop, on which you would have seen our first market-ready digital creature, a robot named AIBO. He (or she) is a long-eared, frisky, four-legged entertainment robot. He walks, crouches, bats a ball, waves his paws, wags his tail, barks, and nods his head quizzically—among other things. And he proved to be an immediate hit with consumers: Offered exclusively at the Sony web site, the 3,000 units available in Japan from our first manufacturing run sold out in 20 minutes. AIBO was all over the evening news and, shortly after, made appearances in the *Wall Street Journal, Business Week,* and many other publications worldwide. We are so grateful for this friendly welcome.

As we introduced AIBO to journalists, we emphasized a number of business points. We made clear our belief that robotics will be an important twenty-first-century industry and our desire at Sony to provide creative, technological, and commercial leadership in the field. We also stated our conviction that no one company can or should dominate; the industry will move vigorously forward only when several companies bring intellectual and financial resources to it.

The journalists were naturally curious to know what comes next. To that inquiry, the director of Sony's Digital Creatures Laboratory, Dr. Toshitada Doi, provided two answers. First, the very name of our lab implies that we plan to develop a digital menagerie of entertainment robots that will be increasingly mobile and fun, and will be endowed with intriguing character design as the technology evolves. Second, Dr. Doi explained that the technologies developed for entertainment robots could be applied to devices that do serious work,

such as rescue and mine clearing. By developing small-scale entertainment robots today, we are laying the foundation of an industry
that will serve some of society's critical needs.

I start with this tale of an entertainment robot because I want to
convey at once that Sony innovates. We take risks for innovations we
believe in, and we put our faith not only in that great impersonal
called *technology* but in gifted individuals who have unique capacities
to imagine, and to engineer and manufacture what they imagine. We
don't place our trust in market surveys or today's business successes.
Our goal is to create new markets by discovering hidden, perhaps
even unrecognized, needs and wishes. We do not imitate: This is the
proudest and most challenging value in our culture.

Designing Products for the Digital Network Era

Sony is a restless organization—we move on—but all Sony employees
respect the company's twin heritage in innovation and marketing,
going back to the two founders. The late Masaru Ibuka was the technology genius, the product innovator. His enormously inquisitive
mind and ability to make the difficult seem easy have passed into our
culture. He retained into advanced old age the curious mind of a
child, a primordial questioner.

The late Akio Morita was the marketing genius, the one who trav-
eled abroad soon after the end of the Second World War to get Sony
into the minds and hearts of customers outside of Japan. He would
have been captivated by the potential of the Internet as a sales channel. As well, he was an organizational innovator. He didn't hesitate to
restructure the company periodically to make it more effective, and
this, too, is an element of heritage we still draw upon.

What we inherit from these two individuals is not the details of
their accomplishments but their values and energy—and the unified
Sony brand. Today's world differs very much from theirs. To my mind,
the watershed events separating the first 50 years of Sony from perhaps the next 50 are the convergence of previously separate technologies and the rise of the Internet.

At Sony we think a great deal about the emerging digital network
era. This concept has two meanings for us, one internal, the other
external. Internally it means that all of us within Sony are engaged in

modifying our business models, R&D, and product designs to take into account that products for today's world must be networked, that is, connected and used together. We expect a PC-centric or an advanced audio-video device to serve as the platform for connectivity and interoperability. Externally, our emphasis on the emerging networked society communicates to the outside world that this is the trend and that Sony is there. We will continue to be a leading player as more and more products gain network capabilities.

Sony focuses on consumer electronics for the home, and we are interested in what you might call "the home network"—a new configuration of devices and functions with the TV as the hub, which has not yet assumed definitive shape. The powerful and novel chips at the heart of our next-generation PlayStation—the Emotion Engine and the Graphics Synthesizer—suggest to many of us applications in the home that go well beyond games. Today, those chips make possible a delightfully realistic new experience of movielike action, generated in real time as directed by the game player. Tomorrow, we shall discover what the wider capabilities of the chips may be.

Some consumers are already experiencing and exploring the emerging home network. For example, users of our new VAIO C1 PictureBook computer can record a digital photograph or video clip on its built-in video camera, edit that content on screen, insert it into an organizational newsletter, a home page, or a personal e-mail, and dispatch it worldwide. The computer is a camera and video recorder; the camera and video recorder are a computer—this is convergence. There is more than a trend here: There is inevitability.

Organizational Innovation: Managing Complexity

I mentioned previously that our cofounder, Akio Morita, didn't hesitate to reorganize Sony as our businesses diversified and grew, and as markets changed. In recent months we have again followed his example through a far-reaching reorganization intended to make Sony an optimally creative, efficient, and profitable participant in the new markets of the digital network era. Our goal is to encourage the independence of our businesses while ensuring that each business helps the others. We have learned that when each independent business influences the others and shares content or technology with them, a new event can occur, for which I've borrowed from science the term *emergent evolution*. Emergent evolution means that important innovations can emerge from the interaction of parts within the complex whole of Sony.

My personal challenge is to create that new business model, a platform for emergent evolution across Sony. The first steps have been taken. In March 1999, we announced our new "integrated decentralized" model. Through this new configuration, I am convinced that our businesses can best serve the networked society of the coming century and generate still greater value for our shareholders. Our electronics businesses are being redefined as network companies, and each is empowered to operate with considerable independence and to develop its own portfolio of venture investments. Sony corporate headquarters has already begun to transfer to the companies essential support functions and R&D laboratories. A somewhat smaller headquarters will provide coordination while operating its own venture portfolio and retaining direct responsibility for certain businesses charged with developing strategies and technologies for the network business model.

Comparable changes are being instituted in our entertainment and other businesses, all to one purpose: to create vigorous enterprises that interact in strikingly creative ways, under the overall direction of a smaller corporate headquarters. Not least among our organizational innovations, we have also revised our board of directors and created a new level of corporate executive officers, to distinguish more clearly between those individuals responsible for oversight and those responsible for management. Sony could emerge in the future as, in effect, a holding company with a portfolio of extremely vital, productive businesses and a more incisive and empowered board. Whatever path we take, it will always be toward managing complex businesses with great effectiveness, relating them creatively to one another, and freeing them to achieve more than ever before.

Delivering Music through the Net

I can best reflect something of Sony's innovation culture by looking, in the following pages, at some of the most intriguing and commercially important developments across our enterprise.

Technologies are evolving with incredible speed, and people are just as speedy to adopt them. This is nowhere truer than in music, where Sony Music Entertainment, with a growing library of more than 500,000 recordings, has an enormous stake. Technology for downloading music from Internet sites has leaped forward in the past few years. A vast library of music is now available online, without payment, from creative talents and performers who wish to have their work heard. However, the same technologies that make possible complimentary distribution can be used illegally to distribute music protected by copyright. The new situation cries out for innovative solutions.

In cooperation with our industry peers and the Secure Digital Music Initiative (SDMI), Sony has been exploring technologies that will accomplish two important objectives: satisfying the legitimate desire of music lovers to download directly from the Net, while safeguarding the commercial structure that has created today's fantastically lively and diverse world of recorded music. Just as we believe that the robotics industry needs many participants in addition to Sony, we believe that the best solutions for delivering music over the Net will be reached through alliances among technology leaders.

In February and May 1999, the SDMI announced an important technology trial in San Diego and a full-fledged technology launch. In San Diego, where broadband cable modem Internet service is available, we are exploring an IBM-developed delivery system that allows consumers to download a 60-minute album in less than 10 minutes—frequently much less than 10 minutes. The system is *end-to-end*, meaning that it not only delivers the music but also includes a credit card payment processing facility and copy control. Consumers can even download album cover art and liner notes.

In a parallel effort, we also agreed with Microsoft to use its new Windows Media 4.0, beginning in the summer of 1999, to deliver singles, rather than entire albums, over today's standard modems. It should take about five minutes to download a hit single.

The pattern I find so interesting here is that one new technology has summoned others: The new capability to distribute music via the Net prompted the major players in the music industry to create orderly channels serving both music lovers and their own corporate purposes. The passion of a technology-savvy consumer group moved an entire industry. I think not for the last time.

Super Audio CD

Sony is historically committed to delivering innovative electronics to mass markets, but one of our preferred pathways to mass markets passes through elite groups of consumers. As we did with AIBO, we often introduce a major new product in a niche market, at a price that reflects our enormous investment in R&D and manufacturing. Our first customers often become, in effect, consultants who help us to take the product in directions they value.

Such a product was announced in mid-1999 after eight years of research and development: Super Audio CD. This is a next-generation audio carrier that not only reproduces the musician's art but also recreates every detail of resonance in the space surrounding the music source. The audience for the product is audiophiles—individuals who will travel with us any distance to achieve the ultimate in sound reproduction. Such passionate audiophiles have long had their ambassador at the highest level in our organization: The chairman of the board, Norio Ohga, is a conservatory-trained singer who played a key role in the development of the original CD system.

The library of Super Audio CDs will develop at a measured pace, but systematically, with an initial release in the United States of 40 recordings, followed by 16 additional recordings each month.

Flat-Screen TV: Market Driven, Innovation Driven

The team that developed our new flat screen CRT television monitor agreed on an interesting criterion as they set to work: Even a three-year-old child would have to be able to recognize at a glance that the new TV was very different and much better. That is a challenge our product development teams can rise to.

Sony has earned a world reputation for the quality of our Trinitron television monitors, both for home and for broadcast and business uses. But nowhere are there laurels to rest upon. Television technology today is dynamic: Who hasn't heard about the advent of high-definition TV (HDTV), pondered the enigmas of old-fashioned analog versus new-fashioned digital signals, or noticed that some new television monitors look different? But if the technology is dynamic, so is the marketplace. Consumers are ready for a new type of television.

Just how this became clear, I find fascinating. In recent years, many of our customers became used to flat-screen laptop computers. As a consequence, the slightly curved screen of a television monitor, with resulting slight distortion at the edges, was beginning to look clumsy to them. At the same time that this consumer perception was taking root, the overall market for television monitors was being rocked by a quiet but relentless price war, such that prices fell to half their prior level. Reason enough to find means of renewing consumers' historical preference for Sony Trinitron and providing value-added content that would reinforce the singular excellence of our brand.

We began to work on flat-screen technology for the consumer market in 1996, the fiftieth anniversary of our company. At the time, every division of Sony had been challenged by top management to develop an outstanding new product to celebrate the milestone. Flat-screen TV was one of the objectives we cared most about, but the product team had to change its ways if it was to come close. This wasn't the first time we had thought about flat screens for the consumer market, and we were actually manufacturing a second-generation flat-screen monitor for air traffic controllers. But there were some missing technologies for affordable color TV. We didn't have the right glass, and we had to overcome the effects of heat expansion in the metal mask fixed to the back of the TV screen, on which the beams of the TV signal are focused.

As I said, we had to change our ways. If this project was to bear fruit within the anniversary year, we would have to shorten our standard 10-month development cycle to 6 months, and we would have to set three concurrent teams in motion: a cathode ray tube (CRT) team, a team to design the complete TV set, and a manufacturing process team. We instituted another timesaving change: In the past we would have looked at three prototypes, but for this accelerated development we decided to eliminate one prototype. This decision saved 3 months—but, paradoxically, it also added expense.

In cooperation with a Japanese glass manufacturer, we developed a new tempered glass some 16 millimeters thick that was perfect for our purpose. And, using advanced computer analysis and design, we solved on our own the challenges of the metal mask. The team delivered its new model on December 10, 1996, just in time to join the celebration. The product is on the market today under the name

WEGA—and even a three-year-old can tell that it's very different and much better.

The Walkman: 20 Years of Innovation

People who think about innovation often point out that it doesn't consist only of breakthroughs; incremental innovation is no less important to sustained business success. The original breakthrough to the Walkman has become legendary (one has one's choice of competing legends at Sony). By the late 1970s, we had been miniaturizing the stereo tape recorder for years, and we were also working on the development of lightweight headphones. One fine day, Masaru Ibuka—as you may recall, a Sony founder—came upon an engineer listening to taped music through headphones while he worked. This seemingly trivial encounter sprang to life in his mind, and he began asking himself whether a fully portable stereo tape player with lightweight headphones might just be a marketable product. We had the basic elements already, including the tape cassette, which had been on the market for some time. What was new was their combination and the concept for their use. We thought that young people might like the product; we couldn't foresee that people of all ages worldwide would adopt it as part of their lifestyle.

In July 1979, we launched the Walkman in Japan, and six months later, in the United States. Our competitors took a wait-and-see attitude toward this innovation—they weren't nearly as sure as we were that we had a winner. And so we had a year to learn the market and refine the product before serious competition appeared. We began at that time, and continue to this day, a process of incremental innovation—of challenges and solutions that keep the product line fresh, expansive, and compelling.

Over the first six years, our engineers targeted the challenge of miniaturization and weight reduction. They decided that the ideal Walkman would be no larger in any dimension than a cassette tape box—a seemingly impossible goal. However, by 1985, that evolution was complete: The electronics had been reduced to a thin envelope surrounding the tape. Over the next five-year period, the Walkman team embraced a second challenge: ultimate user convenience. We developed a small rechargeable battery and remote controls with

LCD displays. We incorporated Dolby C noise reduction. We designed a shutter to protect the controls when users engage in strenuous activity.

And in the 1990s, we focused on a third challenge to incremental innovation: efficiency, especially in the areas of energy conservation and extended play. In 1998, we realized our goal of making available 100 hours of play without battery change or recharge.

As we faced this sequence of challenges, we tried always to articulate our goals in the simplest possible terms, so that everyone involved could easily remember where we were heading. More often than not, "half the size" or "twice as long-playing" was all that needed to be said—simple, direct, and terrifically challenging to engineers, designers, and manufacturing experts.

Walkman's Man: The Wisdom of Kozo Ohsone

Currently Sony corporate advisor for manufacturing operations, Kozo Ohsone played an indispensable role in making the Walkman one of Sony's most popular products. Today's Walkman team still heeds his realistic, challenging, and quietly humorous advice, which he distilled into nine points, every one of which reflects the best of Sony's innovation culture.

1. Believe that everything can be reduced by half.

2. In determining the size, don't worry about what will be housed inside.

3. Set a clear goal.

4. Just say okay, without considering any ramifications.

5. Difficulties can be overcome, but learn to live with what is impossible.

6. Make something up, and demonstrate it before explaining it.

7. Do brainstorming off-site and never come back until your objective is achieved.

8. Keep interesting, funny ideas secret from your boss while you are working on them.

9. When you need someone to do a job for you, choose a person who is very busy.

Green Management

In the excitement of reorganizing our company and launching innovative products, we have not forgotten and must not forget fundamentals. In April 1999, Sony published its latest environmental report covering truly a multitude of issues in our worldwide organization. As well, we opened at corporate headquarters in Tokyo the Sony Eco Plaza, an environmental exhibition that follows the example of the best science museums by offering the visitor opportunities for hands-on experience of some of Sony's green management methods. We are one of the world's major manufacturers, and we intend to be among its most careful stewards of the environment. As I wrote in the new environmental report, "We have identified the environment as one of Sony's central, long-term management themes."

This is an area where innovation greatly matters—and it is also an area where the management of product design, manufacture, packaging, repair, and disposal involves masses of technical detail, and therefore doesn't lend itself very well to inclusion in this chapter. I do, however, want to illustrate our environmental efforts by just one example drawn from research at Sony's Center for Environmental Technologies. All of us are aware of the vast amounts of styrene foam packaging that permits damage-free shipping of consumer electronics. What happens to it after the consumer disposes of it? Our independent research has developed an ecologically sound method for recycling this material. By using liquid limonene, a natural substance extracted from the skins of tangerines and other citrus fruits, we are now able to convert waste styrene foam into high-quality polystyrene, a plastic used in many products. While this is a quite new process, we have already started recycling operations at one location in Japan.

I urge readers interested in the diversified green management program at Sony to read our latest environmental report, which we have published on our web site at www.world.sony.com/eco/.

Teams on Fire: A Conversation

Dr. Doi and I have been colleagues for many years, and in our conversations we sometimes touch on what allows R&D teams to catch fire and become capable of a high level of achievement. He is, as you may remember, the director of our Digital Creatures Laboratory, and he was a principal developer of the compact disc. I suppose he understands as much as anybody about teams on fire with creativity and directed passion.

The surprising thing in a man who has achieved so much of a practical nature is that he doesn't approach the subject strictly from a project management perspective. The inner qualities of team members and their relationships and the capacity for vision and objectivity in the leader matter more to him than anything else. "The team must have a certain purity," he once told me. "This means that it must be free from political distortions—from animosity between team members, from egoistic ambition, and from internal pressure to make technical compromises. It must also be free from top management distortion"—by which I take Toshitada Doi to be warning me to approve worthwhile projects, fund them, and then step courteously away while the real work gets done.

"When this is so," he continued, "all participants can concentrate on the technology, and the team as a whole may catch fire—truly 'switch on' and enter a different state. It's not very logical, but when that switch occurs, everything is possible. We'll face difficulties, but the difficulties will go away. Under these conditions, the team *calls its destiny*. Its fate is different than it would have been. As I said, it's not logical, but I have experienced it many times."

In Dr. Doi's thinking, I detect a convergence between what you might call Asian wisdom and American entrepreneurship. He has expressed admiration for Andrew Carnegie's approach—apply a strong will, and the door will open—and for Theodore Roosevelt's optimistic sense of adventure in the face of challenges.

I once took the position with Dr. Doi that the leader must be close to the team, must mix in and share every burden.

"No," he replied, "the leader must have a certain distance."

I asked him what he meant. "Think of a vehicle moving through unknown territory," he said, "and imagine a bird up above it, looking ahead, seeing what comes next. That is the leader's distance."

It seems best to end here, with two fellows in conversation about the sources of profound and truly useful innovation.

Charles O. "Chad" Holliday, Jr.
Chairman and Chief
Executive Officer, DuPont

DuPont Is a Science Company

The title of this chapter may strike you as obvious—of course, DuPont is a science company. But for us at DuPont the words are strong, and they have navigational power. We are reinventing this great company to encompass new and massively important phases of science, new and massively important twenty-first-century markets. These are not mere words and hopes: In the past 14 months, the board of directors has authorized $32 billion in transactions, primarily acquisitions and divestments, to bring new capabilities into our company and convert noncore businesses into reinvestable cash.

Our company is not quite 200 years old—nearly as old as the republic. DuPont began as a manufacturer of explosives and throughout the nineteenth century led or kept pace with the most advanced technologies in its chosen field. At the turn of the twentieth century, the company went through its first reinvention: Third-generation DuPont family members recapitalized the firm and, through R&D and acquisitions, added a growing number of successful chemicals businesses to the core business in explosives. By 1930 we were manufacturing basic chemicals, fibers, paints and varnishes, dyes, cellophane, photographic film, and many other products of applied science. The invention of nylon in the mid-1930s confirmed DuPont as the leading synthetic fiber company and shaped the public view of who we are—for many consumers, we will always be the company that brought nylon, Dacron®, Kevlar®, and other synthetic fibers into virtually every household, and Teflon® and Corian® into the kitchen. In reality, DuPont has many other businesses—industrial chemicals, pharmaceuticals, agricultural products, and materials for the construction industry, among others.

As we looked at our hand about a year and a half ago, we recognized that we were predominantly a materials business in which the technologies had matured. They retained potential, no doubt about it, but were limited in comparison with the potential of emerging technologies. Similarly, we were in the energy business through our wholly owned subsidiary, Conoco—but size had become critical in energy and we were not among the largest. We elected to exit the energy business in stages, first through an initial public offering (IPO) involving 30 percent of Conoco, which yielded $4.4 billion to reinvest in parts of the company and in new science, where we perceive our real opportunities. We have since split off the remaining 70 percent.

Our reinvestment process is under way. We are keeping chemistry strong, and we are building world-class capacity in molecular biology. We are developing service businesses on a global scale. And in everything we do, we focus on a new value—knowledge intensity, about which, more later.

Chemistry and Biology Converging

Companies cannot afford to ignore valid sources of knowledge. For that reason, we have a number of university partners with which we are engaged in critically important explorations. Our joint program with MIT brings the insights of that distinguished university to our transformative process. The core issue we are exploring with MIT professors is this: how best to take a strong, chemistry-based company and add molecular biology, so as to have not only more tools in our tool kit but tools of a new kind that draw from both sides. A chemical company relies on three disciplines: chemistry, mathematics, and physics. By adding biology, we introduce a fourth fundamental discipline. True, biology has been a component of DuPont for many years, but by acquiring an outstanding biology company (Pioneer Hi-Bred) and a protein technology company, we have recently changed the magnitude of our commitment.

Why did we choose to work with MIT? We perceived it as the institution that recognized the issues we are facing before any of the other leading schools—they are actually reeducating some of their traditional engineering staff to investigate biological solutions to problems that years ago had nothing to do with biology. The institution's freedom from commercial pressure means that MIT people can view challenges freshly; they start with a clean sheet of paper.

And, finally, their energy and enthusiasm for exploring the issues we bring to them genuinely move me. They know, as I do, that the convergence of chemistry and molecular biology *in industry* is a major event, and they want to contribute their good sense, sound values, and ingenuity at this early stage. In practical terms, we are mapping together a strategic timeline reflecting the further development of DuPont's existing capabilities as well as capabilities we will need to develop or acquire as time goes on.

Knowledge Intensity

Knowledge intensity refers to the knowledge content of our products and to knowledge-based services we can provide in association with products or independently. As I have already stated, knowledge intensity is one of our most critical guiding values: Reduced to practice—to real circumstances with customers and markets—it tells us whether we are doing the right things, and doing enough of them to make a difference. Let me illustrate.

DuPont has been producing sulfuric acid, a basic chemical for many industries, for nearly a century. It is a mature business if ever there was one, but in the past seven years, it has grown at an annual rate of 12 percent. Why? Well, this is one of the DuPont businesses that show us the value of the knowledge content of products. We don't just sell sulfuric acid and drive the truck away. We teach our customers how to handle it safely; we design their plants for them; we take the waste streams from their plants and recycle the constituents for other customers. The product is a commodity; however, knowledge-intensive services related to the product are the furthest thing from a commodity. These services represent the state of the art, and they are rooted in DuPont's long internal experience—this is how *we* do it to maximize productivity, promote environmentally conscious industry, and protect our people from the hazards of the chemical workplace. And, of course, we don't have to sell the tank of sulfuric acid to sell knowledge-intensive services.

Things get interesting when you generalize from the practice of our sulfuric acid business to other businesses across the company. I have asked everyone in the company to examine current practices, and we are finding that we have missed opportunities in the past to deliver knowledge content with our products. We often thought that we were just selling products. We often taught safe handling without making clear to our customers how wise it would be to hire us to design a plant that builds safety into every floor plan, every valve.

To formalize and disseminate this new perspective as effectively as possible, we recently turned again to a few outside consultants and a great institution—the Wharton School of Business—to create for us a Knowledge Intensity University. Only a few groups so far have been through its weeklong program, but we are already confident of its value. Participants identify and explore DuPont's knowledge in their specific disciplines and markets, and craft new approaches to adding knowledge content to our products.

Another example of knowledge intensity is safety. We are 12 times safer than the average U.S. industrial company with regard to total recordable injuries and illnesses, and 13 times better in terms of lost workday cases (LWCs). Safety is our heritage, stemming from our long experience with explosives. There was a unique tradition in the old days: When it was time to inaugurate a new process in the explosives plant, a *DuPont family member* was always the first to work the new process. The company would never ask an employee to take the risk because they cared that much about people—and over the years we lost a few family members. That ethic has somehow passed down. You ask, "How in the world could that ethic last 200 years?" I think the answer is that we have insisted on making it a *personal* responsibility rather than an organizational ideal. Every individual has a stake in it, and every employee is individually accountable on a daily basis.

Many global companies today look to us as the world leader in safety. A few years ago we converted that perception—we strive to earn it every day—into a consulting service that now generates some $40 million in annual revenues and has vast potential. There is a problem in the U.S. workplace and worldwide. Every year, the cost of workplace injuries in the United States alone exceeds $60 billion in direct costs. Most of that money is spent after the fact on insurance companies, lawyers—and probably a lot of accounting firms. We maintain that a good percentage of this expense can be eliminated by improved safety practices. And we believe that we have, at most, penetrated but a few percent of the potential market.

To reach that market, we have realistically reshaped our offering. Of course, safety is the right thing for employees, but we're finding that management listens more intently when we spell out that safety helps the bottom line—a business imperative, if you will. We offer a profit-sharing contract: "We'll help you with your safety, we'll make an up-front investment of a well-trained crew—and we'll split with you the savings generated over the first five years." That is our new value proposition. Owing to our leadership in this field and to our willingness to share customers' risks and rewards, it is proving to be enormously attractive.

There is an anecdote behind this new business—sometimes small incidents tell you all you need to know. A few years ago I was visiting with the CEO of one of our top five customers in the world; his company buys annually more than $800 million in DuPont products. I noticed that the CEO could name only a handful of products he bought from us, but he knew our three on-site DuPont safety consultants *by name*. I thought to myself, we're having an impact at the top of this company that we don't appreciate. After two or three experiences of that kind, I realized that we have something of real value here. In the future, when DuPont Safety Resources is fully up and running, I will like the idea of waking up in the morning and knowing that we have some 400 top safety consultants inside major companies, doing their work with exquisite concern and skill—and looking for other DuPont services and products the companies may need. Their advice is sure to influence the products and services we offer, as well as eliminate tens of thousands of injuries per year.

Upgrading the Food Chain

Our Safety Resources initiative is, in our internal language, a "massive project." DuPont's culture, reaching back to the beginning of the twentieth century and earlier, is to welcome massive—and massively complex—projects capable of changing entire industries for the better. Insurers, for example, have taken notice of DuPont Safety Resources, and some anticipate that it will change a major sector of their industry. Similarly, we expect our massive project in agriculture and nutrition to upgrade the quality and quantity of the world's food chain—a huge undertaking, with huge potential benefits for society.

The world population has passed 6 billion, and a conservative number for the year 2050 is 8 billion—and arable land is a finite resource. The world needs to find ways to upgrade the quantity and nutritional quality of food raised on that land. While there may be cyclical farm recessions, over the longer term this is a need and a vast commercial opportunity that will not go away. We are integrating our capabilities in chemistry and molecular biology, and making major acquisitions, to develop offerings for this market.

We recently completed acquisition of a leading agricultural company, Pioneer Hi-Bred, which has tremendous depth of knowledge and capability in the biology, bioengineering, and marketing of seeds. The acquisition will allow DuPont to take a dramatic leap forward in the agricultural applications of molecular biology. Like everyone else, I'm aware of debate in this area, and DuPont is learning from the difficulties that other companies have experienced—by no means with all of their bioengineered products, but obviously with some. Bioengineered medicines have been largely exempt from controversy for the best of reasons: People are getting better or leading longer, higher-quality lives because the medicines work. For DuPont, it has to be that simple in agriculture and nutrition: The value and safety of our products must be evident not just to the farmer but to the consumer.

We have a corn on the market with a guaranteed high oil content that allows the poultry farmer to avoid other, more costly sources of oil in chicken ration. For the farmer, that is a good value proposition. You might ask, what about the consumer who buys that chicken in the supermarket? Has the value moved past the farm gate? And to that I must answer, not yet—but what if DuPont can, through feed enhancements, provide a better-tasting chicken product with lower saturated fat or provide a better-tasting milk substitute with advantages for maintaining healthy cholesterol levels? We do care about risk associated with cardiovascular diseases. These products offer a value choice at the supermarket. These are the types of value-enhanced products that will be reaching consumers.

Our experience with cookware coated with Teflon was a lesson. When we first introduced the product line, there was tremendous uproar: "Cook my food over those chemicals?" But as we learned how to communicate the true and unassailable value of Teflon, the controversy disappeared. "Yes, you can cook on that surface," we said.

"It's perfectly safe—and, by the way, it's incredibly easy to clean and you don't have to cook with butter, so it will help you control your cholesterol level." I'm sure some people still don't buy cookware coated with Teflon, but not many. This experience underlies our model for the agricultural market: Ensure that the product is safe, make clear its singular value not just to early links in the value chain but to the end user, and the consumer will listen.

A DuPont soy product that has been in clinical trials for many years is now being marketed with the U.S. government-backed health claim that it reduces the risks of heart disease. This is a powerful thing; we are keenly interested in the integration of nutrition and medical therapeutics. This is a value sell that all of us can understand and to which we can all respond.

From Corn to Clothing

The integration of chemistry, molecular biology, and agriculture will have a big impact on our traditional synthetic fibers business. Our newest polyester fiber—identified in-house as 3GT and not yet on the market—can be synthesized in part from a starch produced in the field by genetically modified corn. This is an absolute first, and the resulting fiber is by no means an environmentally sensitive, mediocre substitute for something better: It is a first-rate fiber with improved capacity to stretch and recover. This is the most flexible fiber in the world today, and the first wholly new fiber in 40 years. We are extremely optimistic about its market acceptance and more than pleased with its economics—the corn starch is, by orders of magnitude, less expensive than the petrochemical it replaces.

Six Sigma

The reinvention of DuPont—innovation at the scale of an entire global company—also engages our manufacturing and business processes. Like our friend Larry Bossidy at AlliedSignal, who has been so helpful to us in this regard, we have embraced the challenge of *six sigma* performance. On the shop floor, six sigma performance means no more than 3.4 defects per million parts produced. In the business office, it means no more than 3.4 transaction errors per million. And the gist of the six sigma process is to train a company's own black belts—its own manufacturing and business process experts, who learn new process disciplines and then fan out through the company to train others.

The six sigma discipline involves doing not just a dozen or a hundred projects, but literally thousands of small projects that add up. You don't try for a home run, you focus on hitting thousands of singles—and that's how it pays off. We have a tremendous management commitment to this process: One hundred DuPont managers worldwide are specifically responsible for it.

We could have started earlier. Easily 15 years ago, we enjoyed the visit of Dr. W. Edwards Deming, the famed consultant who contributed so much to manufacturing excellence. He would ask us about the manufacture of a certain plastic, for example.

"Hmm . . . How many process improvement projects do you have under way?"

"Well, Dr. Deming," I said, "I think we're up to 30 now."

"You should have 300," he said.

We didn't listen—we may have ramped up to 40 projects. The difference today is that we are engaged in a massive number of projects throughout our manufacturing facilities.

DuPont people are excited. No one likes to work with a process that puts out errors—it doesn't make them want to come to work that day. And, cumulatively, a large number of small projects cuts costs while achieving the most important result of all: improving results for our customers.

Values

We take seriously, and literally, the idea that DuPont reinvents itself each century. As we began our own process of reinvention in 1998, it made sense to check our values. DuPont is an extremely close-knit company, despite our global scale; there really are values among us. How would we express them today, and for our third century? What you'll find in the following differs, I'm sure, from the values charters of most other companies. At DuPont, we aren't wary of strong ideals or of strong words to make them clear and felt. We tested this values charter throughout our company, worldwide. That referendum left them intact. This is what we believe; this is what we are about as a company:

We, the people of DuPont, dedicate ourselves to the work of improving life on our planet. We have the curiosity to go farther . . . the imagination to think bigger . . . the determination to try harder . . . and the conscience to care more.

Our solutions will be bold. We will answer the fundamental needs of the people we live with to ensure harmony, health, and prosperity in the world.

Our methods will be our obsession. Our singular focus will be to serve humanity with the power of all the sciences available to us.

Our tools are our minds. We will encourage unconventional ideas, be daring in our thinking, and courageous in our actions. By sharing our knowledge and learning from each other and the markets we serve, we will solve problems in surprising and magnificent ways.

Our success will be ensured. We will be demanding of ourselves and work relentlessly to complete our tasks. Our achievements will create superior profit for our shareholders and ourselves.

Our principles are sacred. We will respect nature and living things, work safely, be gracious to one another and our partners, and each day we will leave for home with consciences clear and spirits soaring.

In this statement you find all of our values, some of which can be traced to our beginnings in the early nineteenth century: science and innovation, safety and environmental protection, fairness and respect for the dignity of people, uncompromising ethics. No matter how we change or what businesses we engage in, those values make us *DuPont*. The DuPont name—our most powerful brand—has been trusted by commercial customers, individual consumers, and society as a whole for 200 years. Our business will and must change with the times, but we intend to keep that trust.

Knowledge Management

Unifying Knowledge and Action

With the increasingly complex problems that global organizations face every day, intellect has become the infrastructure of competitiveness and success. Knowledge as an asset is beginning to supplant the traditional factors of production—land, labor, and capital—and has become the most important new corporate and competitive resource.

We are witnessing the rise of the knowledge economy. The year 1991 was the first when corporate capital spending on telecommunications, copying, and computer equipment exceeded spending on industrial, construction, mining, and farming equipment combined. More U.S. workers produce and distribute knowledge than make physical goods.

This shift requires that companies become expert in the capture, integration, and use of expertise, know-how, and lessons learned. For today's chief executives, managing the generation, cultivation, and application of knowledge to real-world situations is critical to the ongoing growth and competitiveness of their companies. Prescient chief executives think seriously about intellectual assets. They manage their companies' experience and knowledge in order to solve problems and gain competitive advantage, in part by taking explicit steps to make the organization's expertise available and actionable to each individual.

Knowledge and Knowledge Management

Knowledge is more than explicit methodologies and standards written down in employee guidelines and training programs. If we define knowledge broadly as any intellectual asset, we must then differentiate between different types of knowledge:

> *Explicit knowledge* is recorded. It includes books, manuals, patents, databases, reports, libraries, policies, and procedures. Explicit knowledge can usually be readily identified, articulated, captured, shared, and employed. It may be richly structured or it may be relatively unstructured. In a newspaper, for example, stock price listings are rigidly structured, while most features and editorials are loosely structured by journalistic conventions appropriate to each type of communication.

> *Tacit knowledge* is personal, and in some instances difficult to formalize and communicate. It often takes the form of beliefs and perspectives so ingrained that to articulate or even be conscious of them requires a focused effort. Tacit knowledge is the *wisdom and expertise* in people's heads; it is ideas and know-how that may or may not be proprietary to a business. Tacit knowledge is generally more difficult to extract and codify than explicit knowledge, especially because it is knowledge based in how things are done. It is more commonly shared in conversation rather than in written form. It can be a mix of facts and perceptions, some of these culturally rooted.

The difference between explicit and tacit knowledge is analogous to the difference between the (explicit) rules of golf and the (tacit) spirit of sportsmanship, or the difference between (explicit) patent disclosures and (tacit) trade secrets.

Knowledge management means exercising control over knowledge, acting in such a way that it is used effectively or—as with any business asset—to acquire and then employ it so as to increase the value of the organization. Vast expenditures on the collection of data and information and on a company intranet to share that wealth of knowledge may be largely wasted unless they are aimed at enabling people to innovate, to communicate, to make good decisions efficiently.

CEOs must focus on relevant knowledge. They must act to ensure that the most valuable expertise gets captured and made explicit, that the information technology infrastructure enables staff to find and use relevant knowledge, and that people are encouraged and enabled to acquire knowledge from external sources whenever it is needed. Many companies are good at collecting their explicit wisdom. But effectively capturing and using tacit knowledge is how organizations gain competitive advantage.

Practical Knowledge Management

What follows is a description of steps senior executives can take to begin making the most of their company's tacit and explicit knowledge. These steps demonstrate how different companies are using knowledge management as a practical tool, rather than leaving it on the table as an interesting intellectual concept. They do not comprise a comprehensive, one-size-fits-all list. Solutions should be tailored to the size and type of company. A small company, with all staff on one floor, may not need an intranet to improve visibility: People walk down the hallway to find the expertise that they seek. But they may need a list of common terms and vocabulary. In the medical and pharmaceutical industries, where many scientists have similar backgrounds and share technical terms, vocabulary will already be somewhat normalized. But specialization makes it important to find subject matter experts quickly and easily. Above all, knowledge management demands awareness that intellectual assets are critical components of an organization's power to innovate and overall success.

Focus on the Critical

Much of what has been written on the topic of knowledge management implies—mistakenly—that managers should somehow concern

themselves with all or most of the knowledge existing in their organization. In fact, we all suffer from information overload. As economist Herbert Simon has noted, "A wealth of information creates a
poverty of attention." The amount and scope of knowledge—even
valuable knowledge—exceeds the capacity of any corporation to collect, manage, and use it. Companies that effectively manage knowledge determine carefully what knowledge is vital to their success.
The goal of knowledge management is to enable people to find *relevant* information quickly and easily. Intelligence and discrimination
are fundamental.

What criteria determine critical knowledge? They stem from corporate strategies, core competencies, and, above all, from customers.
Senior management must ask: What knowledge does the organization
need to implement the strategy? What organizational behavior is necessary in order to apply this knowledge? Ericsson, the communications
technology company, determined in 1997 that one of its industry's
value drivers was proprietary technology. As a result, the company
implemented a patent review system that enabled employees worldwide to search and share international patent information. The system's goal was to spread technical knowledge of patents across the
organization, while monitoring the patent activities of competitors.
Patent review has become integral in guiding Ericsson's technology
strategy, and it has contributed to the company's decision to shift its
main business from electromechanical switching and cables to com-
puterized digital switching and cellular mobile communications. (On
this topic, see further Granstrand, Patel, and Pavett, *California Management Review*, June 22, 1997.)

Provide Visibility and Access

In a later discussion in this chapter on knowledge management,
Yahoo! CEO Timothy Koogle quotes Samuel Johnson in words that
bear repeating here. Dr. Johnson recognized more than 200 years ago
that there are two equally important kinds of knowledge: "We know a
subject ourselves, or we know where we can find information upon it."

After determining what knowledge they need, employees must be
able to identify *where* the experts and other sources of knowledge
exist and gain speedy access to this expertise. First and foremost,

expertise must become visible. In smaller offices, this means looking over a cubicle or meeting at the coffee station. In larger organizations, the task is more challenging. Product development managers in Europe and the United States need to "see" knowledge and share it with each other. Financial executives ought to be able to "see" which managers—even those across organizational, geographical, and cultural borders—are expert in the areas of risk, currency hedging, portfolio analysis, and the like. Creating this visibility is more difficult than it sounds. Critical knowledge is something less than splendidly conspicuous at most organizations.

Legal and other professional services firms are largely founded on delivering deep, expert, and timely knowledge to their clients. But visibility isn't just for service firms. As the knowledge economy continues to shape value creation, all types of organizations will need to create more visible knowledge, more visible know-how, more visible experts.

Companies can improve visibility both structurally and technologically. To institutionalize visibility, some organizations establish a network of leaders responsible for harnessing knowledge and illuminating the most visible path to the knowledge most important to the organization. This network need not and perhaps should not resemble the formal corporate management system. Each "champion" in the network should be made responsible for maximizing the capture, organization, and use of the organization's know-how in a given arena. Most important, the leader should be clearly identified. For example, Yahoo! has employees whose sole task is to ensure that information and methodologies from their Santa Clara headquarters are communicated to their satellite offices overseas (and vice versa).

Knowing who knows what can yield results in simple yet profound ways. At one time, different divisions of Monsanto would send people to conferences without knowing who else in the company was going, why the conference was important, and how to use the information gained there. Today, these trips are coordinated: Each attendee is sent with a clear objective and returns with information that must be disseminated to relevant groups and libraries. The result is less duplication of effort and lower costs for the same knowledge.

Technology provides a second critical path to knowledge. Knowledge and the opportunities to use it do not always appear at the same time and place. Telecommunication and information technologies that bring them together are therefore central to knowledge management. As the foundation for communications in today's sprawling organizations, technology can help a great deal in making the hubs of expertise and wisdom visible and accessible throughout the company. Technology is not the only solution, but it is an extremely effective enabler in making knowledge visible.

Technology enables experts to share both explicit and tacit information. Through intranets, companies can collect and distribute explicit knowledge such as presentations and competitor news. At the same time, intranets facilitate tacit exchange through e-mail, bulletin boards, work plans, and real-time communications.

In today's world, the pathways to knowledge often lead to an individual and not—as with information—to a database. Knowledge and information are distinct. Data or information, typically the focus and content of information systems, does not carry the rich context of human interpretation. Data are easily cataloged. Even large amounts of data are made highly visible with modern systems. Most efforts today to make knowledge visible aim to get people in touch with other people—the ones who know something critical. The richest knowledge exchange takes place through human dialogue.

Technologies offer great promise, however, in making even tacit knowledge more visible through such substitutes as simple teleconferencing devices. For example, at BP Exploration, each site is equipped with at least one desktop videoconferencing system, document scanning and sharing tools, and telecommunications network. When a compressor in an oil field in South America broke down, a teleconference with experts in Alaska and Europe enabled a repair in a few hours. (See further Davenport, DeLong, and Beers, *Sloan Management Review*, Winter 1998.)

At a global design company, executives, managers, and designers in three countries use video teleconferencing to work out design details and discuss product developments.

Common Language

Socrates argued that the beginning of wisdom is the definition of terms. How people talk about the world has everything to do with how they understand and act in it—a theme finely developed by Eccles and Nitin in their book, *Beyond the Hype,* from which we draw in part for this section (Harvard Business School Press, 1992). Language is fundamental to effective knowledge management. Imagine a dozen business managers asked to discuss "productivity." One thinks *volume,* a second *profitability,* a third *cost savings. . . .* Without definition, the conversation will be decidedly unproductive.

Establishing a sovereign vocabulary around the use and sharing of knowledge underpins effective knowledge management. An organization has to establish a common terminology that makes it possible to communicate consistently across the entire enterprise as well as with customers and suppliers. This task requires, at a minimum, agreement on the ways in which information should be organized, on key nomenclature, and on standard methodologies. A vocabulary is, of course, more than a list of words: Topical areas can be organized into taxonomies, and relationships among the terms defined. For example, Teltech has a thesaurus of technical terms that allows browsing and searching of the network in ways that make sense to different types of users.

The goal is not merely to avoid experts talking past one another in terms that mean something different to each. A common vocabulary makes it easier to distribute documents and other explicit knowledge and easier to find that knowledge once distributed, much as the Dewey Decimal system makes it possible to browse through topically related books in a library. A common vocabulary also eliminates redundancy and thereby saves money through faster access and decreased storage. Efficient transfer of knowledge enables people in all parts of an organization to locate knowledge that is truly valuable to their work and to distribute knowledge their work has produced.

For some companies, the creation of a common language is the key to competitiveness. Technical Reconnaissance (TRL) is a European provider of health care market information products, recently bought by Skila. TRL has translated the varied languages and terminology of the European health care market into a single common language, through which it provides clients with detailed information on local health care systems, local markets, and other data by country.

What an outstanding exercise in the consolidation of terms into a consistent vocabulary, in a region both enriched and complicated by its many languages.

How to start creating a common vocabulary? It is neither necessary nor desirable in most organizations to impose a new language from the top; an excellent start can be made by identifying communities of people in different locations who can profit from better mutual communication. At one international courier company, an important first step was to agree on common definitions covering "the customer"—which, for a courier company, might designate the individual sender or receiver, corporate accounts, or international delivery affiliates.

Virtual Knowledge

Much of knowledge management has been focused on knowledge embedded in a company—finding the experts, for example, or disseminating lessons learned from projects and processes. But there are other sources. Capturing information from outside through the organization's virtual network—suppliers, customers and ex-customers, expert advisors, industry associations, and regulatory agencies—is no less essential to success. The rise and proven value of the virtual organization is challenging all companies to compete for intellectual assets that they can tap from sources such as alliances with highly sophisticated customers, suppliers, and other business partners. Companies with virtual organizations reaching far beyond their walls develop far deeper understanding of customers, markets, and current products to create new markets, services, and products.

Venkataraman and Henderson have pointed out that companies are becoming virtual in three main dimensions: in the experience offered to customers, in sourcing relationships of all kinds, and in building up expertise (*Sloan Management Review*, Fall 1998). Rather than focusing only on doing a better job of capturing internal information and internally distributing it, companies with leading knowledge management strategies have identified an integrated approach through which tacit and explicit knowledge are combined with knowledge from their vendors, suppliers, and customers.

Yahoo!, the Internet portal whose CEO is a contributor to this book, has a limited number of surfers who organize the immense number of categories in its directory. The company also draws on its customers' knowledge by actively soliciting advice on new and interesting web sites, and how those sites should be classified. In addition, brand loyalty has created open dialogue between the surfers and users of the Yahoo! portal. For instance, a sailing enthusiast recently wrote in to suggest a different (and more logical) way of organizing the sailing site. A customer who knew the ropes willingly added value.

A Learning Culture

While focus, visibility, and language are important enablers of knowledge management, developing a company culture that encourages and rewards knowledge sharing is the best way to optimize a company's intellectual assets.

Culture is the collective name we give to the distinctive values, activities, customs, aspirations, and achievements of a society or group. In a corporation, it is usually a set of shared knowledge, skills, and attitudes applied to any or every element of the business: customers, employees, shareholders, products, service levels, and the like. Obviously, corporate cultures can be influential in fostering growth and innovation, but they can also become obsolete and counterproductive. Management bears great responsibility for constantly reshaping culture to meet evolving corporate goals.

Management fosters a learning culture by creating incentives and processes that encourage teams and individuals to share and capitalize upon the entire organization's intellectual assets. Using and sharing knowledge must be integrated into the fabric of people's jobs. A company mind-set focused on learning *before*, *during*, and *after* actions can be powerful. Actions can be as informal as the bulletin board that one company set up to list the (self-nominated) "Bonehead Move of the Week," that is, a mistake made that week worth publicizing so as to avoid it in the future. It can be as detailed as the U.S. Army's Center for Army Lessons Learned, which conducts detailed postmortems on its missions and actions for distribution among its 1 million troops.

Compensation based on the performance of a group or on the ability of an individual to create knowledge of value to other parts of the organization will quickly dramatize the company's commitment to knowledge sharing. When compensation evaluation is based in part on how often an individual's ideas are used throughout the company, people find ways to contribute. Beyond the carrot and the stick, senior management should find and develop employees who already seize the initiative and are passionate about continually developing the organization's know-how.

Ford Motor Company's Visteon unit, whose 78,000 employees make automotive parts and systems in 19 countries, encourages employees to contribute and harness best-practice knowledge through "Good Samaritan" awards to those who contribute ideas and "copycat" awards to those who use these best practices. But beyond incentives, Visteon seeks to instill a "responsible and accountable" culture among employees regarding their contributions to and use of knowledge repositories. As one company manager explained, "If I go to my management and tell them my equipment efficiency was poor, but I didn't look at the best practices, I'm going to have a lot of explaining to do" (*Computerworld*, February 23, 1998).

Recruiting and retaining people with the right attributes and mind-set to lead an organization through the knowledge management economy requires new ways of developing and rewarding employees. For more on what motivates people to share knowledge and work toward significant innovation, see Chapter 7, "Innovation: New Ideas, Dangerous Ideas."

Measuring Results

Tracking results may seem straightforward—measuring the frequency of use of the knowledge management system and spending time with users to document business benefits, such as closed sales or better solutions. Bob Buckman of Buckman Labs, who spends 3.75 percent of the company's revenues on its knowledge transfer system, dismisses traditional return-on-investment measures: "There are no absolutes. All you can do is increase the probability of success." He chooses to focus instead on speed of customer response—from weeks to hours, for example—as well as the percentage of the workforce that is "effectively engaged with the customer" (cited in *Fast Company*, June 1996).

Specialized consulting companies, such as Celemi, Annie Brookings, and The Technology Broker, take a more formal and comprehensive approach. Celemi focuses on three categories—customers, organization, and people—and monitors the year-to-year changes in such measures as average professional experience, increase in organization-enhancing customers, percentage of repeat orders, and staff turnover. Annie Brookings groups knowledge assets into four categories:

- Human-centered assets (expertise, capability, leadership)
- Intellectual property assets (know-how, patents, design rights)
- Infrastructure assets (technologies, methodologies—elements making up the way the organization works)
- Market assets (branding, market dominance).

The company performs a periodic audit of each of these areas to determine the value of its intellectual assets.

Ultimately, each company will have a different approach to measuring the value of its intellectual assets. As with tracking other kinds of value within organizations, the key is to focus on a few critical measurements and on the long-term value of developing knowledge, rather than on short-term results.

Vision from the Top

The chief executive must convey the expectation that developing knowledge assets is integral to the company's success. The business plan must clearly embody the expectation that knowledge will be stewarded and increased, in the same way that increased revenue is an explicit goal.

Informal information hubs and midlevel champions will not prove to be adequate. A recent internal PricewaterhouseCoopers study of successful knowledge management projects demonstrated that the higher the level of senior involvement, the more likely it is that the project will succeed. Conversely, knowledge management projects with a lower-level champion and no high-level sanction are all but doomed to fail, no matter how motivated or intelligent the champion.

Why is this high level of involvement needed? There are several reasons. The chief executive can allocate the time, money, and resources needed for real actions. More important, changed expectations about sharing knowledge are initially threatening to many in the company, who perceive their value to the organization as rooted in what *they* know that is *not* available to anyone else. Further, only the CEO can champion programs that will affect how the contribution of every person in the company is evaluated.

Ultimately, if an organization is to operate successfully in the new knowledge economy, its CEO and senior managers on down need to develop a culture that values knowledge and, most important, knowledge sharing.

Active Management

Managing knowledge is not a passive endeavor. Senior executives must view the insights and lessons learned by individuals and teams in the organization as resources that need to be fostered, harvested, organized, made accessible, and employed to full advantage. What's more, in light of the worldwide competition among corporations to acquire and make strategic use of valuable, scarce knowledge, companies must increasingly fight for knowledge in several areas. Given the astonishing mobility of today's work, competition for knowledge is especially important as it relates to hiring, developing, motivating, and retaining the best people.

What lies ahead? We believe that information flows, successful applications of knowledge, and innovation will become even more critical in determining corporate success or failure. Only the best, most talented workers will be able to produce a nonstop flow of new products, services, strategies, and business models that provides a sustainable competitive edge. CEOs who can make this happen, who can transform intellect into performance, will be in great demand.

Timothy Koogle

Chairman and Chief Executive Officer, Yahoo! Inc.

Organizing Knowledge throughout the World

Consider the Internet and its rapid development. In 1995, we reached an important junction where several paths of evolution intersected. Personal computers had already developed impressive processing power. They had also become cheap enough to be affordable by large numbers of the public. At the same time, the infrastructure of the Internet had stabilized and software had been created that made it possible to run a vast number of programs. Multimedia technology brought improved sound, sharper color, and sophisticated animation to the PC and the Net.

This conjunction of easy and inexpensive computing completely reshaped the Internet. The costs of new business entry onto the World Wide Web, from sophisticated consulting services to sales of used sporting equipment, dropped lower than ever. Consequently, on the supply side the Internet fostered a truly rich environment for untold numbers of offerings worldwide. On the demand side, this dynamic moved a growing audience now equipped with the computing tools to explore the Internet and use its many resources. This increase in audience traffic in turn stimulated—and continues to stimulate—more authors and more content, thus accelerating knowledge and information creation in geometric proportions. The inexpensive, more powerful PC and its accompanying software have given birth to a pervasive, self-reinforcing cycle.

And there's the rub. The Internet is becoming bigger every day. Sites that have been online for months or years may change daily, while others are abandoned. Imagine going to a library to find a book about dogs, but the books on the shelf are in utterly random order, while trucks pull up to the library and unload thousands of new books hourly. Similarly, millions of people go online daily in search of information that is growing and changing daily. While we are witness to one of the most productive information environments ever created, the riches can easily be overwhelming. People need to make sense of this information. They need a tool that provides context and structure and order.

This is what Yahoo! created. This is why we started our business. We set out to make Yahoo! the only place anyone needs to go to find and connect with anything or anyone, quickly and easily. Nothing in the real world compares.

Connecting and staying connected are real values to people. Further, people perceive value in intelligent uses of knowledge and in having information aggregated for them. Even consumers who are not accessing information in order to make a living are becoming addicted—to the point that they become anxious if there is even a momentary glitch in information access. Today, when there is a pause in access, people get nervous because they are losing contact with a part of their world. They rely on that access. It has become part of their daily lives.

The Knowledgeable Company

We define ourselves as the company that organizes knowledge for the world, but this doesn't necessarily mean that we are knowledge managers in the commonly used sense. To my mind, that term has not been satisfactorily defined. Knowledge management (KM) today typically refers to the technologies that help companies keep information flowing internally. As we are still a small company by head count, knowledge management within Yahoo! means leaning over cubicles and running across hallways to ask questions. The technology-focused definition of KM doesn't have a lot of meaning for us, nor does it describe the compelling part of Yahoo! I want to explore here.

While we have ideas about managing experience and knowledge within Yahoo!, as knowledge managers we are more interested in the role of Yahoo! in the world at large. We are focused on the information needs of the consumer at Yahoo!. *When we talk about knowledge management, we are referring to the way we organize information and knowledge for the outside world.* We enable people, companies, and organizations to discover, harness, and use the vast amount of knowledge that exists on the Internet.

The Path to Intelligent Information

This is the fastest growing, most rapidly transforming industry in which I have ever been involved. We've been running at an astonishingly fast clip for the past four or five years—which amounts to a lifetime in what some call "Web time." But the goal for us at Yahoo! is to make sure that users find at our site a logical, rational presentation of information, and that they are never burdened by this speed or complexity. There is a real danger to information overload. Just as in the case of bug spray.

Bug spray?

I learned the hard lessons of bug spray a long time ago from a mentor at Motorola who was also a neurochemist. He had built his life around studying the structure of the brain and understanding how the nervous system works. Once, when we were attempting to fix a troubled company where people were working feverishly around the clock, he explained the effects of bug spray. Classic bug spray stops the brain from shutting down. If your brain says, "Run," your body sends out chemical nerve impulses. To stop running, another set of molecules must be secreted to suppress these "run" impulses and shut them down. Classic bug spray works by suppressing secretion of the suppressor, so that once a nerve impulse starts to fire, it can't shut down. If you watch a bug that has just been sprayed, you'll see that it just keeps twitching, and it will eventually run out of either oxygen or food, and die.

People and organizations can get into the same syndrome when there is an overabundance of information and no clear map to make sense of it. When this happens, they eventually find themselves, like that dying bug, drowning in stimuli, without any means of sorting out the relative importance of stimuli. We see the Yahoo! directory as anti–bug spray—a rational way of avoiding information overload, identifying their real information needs, and locating that information.

We have been organizing the Internet's information since 1994. During these years, we've learned some guiding principles for making knowledge and information easy to find. These principles enable our users to find information and knowledge more quickly than they would anywhere else:

- Keep the pathways to knowledge visible.

- Keep focused on the information you want, not on the information that will weigh you down.

- Keep vocabulary and terms as clear and objective as possible.

Visibility—The World's Directory

The idea of Yahoo! is classification: Organize web sites into coherent categories; give the Internet a table of contents. In the directory business, we have always focused on navigation from the consumer's point of view, which helps us determine what kind of information and knowledge to build into the directory. We need to understand how consumers look for things on the Internet. It is fundamentally a human issue rather than a technology issue: How do people behave when searching for information?

There are two parts to the answer. First, most people don't know what they're looking for until they see it. They need to look around, sort information, check things out before they find what they really want. Therefore, we need to put information in the logical space where someone would look for it. And we need to do that in a way that reflects the patterns of categorization and selection we observe in people's use of the Internet. At Yahoo!, we actually pay people to surf the Web and help us better understand how users make their choices. The directory is based on knowledge accumulated by the surfers, who make decisions about the quality of thousands of sites, their subject matter, and interconnections between categories. All of this is structured by watching people's consumption patterns and the cross-links they make. If you embrace the evidence that people want to browse by subject and that they will know best how to do this, then study of their behavior will generate a directory that truly works. We're based on the oldest motto in the service business: The customer is always right.

Second, people care much more about the content and services they're looking for than about the technology that delivers it. A woman looking for information about bicycles, for example, cares only about getting the information she needs as easily and as quickly as possible. For us, the goal is to make the means of retrieving content as inconspicuous as possible. This is a very different approach from that of our competitors, who start from a more technological point of view. They have constructed software robots that go out and literally climb inside of sites, extract the text from the site, bring it back, and create a local compressed text database to search. The user constructs a word or a phrase in the form of a search query, which then sends another software robot to enter the database and extract text that may or may not actually be relevant to the user. This is a heavily technocentric solution; it doesn't invite much exercise of human intelligence. Most significantly, it doesn't allow the user to see the context of the information: where it is coming from and how it fits with other possibly relevant information.

Yahoo! has always been a deceptively simple site in technology terms, especially when compared to our competitors, and this approach is successful precisely because it allows for human intelligence. You can see how different the two approaches are if you're shopping for a holiday gift. At a site organized around a search engine, you'll need to type in very specific phrases—usually brand names, rather than gift categories such as wine or mittens—until you hit on some sites that might be relevant. By contrast, the Yahoo! directory always errs on the side of the user. We have a shopping property, Yahoo! Shopping, which is organized by products. Users browse there just as they would in a store—but with infinitely more choices. So you don't just type in J. Crew, you browse in "apparel," which can then lead to categories of apparel, from caps to socks, each of which will offer many different places to go, including J. Crew. Ultimately, there may be thousands of choices even for socks, but they are all organized so that you can look under athletic socks, cashmere socks, and all the rest, rather than a huge jumble of socks, robes, sweaters, and shoes. Or you can move on to chocolate. By showing a table of contents, Yahoo! lets the user find a product or service quickly, rather than spend time typing in search queries.

Stay Focused on the Knowledge You Need

Creating a clear structure for information on the Net requires a deep understanding of the characteristics of the Internet and of people. On the one hand, there is the sprawling, information-rich Web, and on the other there is the human need for organization and selectivity. Successful knowledge management requires juggling the sometimes conflicting needs and requirements of the Web and of people. How much of the Web's content should Yahoo! include on behalf of the user?

The answer is paradoxical: We're extremely inclusive where topics are concerned, but very focused on finding the best web sites. For the directory, we have minimal criteria for the kinds of topics we put in. Basically, if the subject is out there, be it Patty Hearst fan clubs or regional candlepin bowling sites, it's important enough to include in our directory. On the other hand, we are very strict in the editorial process—that is, in deciding which web sites are most relevant, where they should be classified, and how they should link to other categories. As I said earlier, our surfers look through thousands of web sites each day in order to decide whether they should appear in the Yahoo! directory. Yahoo! professional surfers have broad but varied backgrounds in order to overlap user interests and searching styles. By doing a lot of the user's work—by creating classifications and preselecting the most relevant web sites—our surfers enable the user to focus on content rather than wading through hundreds of sites.

Think about a person who is interested in a bicycle trip across Vietnam. By typing in "Bicycling and Vietnam" on Yahoo!, that person will see four site matches with clear directory sections for each site. He or she will clearly see that some sites will give practical advice about the trip, while others offer travelogues about cycling. The user can quickly look through these sites and become more focused on the information that might be needed for a successful trip. Or the user can jump up to the broad category in which these sites appear, so as to direct his or her search more toward information about the country or the activity. The categories preselect and focus on the information the user needs, while allowing the freedom to browse other parts of the Internet. In contrast, typing the same query in a text-based search engine will return a listing of 1,690 sites, including web pages of Vietnam veterans, ecotourism sites, diving vacations, dead sites, and a lot of repetition.

Vocabulary—The Building Blocks of Understanding

Srinija Srinivasan, our vice president and editor in chief, best explains the power and the challenges of vocabulary when she says, "How we choose to name information helps define how users perceive it."

Some of the toughest choices in organizing knowledge boil down to vocabulary: What are you going to call things? There is so much subjectivity and emotion in words. Is a manager strong or tough?

We have two abiding principles that help us resolve these issues. The first is this: While our classification system is an editorial process of selection, when it comes to vocabulary we want to be as objective as possible. We want to present information in the way it was presented to us and pass it on unadulterated. An extreme example that shows the challenges of naming would be a web site devoted to a group who take the Bible so literally that they believe the earth is flat. Whatever our feelings about the subject, we will not put this Flat Earth Society in a category called "Woefully Misinformed"—that is just too editorial. Nor would we categorize these people as "Creationists" because that isn't a term they use; they use the term "Flat-Earthers." So we put their site in the directory under that classification because this is the term that groups of this kind commonly use to describe themselves. We leave it up to the user to decide about the contents.

Surfing with Srinija

Srinija Srinivasan is the vice president and editor in chief at Yahoo!. One of our first employees, she is responsible for maintaining and expanding Yahoo! directories worldwide. Among other things, this means managing and hiring surfers, the people who search out, classify, and categorize the best of the Internet. With millions of web pages added to the Internet every day, she ensures that the knowledge within Yahoo! enables our surfers to organize information in the best way for users. She explains how Yahoo! does it:

Understand the Jobs and Hire Accordingly

There are countless web pages out there, but the challenge of organizing the Web is nothing compared to the challenge of organizing people. It may be a truism, but finding good people and training them is the single most important aspect of developing categories at Yahoo!. The surfers' backgrounds are very different, but they all have something in common—a passion for learning, for organization, and for the Web. We would not be able to survive if we didn't pay enormous attention to recruiting and training.

Training by Feedback (and More Feedback)

When surfers join us, their initial training includes a tremendous amount of feedback. We put them to work from the first day to categorize sites, and for the first three months they get immediate, detailed, and daily comments from several more experienced surfers. Having the experienced surfers review the decisions of new hires adds to the collective wisdom of the group.

Keep People Together

Job candidates are sometimes shocked that we will not allow telecommuting. One of our biggest assets is our collective knowledge. It would be self-defeating if we went out of our way to hire an eclectic group of people and didn't give them instant access to each other to share ideas. Closeness and informality help to create and preserve institutional memory. Low turnover helps keep it.

So far, our turnover has been negligible, and keeping the knowledge within Yahoo! has been fairly easy. People have been through the discussions and the arguments; they understand the way things work. Eighty percent of the time, two different people in Yahoo! will understand and classify the same sites in a similar way.

Apply What Works to the Rest of the Organization

A new producer in Yahoo! now goes through a small surfer training course. Surfer teams have spent so much time refining the best way to find the best information quickly that other teams want to learn the process.

We have a hand in determining what kind of people to look for as we expand overseas. In addition, we have dedicated liaisons based in Santa Clara for each international site, to ensure that these sites are up to date on changes at the main site. This practice is a great communication mechanism for the surfing group. It keeps us alert to developments and changes, and we get good feedback and direction from other parts of the company.

Make Knowledge a Priority

Knowledge managers need to budget time for feedback and discussion. If they understand that time simply must be spent sharing knowledge, they're ahead of the game. Taking that time may be difficult, but it pays off handsomely.

Compounding the vocabulary issue is a language issue. The directory would be much easier to operate (and Yahoo! would be a much smaller company) if we were based only in the United States, with English-speaking users. As of April 1999, Yahoo! actually operates in nine different languages in 14 countries, including Australia, China, and Germany, and 30 percent of our traffic comes from outside the United States. To summarize: We are creating directories in different languages, we must be sensitive and sensible about categories in each language, and we face all the problems of translating from one language to another. To simplify matters, we apply our second principle: We posit that consumers around the globe search for information in the same way—they want to browse categories—and that category concepts, at the highest levels, will be universal. We then apply this rule to the naming process, and the vocabulary is there to serve the underlying concepts.

There is not always a common vocabulary worldwide, and, often enough, several phrases are similar and we must select the most appropriate. When making these decisions in the directory, we apply a set of guiding principles that enable consumers around the world to access information in the same way, no matter the language. We organize our foreign-language directories along the same basic lines as our original English Yahoo! directory. We try to keep as much of the structure as possible when creating other Yahoo!s. For example, there is no nice term for "reference" in German, so we worked with native German speakers to try to find the closest equivalent. We ended up with a fairly long title to get to the "reference" groupings—but the underlying concept remained the same.

Samuel Johnson once said, "Knowledge is of two kinds: we know a subject ourselves, or we know where we can find information upon it." We believe that Yahoo! enables people and companies to increase their knowledge enormously by helping them find information anywhere, at any time.

Once that's been accomplished, there is no limit to what people can accomplish.

Dr. Daniel Vasella

Chairman and Chief Executive Officer, Novartis

Knowledge Focused on Results

I don't have time for wisdom that isn't relevant to the success of Novartis.

The highly competitive dynamics of the health care industry require a focus on results. Our industry is dramatically changing, and costs for health care are driven rapidly upward by an aging population and skyrocketing expenses for hospitals and nursing homes. Insurance companies and governments around the world are trying to contain costs, mainly by exerting downward cost pressure on the prices and reimbursement for drugs.

At the same time, regulators have increased demands for new drug applications, asking for more in-depth clinical studies. In the past 20 years, the number of patients in clinical studies has more than doubled, from approximately 1,500 to 3,500; the number of pages for one new drug application in the United States now reaches close to 100,000, compared to 40,000 in 1980. Research and development expenditures for introducing one drug to the market have increased from about $60 million only 20 years ago to close to $800 million today. The development of new drugs—from discovery to new drug approval—can take 10 years or more, and 90 percent of the projects fail somewhere along the way. The abundance of information implied by these measures requires a ruthless approach to organizing knowledge.

It was this environment that prompted Ciba and Sandoz to merge in 1996, creating Novartis. Our "merger of equals" offered us the opportunity to share the best knowledge and know-how for extraordinary results. At the same time, the merger raised the danger of drowning in a sea of uncertainty, undifferentiated information, competing methodologies, and undefined vocabularies and terms.

We believe in knowledge-based value—brains, not mortar. To succeed, Novartis must be brain-heavy and mortar-light. The keys are:

- *Focus* only on relevant information, and be clear about your priorities.

- Create *transparency* within the organization to discover experts and expertise and to share information.

- Create a company *culture* that is founded on performance and action, and on developing people, respecting the basic human needs for recognition and independence.

Focus

Developing the discipline to say no is as much a key to managing knowledge as it is to managing a company. Without the ability to discern which wisdom will move the company forward, the likelihood of failure increases. Focusing on the right knowledge, while vital, is not something that many companies do well, for all the lip service it gets. I have read that over 95 percent of CEOs thought that knowledge management was going to be critical for their companies' success going forward and that, within their companies, it was easy for people to find the individuals and the information they needed. Frankly, I think this is merely a fashionable answer. I wouldn't be surprised if most chief executives didn't have concrete details about what kind of knowledge sharing occurs within their own companies. Knowledge sharing may happen, but it is often inadvertent and fails to focus on the most important tasks at hand. True, knowledge sharing is important, but it is not my goal in itself. I don't want people just to share knowledge; I want people to produce results.

Knowledge is not relevant unless we translate it into capability. The first task of product development is finding which knowledge should be generated, accumulated, and shared. Knowledge grows stale very quickly unless you keep it continuously flowing and regenerating—a good sign that you're focusing on the correct information. Of course, the challenge is to find the objectives that will lead to the most profitable solutions, the solutions with the greatest potential and need that fit our expertise. Our answer is to create a system to discern the dynamics between the needs of the marketplace and our capabilities (see Figure 8.1).

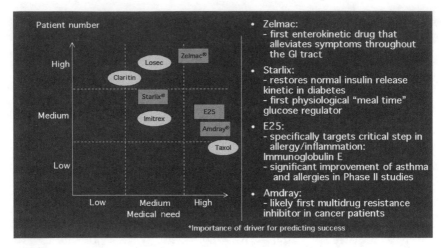

Figure 8.1 Positioning of new launches: high potential for blockbuster.

For example, in pharmaceuticals, we would look at where the untreated or untreatable diseases are, their incidence and prevalence, and the degree of suffering and medical need. The sectors with the highest numbers, the greatest patient pool, and the highest need, with insufficient medical treatments, are the interesting areas to us and offer possibilities for blockbuster drugs. At the same time, we plot through our fields of research, including the specific items in our pipeline and new research concepts such as a new receptor being found or new physiological knowledge, to prioritize those innovative compounds that fit into the high-volume, high-need quadrant of our matrix.

Necessarily, we perform a balancing act between focus and innovation. Scientists by nature create and easily share knowledge; their community defines itself by discourse, interaction, and debate. This type of knowledge sharing is most important to us because we need the interaction of different ideas and opinions in order to stay innovative. We live or die by innovation, and if everybody thinks the same way, without conflicting opinions and ideas, we die.

Transparency

The pitfall for many large science companies, whose research spans several countries and scientific disciplines, is that people do not talk to each other. A breakthrough of little apparent significance in one part of the organization may be the last piece of the jigsaw puzzle in another. To ensure that this communication gap is minimized, we've created an organizational matrix throughout the company.

Organizational Solutions

We developed the matrix system to nudge the far-flung outposts of the group into sharing information. We reorganized our functions—research, development, strategic marketing, and production—so that they are coordinated globally. For example, in development, all projects in pharmaceuticals, whether conducted in Basel, the United States, or China, are responsible to Jörg Reinhardt, head of Development. We therefore can optimally direct, on a global basis, all teams working in cardiovascular and respiratory systems, transplantation, oncology, and so on.

Part of the matrix organization is the multifunctional and cross-geographic project teams that are developed around specific themes. Each team has an expert from a different area within the company—research, clinical research, regulation, toxicology, marketing, and production. Each team member calls on one area of the organization for the relevant know-how and integrates it around a common project. Special teams called Pride (*Proof of Research in Development*) Teams also help rapidly assess the viability of early projects, enabling us to kill nonpromising projects early. We can then focus our resources on full development of the innovative compounds with the most potential to reach market rapidly.

The matrix ensures that we're tapping all of our resources throughout the world and gives us an understanding of how the products fit into the marketplace. It also helps keep us from spending more on R&D than our competitors and wasting money on products that are too costly to manufacture.

Developing drugs demands a paper trail, even if the paper is electronic. There is a file on each project that tracks the experience and wisdom of the development process. It has several roles. It is a contract describing the goals and objectives of the project, as well as a road map outlining the studies and steps, the needed resources. As the project gets under way, the file becomes a living history of what happens, what works, and what doesn't.

Operational Tools — Intranet to Transparency

Technology Enablers to Visibility

A key lesson we're learning from the merger is effectively managing the scope and breadth of our research and development activities. We have gone far past the borders of knowing everything that is going on in research and development. We are too large to operate effectively without using operational tools in order to share knowledge and information across the company. Beyond a group of 100, people cannot interact anymore in the traditional face-to-face way.

One solution is our intranet, the Knowledge MarketPlace, as well as RDS and Pharon, our chemical and genomics databases, all of which contain a broad range of information from professionals at the company, detailing their expertise, research papers, patents, and other information. RDS and Pharon ensure that our internally published scientific publications are globally accessible. Each internal expert knows who the external expert is in his or her research area, and helps other people find additional sources of information and knowledge. Knowledge MarketPlace is valuable for two reasons: for finding expertise, but also for creating a sense of community, since most workers have contact with only 50 to 100 people. In a large, newly merged company, developing norms and commonality between all groups is vital to advancing company performance.

In research, close cooperation between sectors, such as between pharmaceuticals and our seeds business, has the potential to produce substantial benefits. The investments we are making in new technologies such as functional genomics will provide us with better and more targets that can be used in both Pharma and our seeds research. Genomics, mass screening technology, and combinatorial chemistry are all fast, random processes that gather data that we can focus through the lens of functional genomics to provide information. We can share these data across our sectors to look for exciting opportunities in our core businesses.

Visibility has paid off in our development efforts as the different sectors in the company begin to work together. One example is our nutrition and pharmaceutical groups cooperating to create functional food products, an emerging market where we aim to be a strong leader. We've also recently launched a living skin equivalent, combining our expertise in transplantation and dermatology. This product is the only living bilayered skin construct and provides patients who have been suffering from hard-to-heal leg ulcers with an effective solution.

Case Study

How does knowledge sharing work within Novartis? In August 1998, we created a new Consumer Health Division, merging the self-medication and nutrition businesses to focus on functional food and health nutrition. Functional food is food that contains ingredients that have a health benefit—going beyond low-fat cookies, for instance, to cookies that actually lower your cholesterol. It provides an unprecedented platform for leveraging our wisdom and applying our know-how, for building upon our reputation and our relationships with health professionals. Consumers' increasing consideration of retail outlets and supermarkets for health care solutions, including nutritionals for disease prevention and treatment, drives the division.

As an example, let's say that we want to develop a breakfast drink that improves memory. We have two goals: that the drink live up to its promise, and that the drink taste good. Which will be more of a priority? A soft-play approach creates the perception that this drink improves memory. There may also be one or two studies conducted that show the benefit, but the focus will be on the food side, the taste. The hard-play approach, similar to a drug trial, features several rigorous studies that prove that, if you drink our Smart Ovaltine for breakfast, your memory will improve. Our choice would be to blend the best elements of nutrition to create a good-tasting drink, while, in most cases, maintaining the rigor of a hard play. Our ability to do both is our competitive advantage.

Consumer Health allows numerous cross-sector synergies to optimize the flow from prescription to over-the-counter products, and to influence decisions in life cycle product management. Hard-play regulatory knowledge has not been well developed in nutrition. Until now, the nutrition side never had to deal with stringent FDA trials or with complex, long-range project management issues. On the other side, the pharmaceutical people never had to worry whether a pill was tasty, nor did they have to develop a marketing program targeted directly to consumers. The key was to combine the people from pharmaceuticals, who knew how to manage a development portfolio and test products, with the nutrition people, who had a lot of marketing and development experience. Combining these two areas from disparate parts of the company creates something completely new and valuable out of existing expertise.

On the marketing side, Consumer Health brought in knowledge about direct-to-consumer advertising, naturally in greater abundance among our consumer marketers than among our pharmaceutical people. On the other side, we needed the pharmaceutical knowledge about marketing directly to health professionals. By entering the emerging field of functional foods, we have been able to capture the necessary professional marketing experience from pharmaceuticals. The knowledge transfer and experiences of these two sides have been the key to the success of the venture, and our ability to draw wisdom from within the company has been more effective than developing these skills from scratch.

Motivation

The single greatest challenge facing managers is to raise the productivity of knowledge and service workers. You need to help develop people, to give them the opportunity and tools to excel beyond what they can achieve on their own. It requires developing and motivating people within the company, as well as attracting the best people from outside.

What does this mean? I see the new company-employee contract as a split responsibility engaging both parties. Employees must be willing to learn, and the company must provide an environment that promotes and rewards education. We must accustom ourselves to improving knowledge and making it available across groups in all locations.

Let me speak to the first point. By motivating people correctly, we achieve better performance. Motivation can be internal, such as the professional pride that someone takes in doing a job well. Everyone should be internally motivated at Novartis, and we can effect this only by hiring intelligently.

We also spend a lot of time on external motivators, such as recognition and compensation, to focus our employees on relevant knowledge within the company. We have one program called VIVA, which rewards high-performing scientists with access to stock options, additional resources for their research, and recognition as scientific mentors to others in the company. This program emphasizes scientific breakthroughs that move the company forward, rather than the managerial skills of the scientist. The program gives our scientists visibility, internally and externally, in the scientific community.

Other programs include a research symposium that is organized by Paul Herrling, the worldwide Head of Research at Novartis. He invites researchers from our laboratories around the world to present their research at an internal symposium. As at a science fair, scientists can walk around and check other projects throughout Novartis and find out if someone has ideas or labs that can help with their own projects. This occasion shifts the innovation/focus balance more toward innovation.

We tilt back toward focus in our knowledge-sharing incentives. The project groups require teamwork in order to achieve results; therefore, 50 percent of an individual's evaluation may depend on the entire team's performance. In addition, we can greatly increase productivity by more sharing of compounds and ideas. The productivity increase we can anticipate in research alone is greater than 30 percent through this knowledge-sharing process. If an individual has a brilliant mind but was unable to push the project forward, this will be reflected in his or her compensation. Again, we don't reward just for being smart. I don't really care if a scientist knows a lot about world history. It's nice that he or she is knowledgeable, but that's not going to help the company in any way.

Pushing the project forward doesn't necessarily mean that the project will continue. Effectively focused knowledge entails the freedom to say no. We've given awards to project teams that shut down their own projects. It's not bad but, rather, it's necessary to stop a project decisively if you see that it isn't working. From the company's point of view, it's much more important to spend resources wisely.

The second aspect, that of bringing the best people into the company, is vital to our work. We survive on the knowledge of our scientists, so we need to make sure that we're developing a culture and incentives that are attractive to these scientists. Rarely do the issues boil down to compensation, especially in research. Large life-sciences companies usually rank third on a really talented scientist's list of places to work, after universities and biotechnology companies. While employees want to be paid what they're worth, it's just as important that they have decision-making freedom, access to resources, an understanding of the level of bureaucracy and how much paperwork is needed to get a pencil, and so on. These so-called soft things are the hard issues that will bring world-class scientists into Novartis.

Sharing and developing knowledge aren't just for our scientists and our marketing professionals. They must be instilled throughout the company. On the management side, we've had a long-standing alliance with the Harvard Business School. We've developed a program with Harvard that focuses on leadership and change. I've sent most of my top managers to the program—about 420 people so far. We started this project because, when a group of people learns together, its members share a common experience. Moreover, by having the experience outside the company, people have the freedom to speak critically in a way they might not do on-site. The challenge is to push the understanding gained by external training through the rest of the organization, to every individual. The most important ingredient of a knowledgeable community is developing internal motivation to change—not the organization, not others, but you, the individual.

Conclusion: The Knowledge Company at Work

Novartis is about results. We did not install these knowledge-sharing incentives because it was trendy. We did it because knowledge sharing is essential to world-class performance. The results of the increased awareness around knowledge sharing have been striking, from a reinvigorated research pipeline to increased profit margins.

The half-life of knowledge is constantly decreasing. Figuratively speaking, everything that's written today will be irrelevant tomorrow. Our people must constantly replenish and update what they've learned. I realized how important this process was the moment I saw one of our drugs losing market share to a competitor. What bothered me the most was that we could have prevented it, had we given more time and attention to what the customer was looking for. What frustrated me was the lack of energy in the responsible group, energy that would have been needed to break down barriers between ourselves and the customers. A knowledge company means having the energy to surmount these barriers—to listen, to seek input. Knowledge sharing must happen more frequently, so that, for example, our crop protection people will speak not merely to our internal marketing department, but also to the nutrition group, the farmers who buy our goods, the retailers, and so on.

Creating this dialogue is obviously a high priority. At the same time, however, there are so many things to do in a day. People are so absorbed; therefore, unless this motivation for wisdom is instilled within our people, even great products will fail. At the heart of our business, great products and good management provide the essential ingredients for success.

Yotaro Kobayashi
Chairman and Chief Executive Officer, Fuji Xerox Co., Ltd.

Ba
A Place for Managing Knowledge

Today, capital and labor alone are inadequate competitive weapons. Success in the international marketplace comes increasingly from giving employees the tools to express their creativity, to interact with others, and to draw upon the collective wisdom of the organization in order to develop unique products and services.

This process is what we mean by *knowledge management* at Fuji Xerox. The term is becoming common, but I think our view of it is unique. Our version of knowledge management rests on a simple foundation. I am a strong believer in the virtue of patience—allowing ideas, and the products they might become, to develop at their own pace. While it is possible to force an idea along its natural evolutionary path, something is likely to be lost in the effort. Creativity is organic, and it flourishes in what you might call an intellectual ecosystem. If we turn that ecosystem into a hothouse for rapid growth, we will almost certainly damage what we are trying to produce.

I know that many companies take a hard-line approach to knowledge management, in the conviction that only "relevant" knowledge deserves attention and resources. Yet what is irrelevant today may be of critical importance tomorrow. Ideas that are vague and ill-defined right now may harbor in their shadows the revolutionary product of the future.

I suspect that few CEOs today would regard ancient Greek philosophy as knowledge relevant to their business. Joe Wilson, known as the father of Xerox and an extremely important mentor of mine, advised me many years ago to enroll in The Aspen Institute's Executive Seminar. I did so and found that the reading list at Aspen was heavily weighted toward the classics, including Plato and Aristotle. Did the knowledge I gained lead to a new research breakthrough in reproduction science? No. Did the ancient quest for knowledge through dialogue influence my approach to business and the management of Fuji Xerox? Absolutely!

Knowledge management begins with the definition of terms; these definitions inform how the company approaches tasks and goals, even how we speak. Professor Ikujiro Nonaka, one of knowledge management's most influential scholars, and the first recipient of our Distinguished Professorship in Knowledge at UC Berkeley, has drawn the distinction between *explicit* and *tacit* knowledge. Explicit knowledge is the clearly defined, scientific research and information that informs much of our day-to-day business. Tacit knowledge is largely intangible, and harder to define. It is know-how, experience, personal insights, and beliefs. I think that many companies, including Fuji Xerox, have successfully harnessed explicit knowledge, but hierarchies, bureaucracies, and cultures all make it much more difficult to share tacit experience, perspectives, beliefs, and ideas. My personal vision is to go beyond explicit knowledge and share our employees' personal, tacit knowledge with the rest of the organization. Ultimately, I want to create a knowledge-driven company, in both structural and human terms.

Our corporate mission statement recognizes these categories with its use of the Japanese term for knowledge, *Chi*. In Japanese, *Chi* has strong overtones of tacit knowledge; it implies knowledge that has yet to be made specific or assume the form of information. *Chi* suggests something close to wisdom—more difficult to grasp than data, strongly informed by human relationships and experience.

Our commitment to *Chi* is the focal point of that mission statement: Advancing knowledge is at the center of our business objectives. It is worth emphasizing that this statement was not imposed on our company by management. It grew out of a yearlong exploration of our shared values and goals that involved all of our staff, regardless of nationality, language, culture, or location. By consensus, and by passionate commitment, the advancement of *Chi* is our identity. We strongly believe that people wish to be more productive, and they need products to assist them toward that goal. We create these products, and we can only do so at high levels of quality and profitability by constantly advancing our knowledge—and not simply our knowledge of the technical attributes of our products. That is one reason that we took a leadership role in establishing The Aspen Institute Japan in 1998.

Japanese companies have traditionally been very good at generating knowledge. But entrenched hierarchies, combined with geographical and cultural boundaries, have often kept Japanese companies from putting the knowledge they generate at the disposal of the whole organization. Today, all companies need to expand abroad and develop creative corporate cultures to remain competitive. My goal is to break down the barriers of rank, function, and geography that prevent ideas from spreading. To that end, we need to develop a new Japanese management model, which combines the best of Anglo-American with Japanese approaches.

Ba

We have begun this task at Fuji Xerox, but we have only begun. We have started with respect—respect for knowledge, for *Chi*—and regard that as an unshakeable value. At the same time, we have created what we call, for lack of a better term, *spaces* where knowledge can be exchanged freely, where employees and customers alike can become wiser. In Japanese we have a word, *Ba,* which might loosely be translated as this kind of space. At our company we think of *Ba* as a shared space for nurturing the creation of knowledge. These spaces may be physical, such as research and development laboratories, which have always been devoted to learning. They may be virtual spaces, such as intranets and e-mail, in which people can communicate. And they are also mental—an attitude, a climate, in which the exchange of ideas can take place freely, easily, without expectations of application or profit. Above all, these *Ba* enable and support *Chi.*

The challenge now is to work with these elements of our culture to generate tools that facilitate the visibility and accessibility of the collective wisdom of Fuji Xerox. Some tools will harness primarily explicit knowledge. For example, we have created the Virtual Office for our marketing personnel in Japan. It was partially developed by Tokyo's marketing division and further augmented for use by all marketing personnel across the country. The Virtual Office is a series of databases that highlight details on markets and clients, as well as stored proposals. It also gives our sales representatives information—such as a client's uses of Fuji Xerox office equipment, industry trends, corporate performance and affiliations, and R&D efforts. All this is to say that the Virtual Office gives our employees tools to create their own sales approaches to their clients.

Closer to the area of tacit knowledge, with its priceless component of human exchange, is a program called Talknade (a compound word from Talk and Promenade), which was launched in the mid-1980s. It is a way of getting people together with others from all levels and areas to speak their minds. We are trying here to do something that sounds simple but is in fact enormously difficult and rarely attempted: to increase the extent to which people use their minds in highly innovative ways to improve our products and better serve our customers. Innovation is a process that proceeds by its own rules, different in every situation and with every person. The whole idea of Talknade is to encourage people to exchange informally— about serious subjects. Previously, when we brought groups of people together, we would oblige them to arrive with prepared data and statements—you needed definite ideas and plans. There is nothing wrong with that. We would never get anything done if we didn't demand accountability. But we recognized the need to create a *Ba* at an early stage in the creative process, an informal space that fosters interactions between clear-cut know-how and information and tacit knowledge.

Kokomade Yarunoka Xerox

The Talknade program varies in size, composition, and theme. Senior management is always present. We try to encourage informal but clear exchanges of ideas—think of it as the equivalent, in Asian business practice, of sitting around a campfire telling stories and exchanging ideas. When I was president of Fuji Xerox, the largest Talknade group we assembled was some 200 people, who spent the entire day in something like a dozen or more teams engaged in informal exchange. The last few talks, under President Sakamoto's direction, have been clearly centered on our Japanese motto, KYX (*Kokomade Yarunoka Xerox*). The usual translation is "Fuji Xerox is totally dedicated to our customers," or, more loosely, "Xerox, you do this much for me!" But this loses the subtlety of the language. Literally it means, "We will do anything for our customers." It places customers at the heart of our business philosophy.

The Collective Wisdom of Fuji Xerox and Xerox

Fuji Xerox is one of the oldest joint ventures. A pioneering partnership was established in 1962 between Fuji Photo Film and Rank Xerox, itself a Xerox joint venture with Britain's Rank Organisation. The original objective was to enable Xerox to create a presence in Japan and throughout Asia to market copiers. Technology sharing had little place in the original agreement.

Starting as a simple marketing unit, Fuji Xerox would later blossom into a major center of product innovation and improvement. It became what Xerox Chairman Paul Allaire called "a critical asset of Xerox." How did this happen? By the 1970s, Fuji Photo Film and Rank Xerox had become passive partners in Fuji Xerox. This enabled the joint venture to exercise a fair amount of autonomy while it continued to receive a flow of technology expertise from Xerox.

Fuji Xerox did have a technical task—modifying product designs to suit local market conditions. Given its relative autonomy and enormous potential, it became increasingly capable of developing and manufacturing proprietary copiers. Gradually, the division of labor between the companies shifted, and Fuji Xerox acquired more and more responsibility in Xerox's global product delivery strategy.

The turning point may have been in the 1980s, when Xerox was losing market share to Japanese competitors. It took Xerox years to realize that it had the competitive expertise to regain lost ground—resident at Fuji Xerox. Once Xerox recognized its substantial intellectual asset in Fuji Xerox, management acted decisively to ensure that the company used this link well to transfer Japanese best practices, such as the Leadership Through Quality program (adapted from Fuji Xerox in 1983). Over 200 Xerox and Rank managers visited Fuji Xerox facilities to learn about benchmarking and quality management programs—particularly after the highly successful global introduction by Fuji Xerox of the 3500 copier. The year was 1978. In 1980, Fuji Xerox won the coveted Deming Award.

We have had some interesting results from Talknades, which further our wish to blend the best of Japanese and Western wisdom into a new company intelligence. As a result of Talknades, we have introduced a flextime scheme for our employees, and have also created a women's committee to make sure that we are being responsive to all of our workforce. We have created a venture fund that allows our people to develop their own business concepts and spin them off into affiliated companies. These may not seem significant or even new ideas in the West, but they are still rare concepts and practices in Asia. As a result of Talknades, we have set up a special type of customer center, a final gate where our customers can speak to us when all other channels for service in the company have somehow failed to satisfy. It functions both to help the customer and to help us understand how well our services are being used and understood.

Best of all, as Talknade continues, tacit knowledge sharing is creating interesting chemistry among people of different expertise and functions within R&D and headquarters. It is producing solutions and ideas that would be unattainable through a rigidly logical scientific approach. It is leading to new *Bas*, such as satellite offices, located between our main offices and equipped with a full technology infrastructure, Internet access, and library. In Japan, where the commute to work can take as long as two hours each way, these satellites promote work/life balance and increased productivity.

Another program intended to harness tacit knowledge is our employee rotation exchange with Xerox in the United States. Some 10 years ago, all of the Xerox partners agreed to work more closely together. We launched joint projects. Exchanges of personnel and an evolving communication process reinforced research collaboration. Fuji Xerox people spent time as residents at Xerox, and engineers from both companies frequently crossed the Pacific to provide on-the-spot assistance. These exchanges were also an important channel for technology transfer between the companies. Typically, about 10 people from the United States or Europe come to Fuji Xerox, while about 90 of our people from Asia go to Xerox offices around the globe.

The Result

Obviously, it's difficult to measure precisely how these efforts are paying off. That is why some CEOs question their value. Measurable results are probably out there, but further down the line. We certainly see change in the ways that people interact with each other and in the ways that new products, services, and solutions are created and shared within the company. There is no question that we are achieving higher productivity, and I believe that we are creating better products and solutions for our customers. We are working with one of the largest Japanese electronic and entertainment companies to help it develop global solutions for office documentation. For another client, a large automotive company, we are working with its people to manage a vast library of operational manuals. Groups from the United States, Europe, and Japan have joined us in this project to disseminate the new solutions across the client's global organization. This collaboration occurred as a result of our global account management process, and it involved everyone from the CEO down. The solutions combine technology, alterations in work environment, and human factors. And many companies are now benchmarking this as a best practice.

As these examples make clear, we are making the transition from a commodity business to a company with knowledge-based, integrated values to offer our customers. And that is where the payoff is. If you can offer your customers the benefits of your knowledge, you enrich them and at the same time enrich your company. That mutual benefit is the goal, and knowledge is the means.

CEO Biographies

AlliedSignal Inc.
Lawrence A. Bossidy

Lawrence A. Bossidy became chief executive officer of AlliedSignal, an advanced technology and manufacturing company, in July 1991, and was named chairman of the board on January 1, 1992. He previously served in a number of executive and financial positions with General Electric Company, a diversified service and manufacturing company, which he joined in 1957 as a finance management trainee. Mr. Bossidy was vice chairman and executive officer of GE from 1984 until he joined AlliedSignal.

He is on the board of directors of Merck & Co., Champion International Corporation, and J.P. Morgan & Co., Incorporated. He is a member of the Business Council and the Business Roundtable. Born in 1935 in Pittsfield, Massachusetts, he is a 1957 graduate of Colgate University, with a major in economics.

ABB
Göran Lindahl

Göran Lindahl is president and chief executive officer of ABB, a global technology and engineering company of some 170,000 people in more than 100 countries. Under his leadership, ABB is transforming itself into a leading company in the new global knowledge and service economy. Mr. Lindahl is also determined to speed up the rate of technology innovation at ABB by establishing an environment that fosters creativity and challenges people to achieve breakthroughs that overturn conventional ways of thinking.

Mr. Lindahl began his career in 1971 with ASEA AB, the former Swedish co-parent of ABB, and has held a number of senior management positions, including head of the Transmission and Distribution Segment. He has also held regional responsibilities for the Asia Pacific region, the Indian subcontinent, the Middle East, and North Africa.

Mr. Lindahl holds a master's degree in electrical engineering and an honorary doctorate in technology, D.Sc. (Eng.), both from Chalmers University in Sweden. He is a member of the boards of directors of U.S.-based DuPont and LM Ericsson AB of Sweden. He holds appointments on a number of international and multilateral associations, including vice chairman of the board of the Prince of Wales Business Leaders Forum, and member of the World Commission on Dams.

AT&T
C. Michael Armstrong

Since November 1977, Michael Armstrong has been chairman and chief executive officer of AT&T, a provider of voice, data, and video communications services to businesses, consumers, and government agencies. Prior to joining AT&T, Mr. Armstrong was chairman and chief executive officer of Hughes Electronics. From 1961 to 1992, he held a variety of posts at IBM, including senior vice president and chairman of the IBM World Trade Corporation.

Mr. Armstrong is on the board of Citigroup and the supervisory board of the Thyssen-Bornemisza Group. As well, he is chairman of the President's Export Council and the FCC Network Reliability and Interoperability Council. He is a trustee of Johns Hopkins, and a member of the Council on Foreign Relations. Mr. Armstrong received his bachelor of science degree in business and economics from Miami University of Ohio in 1961 and completed the advanced management curriculum at Dartmouth Institute in 1976.

Baxter International Inc.
Harry M. Jansen Kraemer, Jr.

Harry M. Jansen Kraemer, Jr. is president and chief executive officer of Baxter International Inc., having served in that capacity since January 1999. He also serves on Baxter's board of directors.

Mr. Kraemer joined Baxter in 1982 as director of corporate development. His career at Baxter has included senior positions in both domestic and international operations. In 1993, he was named senior vice president and chief financial officer, responsible for all financial operations, business development, communications, Baxter Export Corporation, and European operations. In April 1997, Mr. Kraemer was named president of Baxter International Inc. Before joining Baxter, Mr. Kraemer worked for Bank of America in corporate banking, and for Northwest Industries in planning and business development.

Mr. Kraemer serves on the boards of directors of Comdisco, Inc., Highland Park Hospital, Science Applications International Corporation, and Northwestern University's J.L. Kellogg Graduate School of Management Advisory Board. He also serves on the board of trustees for Lawrence University.

A certified public accountant, Mr. Kraemer graduated from Lawrence University in Wisconsin in 1977 with bachelor's degrees in mathematics and economics. He received a master of management degree in finance and accounting from Northwestern University's J.L. Kellogg Graduate School of Management in 1979.

Bestfoods
Charles R. Shoemate

Charles R. Shoemate is chairman, president, and chief executive officer of Bestfoods. He was elected president and a member of the company's board of directors in October 1988, and became chief executive officer in August 1990 and chairman the following month. Mr. Shoemate joined Bestfoods in 1962 and progressed through a variety of positions in manufacturing, finance, and business management within the consumer foods and corn refining businesses. He was elected vice president of the corporation in 1983, and in 1986 became president of the Corn Refining Division.

Mr. Shoemate is a director of CIGNA Corporation, International Paper Company, Texaco Inc., and the Grocery Manufacturers of America, Inc. He is chairman of the Conference Board and a member of the Business Roundtable. Born in Illinois in 1939, Mr. Shoemate is a graduate of Western Illinois University and holds an M.B.A. in marketing and finance from the University of Chicago.

Blockbuster Inc.
John F. Antioco

Since 1997, John F. Antioco has been chairman and chief executive officer of Blockbuster Inc., the world's leading renter of videos and video games. Before joining Blockbuster, Mr. Antioco was president and CEO of Taco Bell, the leading Mexican-themed quick-service restaurant chain. Prior to Taco Bell, Mr. Antioco was CEO and chairman of the Circle K Corporation, a convenience-store chain, which he also brought public in 1995. In addition, he has held a variety of senior positions, including those at Pearle Vision and the Southland Corporation (7-Eleven), where he began his career.

Mr. Antioco holds a degree in business administration from the New York Institute of Technology.

Corning Incorporated
Roger G. Ackerman

Roger G. Ackerman was elected chairman of the board and chief executive officer of Corning Incorporated, a diversified specialty material, communications, and consumer product company in April 1996. Before this, he had assumed a variety of engineering, sales, and management posts at the company, including president of a Corning subsidiary, Corhart Refractories Co., general manager and vice president of the Ceramic Products Division (1975), and senior vice president (1980). In 1981 Mr. Ackerman became the director of the Manufacturing and Engineering Division, in 1983 the president of MetPath

Inc., and in 1985 the group president of Specialty Materials and a director. In 1990 he was elected the president and chief operating officer of Corning. Mr. Ackerman joined Corning in 1962.

Mr. Ackerman is a director of the Pittston Company, the Massachusetts Mutual Life Insurance Company, and the Dow Corning Corporation. He is president of the Foundation for the Malcolm Baldrige National Quality Award, and chairman of the Business Council of New York State. He is a member of the Business Roundtable, the Business Council, and the Rutgers University Foundation Board of Overseers.

Mr. Ackerman is a graduate of Rutgers University and the P.M.D. program at Harvard, with an honorary doctorate from Rutgers University.

Dell Computer Corporation
Michael S. Dell

Michael S. Dell serves as chairman and chief executive officer for Dell Computer Corporation, the world's leading direct computer and computer systems company. Mr. Dell founded the company in 1984.

He is a member of the board of directors of the U.S. Chamber of Commerce and the Computerworld/Smithsonian Awards. Mr. Dell serves on the nominating committee for the National Technology Medal of Honor and is a member of The Business Council. He is also a member of the Computer Systems Policy Project. Mr. Dell attended the University of Texas at Austin.

DLJ*direct* Inc.
K. Blake Darcy

K. Blake Darcy is chief executive officer of DLJ*direct*, a Donaldson, Lufkin & Jenrette company and one of the first providers of online discount brokerage services. Mr. Darcy began his career in the financial services industry as a retail broker with Lehman Brothers. In 1984, he joined Donaldson, Lufkin & Jenrette, where he was chosen to form a new business unit at DLJ's Pershing division. In 1988, Mr. Darcy introduced DLJ*direct* (originally PC Financial Network).

Mr. Darcy graduated from Hamilton College with a bachelor of arts degree in government.

DuPont
Charles "Chad" O. Holliday, Jr.

Charles "Chad" O. Holliday, Jr. is chairman and chief executive officer of DuPont, the science company. Since joining the company in 1970, Mr. Holliday's career has touched virtually every DuPont business—from fibers and chemicals to agricultural products and biotechnology, and across all key functional areas: manufacturing, marketing, finance, planning, and business management.

Mr. Holliday serves on the board of directors of Pioneer Hi-Bred International, Inc., and Analog Devices, Inc. He is on the Chancellor's Advisory Council for Enhancement at the University of Tennessee at Knoxville and is a senior member of the Institute of Industrial Engineers. He is also a member of the board of Winterthur Museum and Gardens in Wilmington, Delaware.

Born in 1948 in Nashville, Tennessee, Mr. Holliday is a graduate of the University of Tennessee, where he received a bachelor of science degree in industrial engineering. He has an honorary doctor of science degree from Washington College in Chestertown, Maryland.

Eaton Corporation
Stephen R. Hardis

Stephen R. Hardis is chairman and chief executive officer of Eaton Corporation, a global manufacturer of highly engineered products that serves industrial, vehicle, construction, commercial, aerospace, and semiconductor markets. Before becoming CEO in 1995, Mr. Hardis was chief financial and administrative officer and vice chairman of the company. He has also held positions at a variety of other companies, including executive vice president at Sybron Corporation and, before that, with General Dynamics.

Mr. Hardis is on the boards of directors of American Greetings

Corporation, KeyCorp, Progressive, Nordson, Lexmark, and Marsh & McLennan. He is also a trustee of the Musical Arts Association (Cleveland Orchestra), Cleveland Clinic, Playhouse Square Foundation, Greater Cleveland Roundtable, and Cleveland Tomorrow.

Born in 1935, Mr. Hardis received a bachelor of arts degree, Phi Beta Kappa, from Cornell University, and a master's degree in public and international affairs from Princeton University.

EDventure Holdings Inc.
Esther Dyson

Esther Dyson is chairman of EDventure Holdings Inc., a small but diversified venture capital company focused on emerging information technology worldwide and on the emerging computer markets of Central and Eastern Europe. Before founding EDventure Holdings, Ms. Dyson was a securities analyst at New Court Securities and at Oppenheimer & Co. She began her business career as a reporter for *Forbes* magazine.

Ms. Dyson sits on the boards of Scala Business Solutions, Poland Online, New World Publishing, Global Business Network (a consulting organization), ComputerLand Poland, Cygnus Solution, E-Pub Services, Thinking Tools, Accent Software, Medscape, APP (Prague), PRT Group, TrustWorks (Amsterdam), IBS (Moscow), and iCat, and on the advisory boards of Perot Systems and the Internet Capital Group.

Ms. Dyson is also the interim chairman of ICANN, the Internet Corporation of Assigned Names and Numbers, a member of the board of the Electronic Frontier Foundation, and a member of the President's Export Council Subcommittee on Encryption. She also is a member of the boards and executive committees of the Santa Fe Institute, the Institute for EastWest Studies, and the Eurasia Foundation. She is also a founding member of the Russian Software Market Association. She serves on the advisory boards of the Software Entrepreneurs Forum (Silicon Valley), the Poynter Institute for Media Studies, the Russian Internet Technology Center, and the Soros Medical Information Project.

Ms. Dyson graduated from Harvard in 1972, with a B.A. in economics.

EMC Corporation
Michael C. Ruettgers

Michael C. Ruettgers is president and chief executive officer of EMC Corporation, the world's technology and market leader in the rapidly growing market for intelligent enterprise storage systems, software, and services. He has been CEO since 1992, and president since 1989. Since Mr. Ruettgers joined the company, EMC's annual revenues have increased from less than $200 million to more than $5 billion in 1999. Before joining EMC, Mr. Ruettgers was chief operating officer of Technical Financial Services and held senior executive positions at Keane and at Raytheon, where he spent much of his early career.

Born in 1942 in Muskogee, Oklahoma, Mr. Ruettgers received his B.S. from Idaho State University and his M.B.A. from Harvard Business School.

Ford Motor Company
Jacques A. Nasser

Jacques A. Nasser became president and chief executive officer of the Ford Motor Company in 1999. Since joining Ford of Australia in 1968 as a financial analyst, Mr. Nasser has held a number of positions with Ford's international and U.S. operations, including assignments in Asia-Pacific and Latin America. In 1987, he was named director–vice president, finance and administration, for Autolatina, the holding company that oversees Ford and Volkswagen operations in Brazil and Argentina. He was named president of Ford of Australia in 1990 and chairman of Ford of Europe Inc. in 1993. He became group vice president—Product Development, Ford Automotive Operations, in 1994, and chairman of Ford Europe in 1996.

Born in Australia in 1947, Mr. Nasser received his degree in business studies from the Royal Melbourne Institute of Technology.

Fuji Xerox Co., Ltd.
Yotaro Kobayashi

Yotaro Kobayashi is chairman of the board of Fuji Xerox Co., Ltd., a fifty-fifty joint venture between Fuji Photo Film and Rank Xerox (now Xerox Limited), which produces and supplies various kinds of office equipment including color copiers, networked systems, multi-functional machines, and integrated printing systems. Mr. Kobayashi joined Fuji Photo Film in 1958 and was assigned to Fuji Xerox in 1963. He was promoted to president and chief executive officer of Fuji Xerox in 1978 and attained his current position in 1992.

Mr. Kobayashi serves on the boards of directors of Xerox Corporation, Callaway Golf Company, and ABB Ltd. in Switzerland. He is chairman of both the Trilateral Commission and Keizai Doyukai (Japan Association of Corporate Executives). He is a member of the J.P. Morgan International Council and Booz-Allen & Hamilton's International Advisory Board and serves as a trustee of the University of Pennsylvania and Keio University.

Mr. Kobayashi received a bachelor's degree in economics from Keio University in Tokyo in 1956, and an M.B.A in industrial management from the Wharton School of the University of Pennsylvania in 1958. He also received an honorary doctorate in humane letters from St. Peter's College in New Jersey.

HSBC Holdings plc
Sir John Bond

Sir John became group chairman of HSBC Holdings plc in 1998, having been group chief executive since 1993. He is also chairman of HSBC Bank plc, HSBC Bank Middle East, HSBC USA Inc., and HSBC Bank USA, and a member of the boards of The Hongkong and Shanghai Banking Corporation Limited and The Saudi British Bank.

Sir John joined The Hongkong and Shanghai Banking Corporation Limited in 1961 and worked in Asia for 25 years and the U.S.A. for four years, before coming to London in 1993.

Sir John is a member of the board of directors of the London Stock Exchange and a nonexecutive director of Orange plc. He is also chairman of the Institute of International Finance, Washington, D.C., and serves on the Advisory Board of the International Finance Corporation, a member of The World Bank Group.

Johnson & Johnson
Ralph S. Larsen

Ralph S. Larson is chairman and chief executive officer of Johnson & Johnson, posts he has held since 1989. He has been with Johnson & Johnson since the beginning of his business career, where he has worked in a variety of leadership posts across the company divisions, including McNeil Consumer Products and the Chicopee Division.

Mr. Larson also serves on the board of directors of Xerox Corporation and AT&T. He is a member of The Business Council and The Business Roundtable. Born in Brooklyn, New York, in 1938, he holds a B.B.A. from Hofstra University.

Lafarge Group
Bertrand P. Collomb

Bertrand P. Collomb has been chairman and chief executive officer of Lafarge, suppliers of construction materials in North America, since 1989. He joined the group in 1975. At Ciments Lafarge France, he was successively regional director, general manager, and chief executive. He was appointed an executive vice president of the group in 1982. From 1983 to 1985, he headed the group's business in bioactivities as chairman of Orsan, and then took charge of the group's North American subsidiary, Lafarge Corporation, between 1985 and 1988.

Mr. Collomb is also on the board of the Canadian Imperial Bank of Commerce, Crédit Commercial de France, and Elf Aquitaine. Born in Lyon, France, in 1954, Mr. Collomb holds an undergraduate degree from L'Ecole Polytechnique, a law degree from University

Nancy, and a Ph.D. in management from the University of Texas at Austin.

Lloyds TSB Group
Sir Brian Pitman

Sir Brian is the chairman of Lloyds TSB Group, the English banking concern. He began in Lloyds Bank in 1952 and has gained experience throughout the company, culminating in his ascension to chairman in 1997.

Sir Brian is also the governor of Ashridge Management College, the director of Carleton Communication PLC, and the chairman of NEXT PLC. He is president of the Fellow Chartered Institute Bankers. Born in 1931, he holds an honorary doctor of sciences degree from City University of London. He was knighted for his services to banking.

Novartis
Dr. Daniel Vasella

Dr. Daniel Vasella is chairman and chief executive officer of Novartis, a leading global life sciences company. Dr. Vasella was named CEO in 1996, during the merger of Ciba and Sandoz that created Novartis, and was named chairman in 1999. Before becoming CEO, Dr. Vasella held several positions at Sandoz, including senior vice president of worldwide development and head of corporate marketing. Before coming to Sandoz, Dr. Vasella was an attendant physician at University Hospital in Bern, Switzerland.

Dr. Vasella is director of Systemix, and a board member of the Crédit Suisse Group and Siemens. He is also a member of the Business Leaders Advisory Council for the Mayor of Shanghai, the Global Leaders for Tomorrow of the WEF, the Board of Directors of Associates, of Harvard Business School, and he is on the International Board of Governors, Peres Center for Peace.

Born in Fribourg, Switzerland, in 1953, Dr. Vasella received his M.D. from the University of Bern in 1980.

PricewaterhouseCoopers
James J. Schiro

James J. Schiro is chief executive officer of PricewaterhouseCoopers, the largest professional services organization in the world. Prior to the formation of PricewaterhouseCoopers in 1998, Mr. Schiro was chief executive officer of Price Waterhouse, and since 1995, chairman and senior partner of the U.S. firm of Price Waterhouse LLP. In addition to his leadership role, Mr. Schiro has more than two decades of experience serving large multinational engagements throughout the world.

A certified public accountant, Mr. Schiro is a member of the American Institute of Certified Public Accountants, New York State Society of Public Accountants, and the New York Steering Committee of the Accountants Coalition on Liability Reform. He is a member of the board of directors of the United States–China Business Council, a member of the British–North American Committee, and the treasurer and an executive committee member of the United States Council for International Business. He is also a member of the governing board of the Indian School of Business (Mumbai) and a member of the board of directors of the Institute for Advanced Study.

In addition to being a graduate of St. John's University, he also serves as a member of the university's board of trustees. He is a graduate of the Amos Tuck School Executive Program at Dartmouth College.

Sony Corporation
Nobuyuki Idei

Nobuyuki Idei is president and chief executive officer of Sony Corporation, the global electronics and entertainment company. He has been with Sony since 1960 and has held a number of posts, primarily in international marketing, including director and managing director of Sony Corporation, senior general manager of the Creative Communication Division, the Products Communication Group, the Merchandising and Product Communication Strategy Group, and the Advertising and Marketing Communication Strategy Group. His career at Sony has included service as general manager of the Audio Division and senior general manager of the Home Video Group.

Mr. Idei graduated from Waseda University, Faculty of Politics and Economics, in 1960, and has attended L'Institut des Hautes Etudes Internationales in Geneva, Switzerland.

STMicroelectronics NV
Pasquale Pistorio

Pasquale Pistorio has been president and chief executive officer of STMicroelectronics NV, the world's seventh-largest semiconductor company, since its formation in 1987. Prior to this position, he was chief executive officer of the SGS Group, one of the two companies that were merged to form STMicroelectronics. He began his career at Motorola, holding a variety of positions in the United States and Italy, including director of marketing and general manager of the International Semiconductor division. He is a member of the Board of Joint European Sub-micron Silicon Initiative (JESSI), and sits on the board of Microelectronics for European Applications (MEDEA) project.

Mr. Pistorio was born in 1936 in Enna, Italy. He graduated from the Polytechnic of Turin with a master's degree in electronics. He also holds an honorary degree in science from the University of Malta. In 1974, Mr. Pistorio was created *Commendatore al Merito* by the Italian Republic; and *Chevalier de l'Ordre National du Mérite* in 1990 by the French Republic. In 1997, he was named a *Cavaliere del Lavoro* by the President of the Italian Republic.

Texaco, Inc.
Peter I. Bijur

Peter I. Bijur has been chairman of the board and chief executive officer of Texaco, Inc., one of the world's largest energy companies, since 1996. Since joining Texaco in 1966, he has held several positions throughout the company, including assistant to the chairman of the board in 1981, vice president of Texaco, Inc. in 1983, and vice president for special projects in Texaco's Executive Department. Mr. Bijur was appointed president and chief executive officer of Texaco Canada in 1987. In 1990 he assumed the responsibilities of president of Texaco Europe.

Mr. Bijur is a director of International Paper Company and the American Petroleum Institute. He is chairman of The Business Council of New York State, Inc., and serves on the board of trustees of The Conference Board. He is also a member of The Business Council, The Business Roundtable, the National Petroleum Council, and the Council on Foreign Relations. In addition, Mr. Bijur presently serves on the board of trustees of Middlebury College and Mount Sinai-New York University Medical Center. He is a managing director of the Metropolitan Opera Association and a member of the board of The New York Botanical Garden.

Mr. Bijur was born in 1942 in New York City. He graduated with a bachelor of arts degree in political science from the University of Pittsburgh in 1964, and earned his M.B.A. in marketing from Columbia University in 1966.

THOMSON multimedia
Thierry Breton

Thierry Breton is chairman and chief executive officer of THOMSON multimedia, a leading global marketer and seller of consumer electronic goods, posts he assumed in 1997. Before leading THOMSON, he was CEO and vice chairman of the board of directors of Groupe BULL, CEO of Groupe CGI, and CEO of Futuroscope, a science and technology theme park. In addition, he has been a chief advisor to the French Minister of Information and New Technologies, and has been part of an interministerial delegation on teleworking and online services.

Mr. Breton was born in 1955 in Paris. He is a graduate in electrical engineering from SUPELEC, and from the 46th session of the French Institute of Higher National Defense Studies.

Unilever PLC
Niall W.A. FitzGerald

Niall W.A. FitzGerald is chairman of Unilever PLC and vice chairman of Unilever N.V., the global marketer and manufacturer of over 1,000 brands in the food and home and personal care products areas. He has held these positions since 1996.

Since joining Unilever in 1967, Mr. FitzGerald has held a variety of posts including director, financial director, edible fats and dairy coordinator, foods executive member, and detergents coordinator.

Mr. FitzGerald is also a nonexecutive director of the Prudential Corporation PLC and the Bank of Ireland.

U.S. Postal Service
William J. Henderson

William J. Henderson is the 71st Postmaster General of the United States and chief executive officer of the U.S. Postal Service, the world's largest postal system.

Mr. Henderson is the son of a postal clerk and a 26-year veteran of the agency. He has held a variety of jobs, including chief marketing officer and senior vice president, vice president of employee relations, and postmaster and division general manager of Greensboro, North Carolina.

Born in 1947, Mr. Henderson is a graduate of the University of North Carolina at Chapel Hill, and he served in the U.S. Army.

USWeb/CKS
Robert W. Shaw

Robert W. Shaw is chief executive officer of USWeb/CKS, an Internet professional services firm. Before assuming this role in 1998, Mr. Shaw held several positions in the information technology consulting realm, including executive vice president of consulting services and vertical markets at Oracle, partner at Booz·Allen & Hamilton, and managing partner of Coopers & Lybrand's Information Technology Practice. He serves on the board of Portera, a provider of business portals for business professionals, and Quintas, a privately held company offering customer call center solutions.

A certified public accountant, Mr. Shaw holds a bachelor's degree in business administration from the University of Texas.

Yahoo! Inc.
Timothy Koogle

Timothy Koogle is chairman and chief executive officer of Yahoo!, the Internet portal and navigational guide. He joined Yahoo! as president and CEO in 1995.

Prior to joining Yahoo!, Mr. Koogle was president of Intermec Corporation, a Seattle-based manufacturer of automated data collection and data communications products, for a three-year period. Before this, Mr. Koogle spent almost nine years with Motorola, Inc., where he held a number of executive management positions.

Mr. Koogle also serves on the board of Yahoo! and is a member of the American Electronics Association, the American Society of Mechanical Engineers, and the Society of Mechanical Engineers.

Born in Alexandria, Virginia, in 1951, Mr. Koogle has a bachelor of science degree in mechanical engineering from the University of Virginia and a master of science degree and doctorate from Stanford University.

Index